THE SYNAGOGUE

THE SYNAGOGUE

Brian de Breffny   Photography by George Mott

Macmillan Publishing Co., Inc., New York

FRONTISPIECE The façade of the synagogue
in Florence, which was completed in 1882.
This outstanding building in the Moorish
Revival style was commissioned by the
Jewish community to be a monumental
temple worthy of Florence.

Macmillan Publishing Co., Inc.
866 Third Avenue, New York, N.Y. 10022

Library of Congress Cataloging in Publication Data

De Breffny, Brian.
 The synagogue.

 Bibliography: p.
 Includes index.
  1. Synagogue architecture. 2. Synagogues—History.
I. Title.
NA4690.D4   1978   296.6'5   78-7583
ISBN 0-02-530310-3

First American Edition 1978

Printed in Great Britain

Note on dates

The Jewish terms BCE (Before Common Era)
and CE (Common Era) are used instead
of BC and AD
They are directly interchangeable

Note on metric measurements

Metric measurements are used throughout.
For readers unfamiliar with this system the
following guide may be of help:

1 centimetre	0.39 inch
1 metre	3.3 feet (1.1 yards)
1 kilometre	0.6 mile
1 square centimetre	0.155 square inch
1 square metre	11 square feet (1.2 square yards)
1 square kilometre	0.386 square mile
1 hectare	2.5 acres

Contents

Foreword

Since my first visit to the medieval synagogues of Cordoba and Toledo about twenty-five years ago, I have remarked with interest the effects of the prevailing social conditions of Jewish communities on the architecture of their synagogues. My attention was attracted in particular to the way in which their design catered to the liturgical requirements within a framework influenced by the local style and often subject to local restrictions; and my interest was further stimulated by the exhibition of synagogue paintings by Schwarz Abrys in Paris in 1969. In 1973, when George Mott and I were in India, Muriel Spark, who was one of our party, urged us to write a book on the synagogue. This is the book and it is dedicated to her.

I am most grateful for the courtesy and patience of the officers and members of congregations whose synagogues we visited. Our travels took us to the Near East, to the United States and to nearly every country in Europe, from Poland to Spain, from Italy to Sweden. It would be impossible, therefore, to name all the people whose co-operation helped to make this book. I am grateful to them all. Those whose books proved especially valuable I have mentioned in the Bibliography. I would also like to thank in particular the librarian, Virginia Sharp, and the staff of SIDIC, Rome; the Rev. Dr Robert Tamushansky of the Byelorussian section, Vatican Radio, who helped me with topographical problems regarding places once in Greater Poland; Ruth Feldman of Cambridge, Massachusetts; Dr Magdalena Rodzeiger of the Department of Architecture, Warsaw Polytechnic; Barbara Moro, Director of Broadcasting, Chicago Public Library, and Jodey Schonfeld and Phil Loloitis; Sylvia A. Herskowitz, Director, Yeshiva University Museum, New York City, and members of her staff; the Administrator and staff of the Jewish Museum, New York City; Rabbi Schlomo Pappenheim and Ezra P. Gorodetzky, Jewish Museum of Art, Jerusalem; Irene Levitt, Israel Museum, Jerusalem; David Cassuto, Jerusalem; Dr Liesel Franzheim, Cologne City Museum; Dr Hannelore Künzl, Martin Buber Institute, Cologne University; Dr Wulf Schirmer, Professor of Architecture, University of Karlsruhe; Irina Donner, Helsinki; René D. Maduro, Curaçao; and Shelley Donnelly, who sent me useful information from South Africa. The illustration credits appear at the end of the book, but many other individuals and institutions provided me with useful material or allowed us to take photographs. I must also thank those who helped with translations: from German, Irma Elsas, who also typed the manuscript; from Swedish, my wife; from Hebrew, Lina Manor; from Polish, Sister Magdalen (Maria) Morawska, Canoness of St Augustine; from Hungarian, Ursula Kalloy Lazzari. George Mott, who took most of the photographs in

the book, also collaborated extensively on Chapters and 9.

I found no adequate translation of the Hebrew wor 'bimah', for the platform from which the Torah is rea to the assembly in the synagogue and from which th Benediction is recited. Therefore I have used 'bimal throughout my text even in the case of Sephardic syn gogues, although I am aware that these communities us the name 'tevah' for this platform. I thought it coul confuse the reader to employ both terms. However, rath than the Hebrew 'Aron Kodesh' for the Holy Ark, I hav used 'Ark', since I believe that its meaning is widel understood. Other Hebrew terms which are not explaine in the text itself, together with a number of architectur ones, appear in the Glossary at the back of the book.

For a number of reasons ranging from indifference t anti-Semitism, the art and architecture of the synagogu have been widely neglected by both Jews and non-Jew The usually very complete guidebooks of the Tourin Club of Italy, for instance, rarely mention the fine syna gogues in that country, some of which are now in a stat of ruin. In other countries, otherwise comprehensiv national architectural surveys frequently ignore syna gogue buildings of undoubted architectural merit. In th United States, rapidly shifting urban communities hav often, in erecting new houses of worship, discarded earlie buildings which are stylistically and historically wort remembering. There are a number of these on the Lowe East Side of New York City, and I was pleased to lear that an enthusiastic scholar is making a study of them an calling attention to their plight. In fact, in the last decac there does seems to have sprung up a trend towards popu lar interest in Jewish monuments. A German art historia is preparing a study of the Neo-Byzantine and Neo Romanesque synagogues in Germany. The exhibition synagogue models at the New York Yeshiva Universit Museum has awakened considerable interest. The archae ological discoveries at Sardis and Ostia and above all i recent years in Erez Israel have attracted worldwide atten tion, as has the restoration of the old ruined synagogu of the Jewish Quarter in Jerusalem.

It is my hope that this book will stimulate pride in, an care for, synagogues past as well as present, and thereb contribute to the preservation of those in danger of deca In discovering more of the social, cultural and architec tural development of the synagogue, I have inevitabl learned more of Jewish concepts, teachings, practices an observances. For this too I am grateful, because it has in creased my esteem for the vital essence of Judaism an for the Jewish contribution to the world in theology an ethics.

BREFFNY, 197

1 *The Origins of the Synagogue*

Since Jerusalem fell to the fierce besieging legions of Titus in CE 70 and the Second Temple went up in flames, the Synagogue has been the most important institution in Judaism. As an institution it also influenced both Christianity and Islam: they adopted and adapted for their own communal worship the form first organized in the Synagogue.

Early authorities including Josephus[1] believed that the Synagogue existed from the time of Moses. This was also apparently the belief of the author of the Acts of the Apostles.[2] This indicates, at least, how well established the Synagogue was by the first century CE. Some scholars date its origins to the period of the First Temple, built by Solomon about 950 BCE;[3] others claimed it to have been an invention of the Hellenistic Diaspora.[4] It appears, however, that the foundation of the Synagogue as a place of assembly for public worship, prayer and instruction occurred during the period of the Babylonian exile after Solomon's Temple was razed to the ground by Nebuchadnezzar in 586 BCE, when he captured Jerusalem after a two-year siege. The invaders deported a number of Jews to Babylon between 597 and 586 BCE.

For some time prior to the Babylonian victory the people of Israel had been lax in their religious observances, and refused to recognize their moral decadence. They had ignored the admonitions and exhortations of the prophet Jeremiah, but when calamity befell them in the form of a crushing defeat, the consequent dissolution of the sovereign state of Judah, and the deportation of the flower of its inhabitants, they saw their troubles as the punishment of God, divine retribution for their waywardness. Chastened and repentant they turned back to Torah, that is to the Five Books of Moses and their oral explanation and interpretation, the source of God's will. They sought to learn again how to live according to God's will and to learn to know through study his nature and their relationship to him.

The teaching of Torah to the people became of primary importance under the prophet-priest Ezekiel and the scribes who followed him. Without the Temple the sacrificial rites could not be performed by the people assembled to receive instruction. It is a unique Jewish teaching that study is worship: to study Torah is a form of worship. These regular assemblies for study and communal worship were the foundation of the Synagogue. The *bet ha-keneset*, literally 'The House of Assembly', is the Jewish house of worship, whose establishment was without doubt one of the most important and significant events in the history of religion. The English Unitarian theologian Robert Travers Herford has written of it: 'In all their long history, the Jewish people have done scarcely anything more wonderful than to create the synagogue. No human institution has a longer continuous history, and none has done more for the uplifting of the human race.'[5]

From its inception the Synagogue was essentially a creation of the people in response to their needs, and during the exile it grew and developed in its function as a place where the sacred texts were read and the meaning enshrined in them explained and expounded, where the people could gather on the Sabbath to hear God's word and to pray. At the same time it grew as a communal centre, not only of the religious, but also of the social, cultural, and sometimes even the commercial life of the people.

PREVIOUS PAGE Ruined interior of the small synagogue built as part of Herod the Great's hill-top citadel at Masada. This was the place of worship of the heroic patriots who perished there in CE 73.

Eventually the Synagogue was to become to the community what the home is to the individual.

The Temple, in Hebrew *bet ha-mikdash*, literally 'The House of Sanctuary', was the spiritual centre of the people of Israel, the hub of religious life. In the Temple the Jews offered their sacrifices and oblations; as the Second Temple was rebuilt only seventy years after the destruction of Solomon's Temple, which it replaced, those Jews who remained in their land were able to resume these observances. Many Jews from Babylon and Egypt were able to make occasional pilgrimages to the Temple in Jerusalem, but in their scattered communities in foreign countries the children of Israel experienced the need for an accessible centre of worship. The Synagogue, which fulfilled this need, therefore grew in importance in the Diaspora. While religious life in Judaea, which became a theocratic state, actually declined, largely due to lack of adequate teaching, in Babylon a vigorous religious life developed, based on a piety engendered by knowledge. It was from Babylon that Ezra and Nehemiah came to Judaea to institute religious reforms and it is to Ezra and his successors that the Talmud ascribes the formulation of the earliest prayers, the *Amidah*, a collection of benedictions forming the principal prayer of religious services, the *Kiddush*, with which the Sabbath and the Festivals are welcomed, and the *Havdalah*, with which these holy days are closed.

According to tradition the Shef Ve-Yativ synagogue at Nehardea, the great Jewish settlement in Babylon, was actually founded by the first exiles under the dethroned Judaean King Jehoiachin in the sixth century BCE. However, the earliest evidence of a synagogue is of a later date and from elsewhere in the Diaspora, in Egypt. The evidence is epigraphical, an inscription on a marble slab found at Shedia near Alexandria which states that the synagogue there was dedicated by the Jews to Ptolemy III (who reigned from 246 to 221 BCE) and his Queen, Berenice.[6] The Jews enjoyed favourable conditions under the Ptolemies; the Maccabean writings mention the establishment of a synagogue at Ptolemais in the reign of Ptolemy IV (221–204 BCE).[7] Another document of this period, from Alexandru Nesos in Faiyum, west of the Nile,[8] records that one Dorotheos, accused of the theft of a pagan woman's cloak, sought asylum with the stolen article in the *proseuche* of the Jews. This description, *proseuche* (prayer house), was used quite frequently in inscriptions on buildings identifiable as being Jewish at various places in the Diaspora; it did not, however, apply invariably to a Jewish building. A *proseuche* at Arsinoe Crocidilopolis, also in Faiyum, is mentioned in a papyrus of the second century BCE, a register of landed property.[9] The Septuagint, a translation of the Canon from Hebrew into Greek and the first translation of the Jewish scriptures into another tongue, was made by Jewish scholars in Egypt in the third century BCE for the use of the flourishing émigré communities there, because for most of them Greek had become their first language.

Jews who returned from exile to Judaea took the rudiments of the institution of the Synagogue back with them. There is no actual mention of synagogues in Judaea during the persecutions of the Seleucid ruler Antiochus IV, who reigned from 175 to 164 BCE, but it was probably in the synagogues that the teachings of Torah were kept alive and disseminated when the Temple was desecrated and converted to the cult of Olympian Zeus, and ritual prostitution introduced. Antiochus wanted to Hellenize the people so he sought to impose a Hellenistic national culture on them and tried to extirpate the Jewish religion entirely. Jewish rituals and festivals were forbidden. Defence of Torah was the battle-cry of Judas Maccabeus and his followers who revolted against this tyranny. They routed the enemy from Jerusalem, repossessed the Temple and had it reconsecrated in 165 BCE.

In the two centuries that followed these events, until the destruction of the Second Temple by the Roman legions in CE 70, the Synagogue and the Temple enjoyed an organic relationship in harmonious coexistence. The services of sacrifice in the Temple alternated with prayer in the synagogues. The Mishnah, an authoritative digest of oral Torah teachings compiled about CE 200, gives a detailed account of the service on the Day of Atonement in a synagogue before the destruction of the Temple. The hazzan of the synagogue took the scroll of the Torah and handed it to the chief of the synagogue; he handed it to the prefect, who in turn handed it to the high priest, who received it standing and read it standing.[10] While the quorum of priests, Levites and others who were currently due for service in the Temple at Jerusalem were in attendance there according to the weekly rota, the remaining members of the ma'amad who did not accompany them would assemble in their local synagogues to fast and pray. There is ample evidence that by the first century CE the Synagogue had become an integral part of Jewish life, an established and revered institution.

Josephus, relating his experience at Tiberias when he went to the synagogue wearing a breastplate and carrying a sword inconspicuously because he feared an attempt on his life, makes it clear that the people were used to assembling in the synagogue to receive important announcements and for discussions as well as to pray. On the Sabbath there was a 'large crowd' in the synagogue and early the next morning the people had again assembled there although 'they had no idea why they were being convened'.[11]

One passage in the Talmud gives the number of synagogues in Jerusalem at the time of the destruction of the Second Temple as 480, another as 394.[12] It is clear that the synagogues were numerous and most if not all of them must have been small buildings. One stood on the Temple Mount itself.[13] The Talmud mentions synagogues of the Alexandrians and Tarsians at Jerusalem.[14] The New Testament mentions the 'Synagogue of Freedmen' at Jerusalem whose members included people from Cyrene and Alexandria:[15] these were probably descendants of Jews carried off to Rome in 63 BCE and sold as slaves but later released. An anonymous Christian pilgrim who visited Jerusalem in 333 recorded that out of seven synagogues on Mount Zion only one remained.[16] Epiphanius, in the second half of the fourth century, also wrote of the seven synagogues which had remained as huts on Mount Zion, of which one lasted until the reign of Constantine.[17] These synagogues must have been built before the Jews were banished from Jerusalem in CE 135 and probably existed at the time of the Temple. The one which survived until the fourth century may have been used by Judaeo-Christians who continued to assemble in synagogues, and whose practices appear to have differed little from the main body of followers of the Mosaic law except for their recognition of Jesus as Messiah.[18] An epigraph survives from one of these pre-70 CE synagogues in Jerusalem; the Greek inscription reads in translation: 'Theodotos son of Vettenos, priest and archisynagogos, son of an archisynagogos, built the synagogue for the reading of the law and for the teaching of the commandments; furthermore the hospice and the chambers and the water installation for the lodging of needy strangers. The foundation stone thereof has been laid by his fathers and the elders and Simonides.'[19] This inscription indicates that the didactic and social functions of the synagogue were already well established in the first century CE, and that it was exerting its influence even before the destruction of the Temple.

Josephus mentions synagogues at Caesarea, Dora and Tiberias.[20] The New Testament mentions synagogues elsewhere in the country, specifically at Nazareth[21] and at Capharnaum;[22] the references to synagogues in Galilee imply that they were numerous and that many towns and villages had one.[23] Jesus' activity in the synagogues, as recorded in the synoptic gospels of the New Testament, throws an interesting light on their contemporary use. He was able to speak frequently and freely to the assembly in many synagogues, usually on the Sabbath,[24] and it is very evident that it was not unusual for the congregation to be addressed extemporaneously in this way. On one occasion, in his home town of Nazareth, the evangelist records that Jesus 'went into the synagogue on the Sabbath day as he usually did. He stood up to read and they handed him the scroll of the prophet Isaiah. Unrolling the scroll he found the place where it is written. . . .' After reading a passage from the scroll, according to the

Inscription from a synagogue in Jerusalem which functioned prior to the destruction of the Second Temple in CE 70, naming the builder and chief of the synagogue.

account, 'He then rolled up the scroll, gave it back to the assistant and sat down. And all eyes in the synagogue were fixed on him. Then he began to speak to them.'[25] It appears that at that period women frequented the synagogue.[26]

It is interesting to note that at Capharnaum, where Jesus often went to the synagogue, the Jewish elders told him that their synagogue had been built for them by a Roman centurion who was stationed in the town and who was friendly to the Jewish people.[27]

The references to the synagogue in the New Testament suggest a friendly, democratic, bustling assembly where the scholars and the devout, rich and poor, rubbed shoulders with beggars, paralytics, blind men and cripples, where a Jew could address his peers and receive a fair hearing and where there was considerable religious and probably also social and political discussion in addition to formal liturgical worship. Jesus' criticism of people who gave alms in the synagogue 'to win men's admiration' and of those who loved to say their prayers ostentatiously, standing in the synagogue for all to see them,[28] implies that begging, alms-giving and individual declamatory prayer were common occurrences in the contemporary synagogue. James, in his letter written at Jerusalem in the early sixties of the Common Era, upbraided the Judaeo-Christians for seating the well-dressed men in the best places in the synagogues and telling the poor to sit on the floor.[29]

Unfortunately archaeological evidence of the architecture of the Judaean synagogues prior to the destruction of the Second Temple is very scant. King Herod the Great, who reigned from 39 to 4 BCE, was a superbly wily politician and a prolific and grandiose builder. It was he who rebuilt the Second Temple, replacing the modest post-Exilic structure by an important building with sumptuous courts and impressive colonnades. Remains of synagogues have been found in the fortresses built by Herod at Masada and Herodion.

At Masada, high up on bare rock in the barren wilderness forty miles south-east of Jerusalem, King Herod built himself a luxurious royal citadel overlooking the Dead Sea. The stupendous complex, bounded by a casement wall, included a three-tiered hanging palace-villa complete with Roman baths, frescoed walls and mosaic floors, two other palaces, five villas, administrative buildings, a swimming pool, storehouses and an ingenious water-catchment system with immense cisterns. After Herod's death this fortress was garrisoned for sixty years by Roman legionaries until it was captured by Jewish rebel patriots in CE 66. The patriots, called by Josephus *sicarii* (dagger men), managed to hold the fortress heroically even after Jerusalem fell in the year 70. When the Romans finally took Masada in CE 73 they found the bodies of the entire community of 960 men, women and children, who had chosen death at their own hands on the eve of their defeat rather than face humiliation and captivity.

One building at Masada which has been identified as a synagogue dates from the original Herodian construction but it was altered by the patriots during their seven-year period of occupation of the fortress. While there is no absolute proof that the Herodian building was constructed originally as a synagogue, it is likely that the King would have provided one for the Jewish members of his court and family. Moreover, the arrangement of the columns (like those of later Galilean synagogues), the direction of the building towards Jerusalem, and the fact that the patriot community chose this particular building for their synagogue all point to its having been used as such originally.

The patriots were very devout: despite the difficulties of their life on the rock fortress, they adhered rigidly to their religious code. There is evidence that they even paid tithes while there and built *mikveh*, ritual immersion baths, as well as modifying the synagogue.

The building is rectangular in plan with the door facing Jerusalem. The original Herodian arrangement had an antechamber or vestibule, and in the main room along the southern, western, and northern sides there stood five columns, which may have supported a gallery. The patriots demolished the partition wall, thus abolishing the antechamber, and they built walls which created an enclosed cell in the north-west corner of the building. It appears that this was done to provide a place in which to store the Torah scrolls. The patriots also removed the two columns of the western row which had become enclosed by the walls of the cell and replaced them in line with the original northern and southern rows, where the partition wall had been thrown down; in this way the columns could still conveniently support a gallery. Then tiered benches were added along the main walls of the building. In the course of excavation it was found that these benches contained portions of columns and capitals quarried by the patriots from one of the Herodian palaces. On the synagogue floor the archaeologists found coins from the period of the revolt and an ostracon bearing the inscription 'priestly tithe' in Hebrew.

Before voluntarily accepting death the defenders of Masada set fire to most of their valuables. In the cell of the synagogue, in addition to a large number of soot-blackened lamps in a corner of its main room, the members of the archaeological expedition of 1963-5 found evidence of a great fire and the charred remains of glass and metal vessels. The sanctity attached to sacred documents prohibited their destruction so it was orthodox Jewish custom to bury unwanted manuscripts in a hiding-place, called a *genizah*. Two such places were uncovered beneath the floor of the cell in the corner of the Masada synagogue. In one pit was found a rolled scroll containing the last two chapters of the Book of Deuteronomy; in the bottom of the other pit were found the remains of a scroll containing parts of the Book of Ezekiel, including the portion of Chapter 37 describing the prophet's vision of the dry bones. It is likely that such elements as a storage-place for the Torah scrolls and tiered benches around the walls were usual in the early Judaean synagogues.

Josephus mentions the custom among Hellenic Jewish communities of the Diaspora of building their places of worship near the sea. At Halikarnassos a decree was passed on the motion of one Marcus Alexander that 'these Jewish men and women who so wish may observe their Sabbaths and perform their sacred rites in accordance with the Jewish laws and may build a place of prayer τὰς προσευχὰς ποιεῖσθαι near the sea in accordance with their native custom.'[30] This may have been to obviate the need for constructing a *mikveh*' which had to have some 'pure' flowing water, or facilitate its water supply. At Philippi in Greece the people customarily met to pray on the Sabbath at a spot along the river outside the city gates.[31] It would appear that there was not then a synagogue building at Philippi, although throughout the Diaspora the Synagogue was already a widespread, well-established institution in the first century CE.

The largest synagogue building in the Diaspora, perhaps indeed in the world, prior to the destruction of the Temple, must have been the Great Synagogue in Alexandria in which Caligula wished to have his effigy set up to be adored as a divinity, as it was in the pagan temple. It was destroyed during the reign of the Emperor Trajan (CE 98–117). According to Philo this synagogue, which served a large and powerful Jewish colony, was only one of many in the city.[32] There is an account of it, given about forty or fifty years after its destruction, by the Galilean Talmudist, Rabbi Judah:

He who has not seen the double stoa of Alexandria in Egypt has never seen the glory of Israel. It was said that it was like a huge basilica, one stoa within another, and it sometimes held twice the number of people that went forth into Egypt. There were in it seventy-one cathedras of gold, corresponding to the seventy-one elders of the Great Sanhedrin, not one of them containing less than twenty-one talents of gold, and a wooden platform in the middle upon which the attendant of the Synagogue stood with a napkin in his hand; when the time came to answer Amen he waved his napkin and all the congregation duly responded. They moreover did not occupy their seats promiscuously, but goldsmiths sat separately, silversmiths separately, blacksmiths separately, metalworkers separately and weavers separately, so that when a poor man entered the place he recognized the members of his craft and on applying to that quarter obtained a livelihood for himself and the members of his family.[33]

Even allowing for a certain rhetorical exaggeration, this must have been a splendid building, Hellenistic in style, with lavish furnishings such as the golden chairs, and so large that it was necessary for the hazzan to give a signal for the responses as the precentor's voice was not audible to the entire congregation. Rabbi Judah's account also makes clear the social role of the Synagogue, which was not only a place of prayer but also a useful 'employment exchange' for the community.

Although the little windswept holy island of Delos, one of the Cycladean group in the Aegean Sea, only covers an area of five square kilometres, it enjoyed very considerable religious, political and commercial importance and in the second and third centuries BCE it was at the height of its fame. Besides being the sacred pagan sanctuary of Apollo, which gave the island importance and to which gifts poured in from all over the Hellenistic world, Delos flourished as a busy commercial centre with long lines of warehouses and quays. Many foreign merchants lived there. The Egyptian traders built their own temple to Serapis, the Syrians built their own sanctuary, the Italian merchants built an impressive agora, while the Jewish community, it seems, erected a synagogue. There is epigraphical evidence of a Jewish community on Delos in the second century BCE,[34] and in 139 BCE the government of Delos was one of the recipients of a Roman consular recommendation regarding the treatment of Jews. When the Jewish ambassadors returned to Judaea from Rome in that year they carried with them letters to King Ptolemy VI from the Roman consul,

View of the ruins of the synagogue at
Delos, from the south-west.

which began, 'Lucius, consul of the Romans to King Ptolemy, greetings.
The Jewish ambassadors have come to us as our friends and allies to renew
our original friendship and alliance in the name of the high priest Simon
and the Jewish people. ...' and continued '... we have decided to write
to various Kings and states, warning them not to molest them nor to attack
them or their towns or their country....'[35] The Roman consul sent this
same letter to the Seleucid ruler, King Demetrius, to Delos, and to other
states: Rhodes, Sparta, Cyprus, Kos, Pamphylia, Lycia, Samos, Halikarnassos and Cyrene. The Jews of Delos are again mentioned about 49 BCE
in a decree of exemption from military service cited by Josephus.[36]

A building excavated on the eastern side of the island of Delos where
there was a suburb of houses, a stadium and a gymnasium, but standing
off from them near the shore, has been tentatively identified as the synagogue of the Jewish community because of inscriptions referring to 'God
the Most High', 'the Most High', and to the building itself as a *proseuche*.
E. L. Sukenik revised his earlier opinion that the building was a Jewish
place of worship and decided that it was a pagan place of assembly.[37]
Some time after the original construction the main part of the building
was divided into two adjacent halls by a partition wall; the materials used
for this were salvaged from the gymnasium, which was destroyed in 88
BCE. The palaeographic evidence of the inscriptions points to a date in
the second century BCE for the original building and it appears that the

synagogue hall was divided after 88 BCE. A row of marble benches are arranged on either side of the presidential cathedra on the west wall of the most northerly of the two rooms.

In the kingdom of Bosphorus, north of the Black Sea, epigraphic evidences of *proseuche* have been found, dating from the first century BCE. Greek inscriptions at Berenice in Cyrenaica, North Africa, with reference to the Festival of Booths (*Sukkot*), can be identified with a Jewish community there.[38] One of the inscriptions, of the year CE 56, contains the word συναγωγή, which signifies the community as well as the synagogue building: another pays tribute to a Decimus Valerius Dionysius, son of Gaius, because he had the floors of the 'amphitheatre whitewashed and the walls frescoed in the good Greek manner'. It may be inferred that this amphitheatre was a meeting-place of the Jewish community at Berenice.

Philo mentioned synagogues in Rome.[39] The names of some of these early Roman synagogues indicate the period of their foundation. The synagogue of the Augustesians was presumably established under the patronage of the Emperor Augustus, who reigned from 27 BCE to CE 14. This emperor and his family were benevolent to the Jews; the Roman synagogue of the Agrippesians was most probably named for his son-in-law, Agrippa, while the synagogue of the Volumnesians appears to have been named for Volumnius, the contemporary Roman procurator of Syria. The synagogue of the Herodians commemorated Herod the Great, King of Judaea and friend of Augustus.

The synagogue at Antioch in Syria is mentioned by Josephus.[40] It must have been established by the second century BCE because the Seleucid ruler Antiochus IV Epiphanes, who reigned from 175 BCE, presented it with consecrated pottery vessels plundered from the Temple in Jerusalem. Josephus also records a decree by which the council and people of Sardis, on a notion of the magistrates, decreed that a place be given the Jews of the city to 'gather together with their wives and children and offer their ancestral prayers and sacrifices to God ... to come together on stated days to do those things which are in accordance with their laws and that a place shall be set apart by the magistrates for them to build and inhabit which they may consider suitable for the purpose'.[41]

Damascus, in Syria, had several synagogues in which Paul preached and,[42] according to the author of the Acts of the Apostles, created confusion among the Jewish community there by his arguments that Jesus was the Messiah. On their missionary travels Peter and Paul usually made at once for the synagogue, where they addressed the assembly. Paul and his companions went to the synagogue at Antioch-in-Pisidia 'on the Sabbath and took their seats', an occasion on which the democratic nature of the institution was again made clear: 'After the lessons from the Law and the Prophets had been read, the presidents of the synagogue sent them a message, "Brothers, if you would like to address some words of encouragement to the congregation, please do so."[43] Paul stood up, held up a hand for silence and began to speak.'[44] Paul spoke in the synagogue at Ephesus for three months until opposition from the congregation caused him to shift his activities to a hall, where he continued his arguments daily.[45] At Iconium, too, there was a synagogue where Paul addressed the assembly[46] and at Thessalonika in Greece, having in-

troduced himself, Paul was able to preach in the synagogue on three consecutive Sabbaths.[47] Paul also preached in a synagogue at Beroea[48] and in one at Athens.[49] At Corinth he held debates in the synagogues every Sabbath, 'trying to convert Jews as well as Greeks'.[50] Corinth was a splendid city at that time; it had been majestically rebuilt by Julius Caesar in 44 BCE and besides the theatre, which held 15,000 people, boasted a fine agora with long colonnades of shops and expensive public buildings. A marble block with the inscription '*Sinagoga Ebraion*'[51] was found by archaeologists at the foot of the steps which led to the ancient propylaeum, or gateway of the city. On the island of Cyprus Paul found synagogues at Salamis[52] and presumably at Paphos.

Unlike the Temple, which non-Jews were barred from entering, the Synagogue was accessible to sympathetic pagans. Judaism drew a number of proselytes in all parts of the Hellenistic world, men and women who were attracted by the social and moral ethics of the Jews and who admired their monotheistic belief and their culture. One of these was Helena,

ΕΝΘΑΔΕΚΕΙΤΕ
ΚΑΙΛΙϹ ΠΡΟϹΤΑ
ΤΗϹΑΓΡΙΠΠΗ
ϹΙΩΝΕΝΕΙΡΗ
ΝΗΚΟΙΜΑϹΘΩ

ΕΝΘΑΔΕΚΙΤΕΛΛΑΡΟϹ
ΑΡΧΩΝΑΠΟϹΥΝΑΓΩ
ΗϹΒΟΛΥΛΩΝϹΙΩΝ
ΖΗϹΑϹΕΤ+ΛΕΕΝΙ
ΡΗΝΗ+ΚΟΙΜ ϹΙϹ
ΑΥΤΟΥ ΛΙΝΙΑΥ ΙΟΥ

ΕΝΘΑΔΕϹΚΕΥΘΑΙΝ
ΠΟ ΛΠΩΝΙϹΟΔΙϹ
ΑΡΧΩΝΤΗϹϹΥΝΑ
ΓΩ ΒϹΚΑΛΑΡΗϹϹ
ΖΗϹΕΝϹΤΩΝ Ζ ΕΝΙΡ
ΗΝΗ ΚΥΜΗ
ϹΙϹΑΥΤΟ

ΕΝΘΑΔΕΚΕΙΤΕΠΡΟ
ΚΛΟϹΑΡΧΩΝϹΥΝΑΓΩ
ΓΗϹΤΡΙΠΟΛΕΙΤΩΝ
ΕΝΕΙΡΗΝΗΚΟΙΜΑϹΘΩ

Queen of Adiabene, beyond the Tigris, who was converted to Judaism with her two sons about CE 35–40 and had a burial vault for the family constructed at Jerusalem.

The synagogues of the Hellenistic Diaspora were frequented not only by émigré Jews and their descendants and by converts to Judaism from the local pagan population, but also by Gentile sympathizers who were attracted to Judaism but balked at the necessity for meticulous observance of the Mosaic law which actual conversion entailed. It is not surprising, therefore, that a number of these pro-Judaic pagans – the 'God-fearing' or the 'Proselytes of the Gates' – joined the ranks of the first Christians, embracing a Jewish sect which did not impose exacting requirements alien to their own ethnic origins. Along with those Jews in the Diaspora who accepted Christian teachings, these proselytes continued to frequent the synagogues until their beliefs and practices so separated them from the mainstream of Jewry that they met and worshipped independently. This separation was hastened by the Jewish defeat and the fall of Jerusalem in CE 70, when the Hellenistic Christian communities disengaged themselves socially and politically from Judaism. The Greek word *ekklesia*, used in the Septuagint for the collectivity of Israel as God's People as well as for a worshipping community, and interchangeably with *sunagogè* as a translation of the Hebrew HQL, became the technical term for the Christian community or assembly. The congregational worship of these assemblies was based on the pattern of the synagogue, with the reading and explanation of God's word, praise, prayers of supplication and thanksgiving, and religious exercises. The Eucharist, which became a fundamental part of Christian worship, can be seen as the continuation of an established Jewish custom, the meal of religious character which celebrated both men's own fellowship and their fellowship with God, and was essentially eucharistic, being an expression of thanksgiving.

OPPOSITE Roman funerary epitaphs of synagogue dignitaries mentioning the synagogues of the Agrippesians (ABOVE), the Volumnesians (LEFT), the Calcarenses (RIGHT), and the Tripolitanians (BELOW).

In Palestine where the Christians, or Nazarenes as they were then called, were regarded by the orthodox as just another Jewish sect which observed peculiar rites of its own, the Judaeo-Christians withdrew from Judaism and customary Judaic practice much more slowly than their fellow believers abroad. The deliberations of the so-called Council of Jerusalem of about CE 50 barely affected them and at least until the time of Hadrian, nearly a century later, the Hebrew Christian community in Jerusalem was composed of practising Jews;[53] Eusebius referred to their first fifteen successive Hebrew bishops there as 'the bishops of the circumcision'.[54] Until its destruction in CE 70, the Judaeo-Christians in Jerusalem attended the Temple assiduously and, of course, observed the law of circumcision. Even though many Judaeo-Christians fled when the Temple was destroyed, and again during the persecutions under Hadrian in CE 135, some vital communities of them persisted in Palestine and the surrounding countries. It has been suggested[55] that the Tomb of David on Mount Zion was a synagogue. The main room, which has undergone many changes, had an apse or niche 1.92 m above the floor level, 2.44 m in height, 2.4 m in diameter and 1.2 m in depth. This niche is pointed exactly towards the Temple Mount, north with a slight easterly deviation: it could well have been constructed to hold the Torah scrolls. On the floor above and to the west is the room called the Cenacle, according to tradition the 'upper room' (*hyperoon*) where the followers of Jesus, about 120 in number, assembled for prayer in the period just after his death.[56]

It has been estimated that in the year CE 60 there were less than two million Jews in Palestine and about three million in other countries. There were communities in Babylon, in many places in Asia Minor and North Africa, in Egypt, in Greece, in what is now Yugoslavia, in Italy and in Spain. They all looked to the Temple in Jerusalem as their ultimate spiritual centre; desire to attend there was paramount among all believing Jews and in their distant homes they yearned and aspired to make a pilgrimage to the Temple in the Chosen Land.

With the destruction of the Temple in the year CE 70, and the consequent abrupt cessation of the service of sacrifice, the Synagogue immediately acquired a new and more important role in Jewry, for it stood without any rival as the nucleus of religious activity. Prayer, which had previously accompanied the rite of sacrifice, came to be regarded as a provisional substitute for it. In addition, some of the other Temple customs and rituals were deliberately transferred to the Synagogue, thus increasing its importance. To ensure its effective continuity, uniformity of cult became an essential factor, so divergent practices were at first discouraged and then extirpated. Jews everywhere prayed and hoped for the restoration of the Temple; until that day the Synagogue would be their bond, the pivot of their religious life and eventually also of their social life.

2 *The Patriarchate and the Exilarchate*

The maladministration of a series of short-sighted Roman procurators and the rapacious tactics of their tax-collectors brought the former kingdom of Herod the Great to a state of overt rebellion within twenty years of the death of Herod's grandson in CE 44. Following the loss of 6000 of the Roman army trapped in the gorge of Beth Horon in that year in an attempt to quell the insurgents, the Emperor sent his general Vespasian to direct operations. Titus, son of Vespasian, joined his father with a Roman legion from Egypt. When Vespasian became Emperor in 69 he again recalled Titus from Egypt to complete the conquest of Judaea. In the campaign which ensued, Titus, enraged by the resistance of the besieged defenders of Jerusalem, retaliated with slaughter and destruction. The Temple, in which daily sacrifice had had to cease on the seventeenth of Tamuz, was stormed and burned on the ninth of Ab, 70.

Leaving one legion in Jerusalem to help maintain Roman supremacy and to quash any possible further attempts at insurrection, Titus returned triumphantly to Rome. With him he brought Jewish captives, among them John of Giscala (Jochanan ben Levi), a leader of the revolt, and trophies ransacked from the Temple including the Menorah, the great seven-branched candelabrum which had provided its central illumination, the table of the Shewbread, the sacred trumpets, vessels, censers, and scrolls of the Torah. On the relief of the triumphal Arch of Titus in Rome (completed after his death by his brother, the Emperor Domitian, to commemorate the victory), the Romans are depicted returning home bearing some of the sacred loot. Pious traditions would have it that Jewish refugees who fled from Jerusalem also brought away remnants salvaged from the Temple: one of the doors, for instance, is said to have been walled into the Ghriba synagogue on the island of Djerba, Tunisia.[1]

The vanquished Jews who remained in Erez Israel after their cataclysmic defeat were enabled to overcome the delusion and discouragement caused by the loss of the Temple thanks to the assiduous ministry of the scholarly Perushim (Pharisees) who undertook the arduous task of repairing the shattered fabric of Jewish spiritual life. The High Priesthood had come to an end with the destruction of the Temple and with it too the importance of the Zadokim (Sadducees) diminished. Already, even before the war, the Pharisees, who were by tradition eclectic and democratic, had counselled disengagement in the political sphere. Unlike the other sects they were prepared to seek peace through reconciliation with the Imperial Roman hegemony and they promoted study and observance of Torah as a remedy in a troubled world.

Rabbi Jochanan ben Zakkai, who had managed to leave Jerusalem just before the final disaster, founded a school with the permission of Titus in the coastal town of Jabneh. Other erudite teachers joined him there after the catastrophe and an academic Sanhedrin was reconstituted with an elected head. This developed into the central Jewish authority, not only in Erez Israel, but for all the Jewish Diaspora. Within the framework of limited freedom and autonomy which the Jews could enjoy under the Roman administration, the Jabneh scholars regulated matters of religious observance, custom, education and law.

The first important task and achievement of the energetic Jabneh rabbis was the recasting of the divine services and liturgy. These were

PREVIOUS PAGE Prophet reading a scroll. Fresco from the third-century synagogue discovered at Dura Europos Syria.

Detail of the Triumphal Arch of Titus, in Rome, depicting the victorious return of the Imperial army with Jewish slaves and sacred loot from the Second Temple in Jerusalem.

adapted to accommodate specific prayers in place of the animal sacrifices of the Temple, prayers for the restoration of the Temple, and also some of the actual Temple customs and rituals. Rabbi Akiba (c. 50–135) also undertook the arrangement by subject matter of the Halakhic teachings, a work which was continued by his disciples, organizing the digest, codification and compilation of the body of law of the Oral Torah in the form of the Mishnah. Akiba also cultivated the preparation of Midrashim, homiletic literary interpretations of the Bible, and in this field he evolved and promoted a method of interpretation which was based on the paramount importance of attention to the minutiae of the biblical text. Furthermore, the Jabneh rabbis considered the various Hebrew texts of the Bible, pronounced on which were authoritative, and brought the process of canonization to completion. When they had determined the final canon they commissioned a convert to Judaism, one Aquila from Sinope, to translate it into Greek.

Through the rabbinical teaching which emanated from Jabneh, the concept of holiness which had been exclusively attached to the Temple came to be extended to embrace to some extent the Synagogue, and so the synagogues of the Diaspora came to be considered by the Jewish congregations who gathered around them as something akin to extra-territorial units of Erez Israel. Consequently the Synagogue, the house of study and prayer, assumed an increasingly important and focal role in Jewish life.

The Emperor Hadrian, who began his reign in CE 117, was at first favourably disposed to the Jews, who were led therefore to hope that the delicately re-woven tissue of Jewish religious and social life that had been achieved in the preceding half-century might be maintained, strengthened and consolidated. However, like some of his Imperial predecessors, Hadrian embarked on a programme of cultural and religious uniformity throughout the Empire. When he erected a Temple dedicated to Jupiter on the venerated site of the ruined Temple in Jerusalem, his Jewish subjects were outraged. The popular revolt led by Bar Kochba which ensued in 132 was encouraged by Rabbi Akiba against the counsel of many of the religious leaders. This rising, at first successful, was quelled in 135 and the Emperor then clamped down on the Jews, rescinding measures of autonomy which they had gained; he had Rabbi Akiba put to death, closed the Jabneh academy, suppressed the Sanhedrin, and forbade by formal decree not only the study of Torah but even the observance of its precepts. Moreover, Jews were barred from residing in and around Jerusalem and even restricted from entry to the city except for one day a year when, on the anniversary of the destruction of the Temple, they were permitted to come and weep beside its ruined wall. The centre of Jewish national life moved north to Galilee, but a number of Jews, faced with Hadrian's restrictions, left the country to live abroad.

In Galilee, where religious activity had continued unobtrusively during the Hadrianic wars, there was a flowering of Pharisaic activity again during the reign of Hadrian's successor, Antoninus Pius, who was more lenient. He revoked some of the harshest anti-Jewish decrees but permitted circumcision only for those of the Jewish race, thus curtailing Jewish proselytizing activities and indeed making conversion a capital offence. The ban on Jews living in Jerusalem was not lifted. A new academic Sanhedrin was founded at Usha in Galilee and its *Nasi* (President), Rabbi Simeon ben Gamaliel, was recognized by the Emperor as the Patriarch, the accredited representative of all the Jews in the Roman Empire.

Rabbi Simeon was succeeded as Patriarch by his son Judah (135–217) who ruled in that capacity for over half a century. He imposed his authority over the Sanhedrin, obtained the right to nominate all rabbis and dispatched his special envoys or *apostoloi* throughout the Diaspora to inspect communities, depose functionaries when and where necessary, and solicit and collect voluntary contributions for the maintenance of the Patriarch. In exchange for the recognition of his office by the Romans, with whom he remained on good terms, the Patriarch saw to it that there were no Zealot uprisings. The patriarchal circle also encouraged the study of Greek language and culture, because familiarity with these would be an asset to the Jews in their dealings with the Roman authorities. Under the patriarchate of Judah the academic compilation of the Mishnah was finally completed, being divided into six orders (Seeds, Appointed Seasons, Women, Damages, Holy Things, Purifications) each containing sixty-three tractates, and its authority as a standard work was established throughout Jewry.

Because of a renewed spate of harassment and persecution following Judah's death, which provoked the decline of his school, one of his disciples, Rabbi Abba Arika (175–267), emigrated to Babylon, where Jews had lived during the time of the second Temple and where more had arrived during the Hadrianic persecutions, some as refugees, some as deportees, the unluckiest as slaves. In Babylon, at Sura, Abba Arika founded a new school where he expounded his late teacher's Mishnah. This academy at Sura, together with others in Babylon, Pumbeditha (founded by Judah ben Ezekiel, who died in 279) and Nehardea (founded by Samuel, an expert in civil law who died in 250), attracted thousands of students.

Another of the Patriarch Judah's disciples, Rabbi Jochanan ben Nappacha, who died in 279, founded an academy about the year 250 in the Galilean town of Tiberias, famed for the medicinal qualities of its hot springs. Tiberias became the principal seat of Jewish scholarship in Erez Israel and there the Palestinian Talmud, the great compendium of the deliberations and discussions of the sages, was begun. There was a steady flow of ideas back and forth between Tiberias and Babylon, where the scholars compiled a separate Talmud, which, on completion, was three times the size of the Palestinian one.

Tiberias remained the seat of the Patriarchs, who maintained their little court there with some display of state, thanks to the contributions which poured in from world Jewry. The office became hereditary; in consequence the academic and spiritual qualifications of the Patriarch were often scant, but this did not diminish his authority. The Patriarchate survived the conversion of the Emperor Constantine to Christianity and its consequent imposition as the official religion of the Empire in the fourth century, and the Patriarch Hillel II was briefly favoured by the next Emperor, Julian the Apostate, who reacted against Christianity. In a letter in which he addressed the Patriarch as 'brother', Julian promised to rebuild the Temple at Jerusalem.[2] However, he reigned for only three years and when he was slain in battle in Persia in 363 he was succeeded by a Christian Emperor, and Hillel II foresaw the deterioration of the patriarchal apparatus and the eventual demise of its jurisdiction. He therefore distributed a permanent calendar for the use of all Jewish communities, to replace the one which had hitherto been dispatched annually from Tiberias and on which they had depended. In 364, a year before the death of Hillel II, the Roman Empire was split into the Eastern and Western Empires, and in 399 the Patriarchate received a grave financial blow when the Western Emperor, Honorius, disallowed the transmission of funds from Italy to the Patriarch in the Eastern Empire. Not long after this, the office of Patriarch was abolished by the Eastern Emperor, Theodosius II, who seized the occasion to do so on the death without male issue of Patriarch Gamaliel IV in 425.

Halakah, the laws, rules and regulations which govern every phase of Jewish life and human relations, not only religious but also domestic, social and political, govern only some specific aspects of synagogue design and are silent regarding the style and plan of the building. Therefore no conventional style was imposed. According to the Tosefta, the synagogue ought to be built on high ground and rise above the other buildings of the place.[3] Halakah requires that the synagogue must have windows:[4] this rule is based on Daniel 6:11, which relates how the prophet, in exile in Babylon, fell to his knees thrice daily and prayed and praised God in his upstairs room which had windows facing Jerusalem. The Tosefta states, concerning the container in which the Torah scrolls were kept: 'When the chest (תיבה) is set down, it has to stand with its front toward the people and its back toward the sanctuary (קודש).'[5] By sanctuary it appears that the Temple in Jerusalem is meant. This injunction clearly refers to the use of a mobile Ark. A solitary injunction in the Tosefta regards the architectural arrangements of the synagogue: 'Synagogue gates should open toward the east as did the gates of the tent of meeting for it is written "round about the tent of meeting ... those that pitch on the east toward the sunrising".'[6]

The pagans observed a sacred direction in their temple building.

According to Vitruvius: 'The holy Temples of the immortal Gods have to be so built that, temple usages permitting and no obstacles interfering, the divine statue in the cella should appear to be looking westward, so that those approaching the altar with their offerings should direct their gaze toward the eastern heaven and, at the same time, toward the temple statue.'[7]

It is uncertain whether the principle of a sacred direction in Christian churches derives from the pagan temple through the Gentile converts to Christianity or from the synagogue through the Jews. For the early Gentile Christians the East represented both Jesus and Paradise. Tertullian wrote as early as the second century of '... *Orientem, Christi figuram*'[8] and the third-century Syrian church discipline, the *Didaskalia*, instructed: 'For we must pray toward the East inasmuch as it is written "Sing to God that rides on the heavens of heaven, eastward."'[9] In the fourth century Basilius of Caesarea explained the reason for looking towards the sunrise during prayer as seeking man's ancient home, Paradise, 'which God planted in Eden toward the sunrise'.[10] In the same century Gregory of Nyssa wrote: 'If we turn toward the east, it is not in order to search for God for He is everywhere, but because the orient was our first fatherland. It was our abode when we lived in Paradise whence we were ejected. God established Paradise toward the east.'[11] Christian sacred directionality was certainly to the east and thus it has come to be called 'orientation'. About the year CE 100 a Jewish preacher, Elkasai, already found it necessary to remind the faithful to continue to pray towards Jerusalem and not towards the east.[12]

In Jewish practice there was, it seems, some ambiguity about sacred directionality in the first centuries following the destruction of the Temple. In the synagogue the sacred scrolls became the focal point of reverence and as long as they were carried in and out in a portable Ark their presence did not affect the directionality of the house of prayer. The Babylonian Talmudists, Rabbi Oshaia and Rabbi Ishmael, expressed the opinion in the second century that a prayer direction was superfluous inasmuch as the Divine was everywhere. However, when and where the scrolls were conserved in a permanent receptacle in the synagogue, the wall which contained it or against which it stood, the 'Torah wall', was the one which pointed to Jerusalem. This is quite clear in those early synagogues of Erez Israel built with a niche or apse to house the Torah scrolls: in the buildings south of Jerusalem the Torah wall was the north wall; in those to the north, the Torah wall was the south wall. In the early third-century synagogue of Dura Europos on the Euphrates the wall containing the niche for the scrolls also faced towards Jerusalem.

In some synagogues of Erez Israel under the Patriarchate the sacred direction was that of the entrance wall, which pointed towards Jerusalem. This principle also obtained in the majority of Christian churches until the fifth century: the sacred direction, east, was vested not in the altar but in the portal. This was the case of the first basilica of St Peter at Rome, and of the Constantinian basilica of the Holy Sepulchre at Jerusalem, of which Eusebius wrote: 'Three well-established doors toward the rising sun admit the entering host.'[13] As the sacred direction in the synagogue switched from the entrance wall to the Torah wall, so it was trans-

Zenobia, Queen of Palmyra, seized Egypt and ruled it from 269 to 272. This inscription records the bestowal of rights of asylum on a synagogue there by Zenobia and her son.

ferred in the church to the altar wall at the choir end of the building.

The change in the synagogue did not take place at one time – different practice obtained for some centuries. Where the sacred direction was that of the entrance wall, as for example at Bar'am (K'far Birim) in northern Galilee, presumably the worshippers turned and faced the doors and windows which pointed towards the Holy City when they prayed, thus fulfilling the requirement to pray before windows facing Jerusalem. At Capharnaum, where the entrance wall of the synagogue pointed towards Jerusalem, Father Virgilio Corbo, who has carried out excavations and reconstruction on the ruin, has noted the foundations of platforms where the Ark may have stood on each side of the main door of the entrance wall. While this is possible (cf. synagogue of Sardis, p. 31) it is by no means certain. The whole plan of the building seems to call for the scrolls of the Torah to have been placed at the centre of attention in the middle of the nave, in a mobile Ark. If there was a platform or construction against the entrance wall it seems more likely that it was the bimah from which the law could have been read with all the congregation turned to it and towards the Holy City. The addition to the synagogue of an axial courtyard, the counterpart as an architectural expression of sacred directionality in the atrium and narthex of Christian basilicas, served to emphasize the sacred direction by prolonging the axis. This took place in the early Diaspora synagogues of Dura Europos, Miletus, Priene and Sardis, and in Erez Israel in the Beth Alpha synagogue, Hefzibah.

Remains of synagogues dating from the era of the Patriarchate have been discovered in different countries of the Diaspora and it seems likely that more may yet be found. All these buildings belong to the Hellenistic artistic and architectural tradition.

A British army patrol discovered the site of the city of Dura Europos quite accidentally in the course of manœuvres in Mesopotamia during World War I. In 1928 a Franco–American expedition began excavations and in 1932 the remarkably well-preserved synagogue of the town was discovered. The early commercial importance of Dura was due to its location. It was a caravan town without academic distinction where goods from the East could be brought up the Euphrates and repacked on camels for transportation to the Mediterranean via Palmyra. The Parthians wrested Dura from the Seleucid rulers in 140 BCE, and except for a brief interlude of Roman occupation under Trajan they held it until CE 165, when the Roman forces captured the city. Dura then became for almost a century an outpost of the vast Roman Empire until it fell to the Sassanids who stormed and destroyed the city in CE 256. Dura retained some of its Hellenistic character deriving from the Seleucid period throughout the three centuries of Parthian rule, so that its cultural tradition was a hybrid one. A provincial city of the Hellenized Orient, it stood on the frontiers of the West and the East. Excavations have shown that its population included minority groups of Christians and Jews as well as the pagans. There existed a sizeable Mithraeum, a small Christian church and a small synagogue under the Roman administration in the first half of the third century. The Jewish community was most probably primarily engaged in mercantile activity and victualling the Roman garrison.

The synagogue was built against the city wall in 245. When the

Sassanids attacked only eleven years later the townspeople unroofed the building and filled it with sand to strengthen the wall against the assault of the enemy forces. Consequently the almost new frescoes were buried and preserved under the sand until they emerged practically undamaged when it was removed in the course of the archaeological excavation nearly 1700 years later. The building date is testified by an inscription in Aramaic recording that the synagogue was completed in 244–5; another inscription, in Greek, records that it was built by Samuel ben Idi, elder of the Jews, with the support of some of the congregation. The remains of another smaller, simpler, earlier synagogue were discovered underneath.[14]

The synagogue at Dura Europos remains to date a unique example of such a building east of Israel in the period of the Patriarchate. It is, therefore, impossible to determine whether it is representative of other synagogues of eastern Syria and upper Mesopotamia which have vanished or are as yet undiscovered. It is, however, doubtful that it could have been an isolated example because it appears to represent a developed stage of a decorative style.

The minority Jewish community in the third century presumably had the usual contact of the Diaspora congregations with the Patriarchate in Tiberias, and they were possibly also in touch with the great Babylonian academy directed by Rabbi Samuel at Nehardea, 400 kilometres away, but they may nevertheless have been outside the mainstream of Jewish life, thought and teaching, in the hybridized environment of Dura. The inscriptions in the synagogue in Aramaic and Greek indicate that the Jewish community was bilingual or at least that its membership included speakers of both languages. A duality of cultural influence is very evident in the costumes of the biblical characters depicted in the tiers of pictorial frescoes on panels which decorate the walls of the synagogue prayer-room: some are dressed in draped white Greco-Roman robes, the women resembling Hellenistic city-goddesses; the Israelite host like Roman legionaries; others are shown in tailored Parthian costume – a belted knee-length tunic with side-slashes and trousers tucked into soft boots. In one scene the souls of the dead are depicted as Greek Psyches with butterfly wings; in another, Aaron the High Priest is very oriental in trousers and an embroidered cloak with a large clasp.

Under the synagogue an earlier one was found, apparently dating from the second century. When the new synagogue was built in 245 the earlier one was partially demolished. Both synagogues were realized by the adaptation of private dwellings; their architectural idiom is local and domestic, box-like, with high walls and a flat roof. The prayer-room of the earlier synagogue measured 10.85 × 4.6 m; it was frescoed with geometric designs and fruit and floral motifs. A bench ran along the walls and in the west wall was a niche which could have been the Torah shrine. Off the courtyard was a larger room with benches which was probably a school. The main prayer-room was enlarged by incorporating part of another house, so that its dimensions became 13.65 × 7.68 m; the prayer-hall was 7 m in height. The wall-benches were extended in the new building and a small, stepped bimah was constructed adjacent to the Ark niche on the west wall; the entrances were in the east wall. It has been calculated that the synagogue could seat about sixty-five persons. There is no satis-

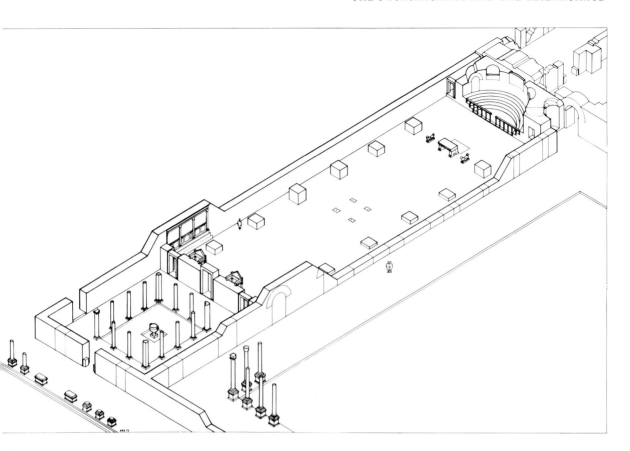

ardis synagogue, Turkey.
ometric reconstruction.

factory evidence that any accommodation was provided for women although it has been suggested that the benches with foot-rests were for the men and a section without were for women. Such an arrangement seems unlikely.

Painters of modest artistic ability but adept in projecting complex visual narratives decorated the walls. Their work, which has its origins in diverse pictorial traditions – Palmyrene, Roman and Parthian (Iranian) – reflects the importance of imagery in this place of worship. The community appears to have had no inhibitions about decoration which included human figures in their synagogues. The biblical scenes are vivid, especially Ezekiel and the dry bones and the story of Queen Esther, but they do not follow any apparent theological sequence. A menorah and a representation of the Herodian Temple painted above the niche draw attention to the shrine as the synagogue's focal point.

The synagogue discovered at Sardis in Turkey was already in use by the third century. Unlike the Dura synagogue which was built in a residential quarter and was externally inconspicuous, the Sardis synagogue, which served a large and influential Jewish community living under the Roman administration in Anatolia, was located in a prominent situation in the civic centre and was remarkably elegant. According to a decree recorded by Josephus, the city authorities had already agreed to allocate a place for a synagogue to the Jewish *politeuma* about 45 BCE (see p. 16). In Anatolia in the third century the Jews participated fully in the economic, social, political and cultural life of the country of their residence. Nine of the donors mentioned in mosaic inscriptions in the synagogue

were civic authorities, *bouleutai* (city councillors); two others were civil servants in the Roman provincial administration, *boethoi taboulariou* (record keepers); another had held the important post of procurator, *apo epitropon*, while yet another was described by the title of *comes* (Count).[15]

When Sardis was rebuilt after an earthquake in CE 17 the foundations of the ambitious building complex, a monumental Roman bath-gymnasium, were laid in a choice section of the city with an adjacent elegant colonnaded avenue of shops. The sizeable and obviously affluent Jewish community was able to procure the south-east corner of the complex – three rooms which had been destined to serve as part of the gymnasium palaestra. The extant Roman structure was converted into a basilical assembly hall with an apse and a small vestibule. By the third century the completed building was certainly in use as a synagogue without the dividing wall of the vestibule. In the latter half of the fourth century the building was further modified: an axial peristyle forecourt was created at the entrance end.

Originally the synagogue had three external doors; after the creation of the forecourt two of these were blocked in and three internal doors were made in the new wall between the forecourt and the prayer-hall. In this final form the synagogue measured 54 m in length from the entrance wall to the apse; it was symmetrical about its long axis, with two rows of columns placed near the long walls creating a broad nave and very

Ruins of the synagogue discovered in 1961 at Ostia Antica near Rome.

narrow aisles. Three concentric tiers of benches in the apse must have served for the Elders of the synagogue, who would thus have faced Jerusalem when seated there. No other trace of masonry seats or benches has been found. It appears that the rest of the assembly stood or were seated on the ground, unless there were movable wooden benches, which seems unlikely. The synagogue, which could accommodate a thousand people, had no single focal point; some of the inscriptions are read facing east, others facing west, which indicates that in the original building a portable Ark was used. Two aedicular shrines built against the Jerusalem-oriented entrance wall at the time of the fourth-century modifications may have been made to serve as a permanent repository for the Torah scrolls. Four marble slabs in the centre of the basilica which also date from the fourth-century modifications apparently supported a bimah.

The synagogue floor was paved with mosaic, the lower part of the walls was decorated with panels of marble intarsia, and there is epigraphical evidence of paintings in the synagogue, presumably frescoes on the upper part of the walls. The function of the massive marble table with eagles carved on its supports and flanked by free-standing lions is uncertain; it stood in the first bay in front of the apse. No counterpart of this table has been discovered in other early synagogues. If the hall was also used by the community for purposes other than worship, the table could have served a tribunal.

As at Dura, there is no trace of any permanent partition for women; there were no formal arrangements for classrooms or guest accommodation except for a suite of rooms to the west reached through a small chamber and a narrow passage, seemingly of late date, roughly hewn through the thick wall. Water installations in one of these rooms indicate that it may have served as a *mikveh*. This synagogue served the Jews of the community for nearly two centuries after the demise of the Patriarchate, until CE 616 when Sardis was raided and devastated by the Persians.

In the spring of 1961 during the construction of a new *autostrada* to Rome's Leonardo da Vinci International Airport, near the coast at Fiumicino, the remains of an important building which proved to be a synagogue were discovered. Its site was on the edge of the ancient port-town of Ostia, near the water and beside the Via Severiana. Careful excavation and examination of the ruins enabled the archaeologists to determine the original ground-plan of a building of the first century CE and the disposition of subsequent modifications and additions, and they were able partially to reconstruct the synagogue. The first-century date for the original building is evidenced by the workmanship of its walls in *opus reticulatum*;[16] the alterations of the fourth century were in *opus vittatum*, horizontal rows of small tufaceous bricks. A coin of the reign of the Emperor Maxentius (CE 306–312) found in a wall which was part of the modification work between the vestibule and adjacent hall indicates that the changes were made after that date.[17] While there is no proof that the first building was constructed as a synagogue, it is likely that this was the case; the entrance front is directed to the south-east, precisely in the direction of Jerusalem.

The first building was a spacious rectangular hall, slightly curved at the end, measuring 24.9 × 12.5 m; beside it and communicating with it at the front end, was another hall, 10.5 × 6.2 m, which once had masonry benches against the walls. The doors at the front gave access to the side hall and a tripartite entrance with a larger central doorway gave access to the main hall, which was divided at about one-third of its length by a propylaeum and flanking transverse walls so that the front part of the hall formed a vestibule and the back part, beyond the propylaeum, the prayer-room proper. The adjacent hall would have been a *bet midrash* (study-hall) and may also have served as a *bet din* (rabbinical court). In front of the building was a sort of narthex from which, through an important entrance at one side, a flight of steps communicated with the Via Severiana. There was also a well in the narthex. At the end of the hall against the curved wall and facing the propylaeum was a podium with steps, 79 cm in height. This appears to have been the bimah. The propylaeum itself was a monumental element of the building, 4.3 m in width and 3.2 m in length; four marble columns 4.7 m in height with Corinthian capitals stood at the angles of this imposing entrance-way.

Presumably before the modifications the Torah scrolls were brought in and out in a mobile Ark. A slab with an inscription in Latin and Greek was discovered in the *opus sectile* floor of the vestibule; it appears to date from the second century, and must have been laid in the floor when a permanent Torah repository in masonry was built at the time of the fourth-century modifications. The inscription reads '*Pro Salute Aug ...* οιχοδομησεν χε αιπσησεν εχ τῶν αυτου δοματων χαι την χειβωτον ἀνέθηχεν νόμῳ ἁγίῳ. Μινδις Φαῦστος'.[18] (For the health of Aug ... I constructed and donated at my own expense the Ark placed for the Holy Law. Mindis Faustos.) Here the Greek word χειβωτος used for the Ark implies that it was a wooden cabinet.

When the fairly extensive modifications were carried out in the fourth century the original vestibule was divided laterally into three chambers. The central one between the main entrance and the propylaeum, measuring 5.37 × 4.15 m, became the new vestibule. The chamber to the right, measuring 5.85 × 3.37 m, must have been the *mikveh*, as it contains a basin which could have been used for ablutions. The chamber to the left, 7.4 × 3.35 m, was paved with a mosaic floor: its use is uncertain but it communicated with the original side hall and, by a narrow corridor, with a large hall with built-in benches which was added at the side of the building. Changes were made to the original side hall; its benches were removed and a bread-oven was built in one corner. Professor Maria Floriani Squarciapino has suggested that this room was used by the communities for various purposes including the baking of the unleavened bread.[19] The new hall presumably became the study-hall.

Inside the prayer-hall changes were also made. A door was opened in the dividing wall to one side of the propylaeum to make an entrance to a small chamber which backed on to the *mikveh*. On the other side of the propylaeum the dividing wall was demolished to allow for the construction of an apsidal niche on a raised podium with steps, its back forming the rear wall of the chamber to the left of the vestibule. A sort of prostyle portico was constructed in front of the niche, projecting over its steps and consisting of two marble columns of the composite order supporting architraves on which are sculpted Jewish cult objects, the

OPPOSITE The reconstructed remai
of the imposing synagogue whi
dominated the little fishing town
Capharnaum in Galilee. Built at the e
of the fourth century, it replaced
earlier synagogue frequented
Jesus and Pet
FOLLOWING PAGES The façade of th
splendid ruined synagogue at K'
Birim in northern Galilee has a wea
of finely carved classical deta

ΖΩΙΛΟC
ΕΥΧΟΜΕ
ΝΟCΕΠΟΙΗ
CΕΝΖΗCΗ
ΚΑΛΙΝΙΚΟ
ΕΥΧΟΜΕ
ΝΟCΕΠΟΙΗ
CΕΝΖΗCΗ

menorah, the etrog, the lulav and the shofar. The inner architrave had to be cut so that it would fit against one of the columns of the already extant propylaeum. Undoubtedly this masonry construction was a fixed repository for the sacred scrolls. Its appearance as a fourth-century modification to the Sardis synagogue is of particular interest in the development of synagogue architecture and may help in understanding the arrangement for the Ark in contemporary synagogues in Erez Israel.

The synagogue complex at Ostia with the fourth-century additions covered 856 square metres and obviously served a prosperous community of several hundred persons. With its annexes it may have been the '*universitas Iudeorum*' or the '*col[onia] Ost[iensi]*' (university of the Jews of the col[ony] of Ost[ia]) mentioned in an inscription found at Castel Porziano. From inscriptions in the catacombs it is known that the Roman Jews under the Patriarchate enjoyed a well-defined administrative establishment with a gerusiarch, presbyters, archons and an archisynagogue.

At Stobi, in what was the Roman province of Macedonia, now part of Yugoslavia, the ruins of a synagogue were discovered, partly incorporated in a church which was built in the fifth or sixth century. On a column is a Greek inscription of which the first line, which may have contained an exact date, is unfortunately missing. The remainder of the thirty-two line inscription,[20] which appears to date from the end of the third century, is of interest as it illustrates the authority of the Patriarch in the scattered communities of the Diaspora. It reads in translation:

... KL. [CLAUDIOS] TIBERIOS POLYCHARMOS, ALSO NAMED ACHYRIOS, FATHER OF THE SYNAGOGUE AT STOBI, HAVING CONDUCTED MY WHOLE LIFE ACCORDING TO JUDAISM, IN FULFILMENT OF A VOW [ERECTED] THE BUILDINGS FOR THE HOLY PLACE AND THE TRICLINIUM WITH THE TRIPLE STOA WITH MY OWN MEANS WITHOUT IN THE LEAST TOUCHING THE SACRED [FUNDS]. THEREFORE, THE RIGHT OF DISPOSAL OF ALL THE UPPER CHAMBERS AND THEIR PROPRIETORSHIP SHALL BE RESTED IN ME KL. TIBERIOS POLYCHARMOS AND MY HEIRS FOR LIFE AND WHOSOEVER SHALL TRY IN ANY WAY TO ALTER ANY OF THESE MY DISPOSITIONS SHALL PAY UNTO THE PATRIARCH 250,000 DENARII. FOR THUS I HAVE RESOLVED. BUT THE REPAIR OF THE TILED ROOF OF THE UPPER CHAMBERS SHALL BE CARRIED OUT BY ME AND MY HEIRS.

OPPOSITE Detail of one of the panels of fourth-century mosaic floor in the synagogue at Hammath-by-Tiberias, Israel, showing one of the pair of lions which flank a Greek inscription.

It seems that by the 'triclinium' the donor meant a room with built-in benches along three of its sides and it may be inferred from the term 'triple stoa' that the prayer-hall itself was basilical and divided into a nave and flanking aisles by two rows of columns.

This plan recalls that of the synagogue whose foundations were discovered at Miletus in Greece; it had an axial peristyle courtyard with benches along three walls. Originally this building had had three doorways at the east end off the courtyard. The central doorway was larger than the side ones, which were blocked by the end columns of the two rows when these were added to the original building. In the absence of epigraphical or other evidence the date of this ancient synagogue remains uncertain, as does that of another synagogue discovered in Ionia, at Priene – a basilica, of which the stylobates survive, with a small forecourt. Along the north wall there was a masonry bench and in the east wall, directed towards Jerusalem, a niche for the Ark. A sculpted stone slab with a menorah, etrog, lulav and shofar, discovered in the course of excavation, must have belonged to this synagogue.

The locations of many other synagogues of the Diaspora under the Patriarchate are known from documentary and epigraphical evidence, in Asia Minor, in Greece and the Balkans, in Sicily and in Italy, and in North Africa as far as Tipasa in Mauritania. Archaeologists have discovered others, like the synagogue at Leptis Magna in Libya or the one at Apamea in central Syria which was found beneath a Christian church and which has a Greek inscription in its mosaic floor[21] reading (in translation): 'IN THE TIME OF THE MOST ILLUSTRIOUS PRESBYTERS ISAKIOS, SAULOS AND THE OTHERS, ILASIOS ARCHISYNAGOGUE OF THE ANTIOCHIANS MADE THE ENTRANCE OF MOSAIC ... IN THE YEAR 703, THE 7TH DAY OF AUDYNAIOS. BLESSINGS UPON ALL.' This corresponds to the year CE 391.

Unfortunately few dated inscriptions have been found in early synagogues although there are very numerous inscriptions naming donors. An inscription in the mosaic floor of a synagogue at Gaza bears a date corresponding to the year CE 508–9;[22] an Aramaic inscription in the floor at Beth Alpha, Hefzibah, records its construction in the time of the Emperor Justin, which could mean either ruler of this name, therefore CE 518–27 or CE 565–78.[23] A third dated inscription found in a synagogue in Erez Israel is on a lintel of the synagogue of Nabreten in Galilee;[24] it records that '... FOUR HUNDRED AND NINETY–FOUR YEARS AFTER THE DESTRUCTION [OF THE TEMPLE] THE HOUSE WAS BUILT DURING THE OFFICE OF HANINA SON OF LEZER AND LULIANA SON OF YUDAN'; that is to say in the year CE 564. A later date appears on a marble slab found at Ascalon[25] where the inscription in Greek names the benefactors of a holy place, apparently a synagogue; the date corresponds to CE 604.

Slab sculpted with a menorah discovered in the course of excavations on the site of the ancient synagogue at Priene, Greece.

The dating by archaeologists on stylistic grounds alone has been proved unsatisfactory in the case of some excavations in Erez Israel. The discovery of many coins of identifiable regnal years under the floor and foundations of the synagogue at Capharnaum has proved that it was built in the last years of the Patriarchate, at the very end of the fourth century if not at the beginning of the fifth. Previously it had been considered on stylistic and historical grounds to have been built at least 100 or even 200 years earlier than that. Imaginative guides who have read only the conclusions of the earliest investigators may still be heard occasionally assuring parties of visitors that the ruins are those of the first-century synagogue associated with the ministry of Jesus. It is now clear that different styles were adopted concurrently, that the choice of style was arbitrary, and that not infrequently anachronistic synagogue buildings were constructed in an archaic style. It is also true that differing practices regarding sacred directionality obtained at the same time, as did differing practices regarding the placing of the Torah scrolls and the Ark. Therefore it is rash in the absence of any incontrovertible evidence to be dogmatic about building dates or stylistic sequences.

Synagogue building did not come to an end in Erez Israel with the abolition of the Patriarchate, nor did it decline. Indeed, many imposing synagogues were built after the beginning of the fifth century by Jewish communities who managed to survive the restrictions on synagogal wor-

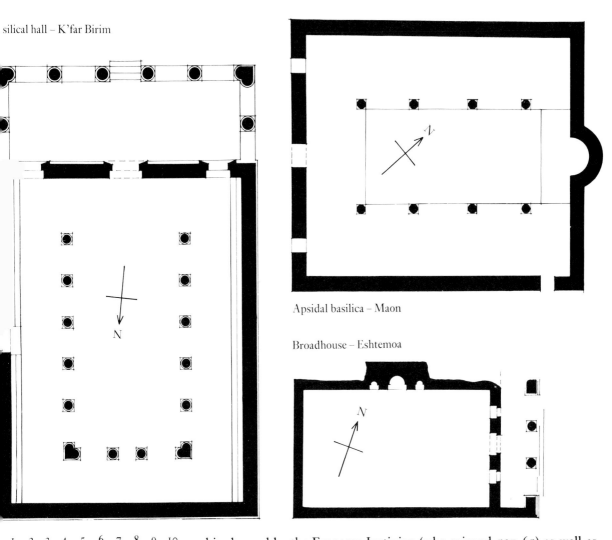

Apsidal basilica – Maon

Broadhouse – Eshtemoa

1 2 3 4 5 6 7 8 9 10
metres

arly synagogue types in Erez Israel.

ship decreed by the Emperor Justinian (who reigned 527–65) as well as the general interference by the Christian Byzantine rulers in internal Jewish affairs and even in the synagogue service. The architecture, and in particular the Byzantine mosaic floors, of the fifth- and sixth-century synagogues do, however, reflect the omnipresent alien culture in a period when the remnants of the pagan deities contended against Christianity, Judaism and the mystery faiths as the classical world slowly faded away.

Three main types of ancient synagogues can be distinguished in Erez Israel: an oblong building like that of the Babylonian synagogue of Dura Europos, usually with a Torah niche in one long wall directed towards Jerusalem (this type is usually referred to as a 'broadhouse'); a rectangular basilical hall with a nave and flanking aisles, usually with the entrance wall directed towards Jerusalem; and an apsidal basilica often with an atrium and a narthex, the building type adopted for Christian churches but with the apse directed towards Jerusalem and not to the east. The broadhouse has been described as a transitional style but the revised dating of the Capharnaum synagogue indicates that the broadhouse (which was used at Dura in the third century) was in fact a parallel type, a contemporary alternative to the basilical hall and the apsidal basilica.

Two good examples of the broadhouse synagogue are to be found south of Jerusalem in Judaea, perched on hill-tops only three miles distant from one another as the crow flies, at Eshtemoa (Es-Samu) and Khirbet

Susiya. At Eshtemoa the entrance was through a colonnaded portico and three doors in the east wall. A niche in the north wall pointing towards Jerusalem apparently housed the Torah scrolls; thus both the requirements of the Ark being in the direction of the Holy City and of an eastern entrance were fulfilled: the floor was paved with non-figurative mosaic. It appears that this synagogue was built in the sixth century and remained in use as such at least until the tenth, but hardly until the arrival of the Crusaders, who left their mark at Eshtemoa. The same plan was used in the synagogue at Susiya which also remained in use until a late date; here the Ark repository was on a monumental stepped podium and the decorative mosaic floor included a representation of a classical pedimented Ark between two menorot.

On a panoramic mountain top near Meiron in Galilee, a few metres from the tomb of Rabbi Shemai who lived in the first century BCE, are the remains of another broadhouse synagogue but with interior columns and entrances on the north and west walls, stone benches against the walls, and a stone platform near the south wall which appears to have been the bimah. A synagogue of the broadhouse type, later drastically changed, was built at Hammath-by-Tiberias under the Patriarchate and apparently before the end of the fourth century.

Of the Galilean synagogues undoubtedly the most renowned is that of Capharnaum and it is unfortunate that it has been subjected to some heavy-handed restoration. The early misconceptions about its plan have

Section of a cornice of the Capharnaum synagogue carved with the Magen D

Stone cathedra, the seat of honour from the ancient synagogue of Chorazin in Galilee.

not been entirely dispelled, and while some of the wall which was incorrectly reconstructed some years ago is still *in situ*, further reconstruction has gone ahead with a bold and lavish use of cement so that it will be increasingly hard for future generations to understand the true original arrangements or to correct any errors that may have been made. The site of the ancient town of Capharnaum including the synagogue was purchased by the Order of the Friars Minor of Saint Francis, so most of the excavation and restoration of the site has been handled by Italian Franciscan archaeologists with some financial assistance from the Italian government. It did not perhaps augur well when the name and achievements of Father Orfali, who directed the work for many years, were inscribed on one of the columns of the synagogue with more sentiment than discretion. Father Virgilio Corbo has, however, made some invaluable discoveries in trenches cut under the floor and foundations of the synagogue with his colleagues Father Stanislao Loffreda, who classified the ceramic finds, and Father Augusto Spijkerman, a numismatist who catalogued the coin finds.[26]

As a result of their work it seems indisputable that the synagogue must have been built at the close of the fourth century and probably not completed until the beginning of the fifth. This means that it was erected under the Christian Emperors, and only a few paces from the house of the apostle Peter which had been converted into a church and was so described by Etheria, a Spanish Christian pilgrim who visited Capharnaum at the beginning of the fifth century[27] when the synagogue had just been built or was being completed. In the middle years of the fifth century an octagonal Christian basilica was built on the site of Peter's house.[28] The rift between the Jewish and Christian populations in this small town was not therefore serious at the beginning of the fifth century despite the presence there of Judaeo-Christians, referred to in rabbinical sources as *minim* (heretics), who exasperated the Jewish and Christian authorities alike. It is not clear where the Judaeo-Christians would have assembled to worship in a small town like Capharnaum in which a synagogue and a *domus-ecclesia* stood in close proximity to one another. St John Chrysostom pronounced homilies at Antioch in 386 condemning Christians who frequented the synagogues on Jewish feast-days, observed the Jewish Sabbath, practised circumcision, and celebrated Easter on the fourteenth of Nisan.[29] Other Christian authorities of the period were obliged to exhort the faithful not to frequent Jewish synagogues. St Gregory of Nyssa reported from Jerusalem that he had met Christians there who believed in the restoration of the Temple and of the blood sacrifices.[30] It is likely therefore that at Capharnaum in the fifth century the Judaeo-Christian population frequented the synagogue, especially on feast-days, as well as assembling in the *domus-ecclesia* on the site of Peter's house in which a Judaeo-Christian interpolation has been found among the graffiti,[31] of which there are 110 in Greek, ten in Aramaic, nine in Estrangelo script and two in Latin. A Greek inscription on a column of the synagogue records that it was erected by 'Herod [son] of Monimas and Justus [his] son together with their children'[32] and an Aramaic inscription on another that it was made by 'Halfu [Alphaeus] the son of Zebidah the son of Yochanan [John]'.[33]

Both in size and in the elegance of its decorative elements the Caphar-naum synagogue stands out as the most splendid yet found in Erez Israel. A rectangular basilical hall 20.4 × 18.65 m with rows of columns parallel to its east, west and north walls, it was constructed in a densely populated residential area of the ancient town on an artificial platform raised over dwellings which were demolished after the middle of the fourth century, certainly not earlier than 341.[34] The synagogue was conspicuous not only because of its height and dominant position above the insignificant dwell-ings of the streets which immediately surrounded it but also because it was constructed not of the local black basalt but of white limestone which resembles marble. Side benches ran along the east and west walls and a door in the east wall gave access to an enclosed courtyard with a sur-rounding roofed portico on three sides; it may have served as a *bet midrash*. At one time it was thought that the prayer-hall had a gallery, but this idea must be practically discarded as the foundations were not strong enough to support an upper storey. The main access to the syna-gogue was through three doors with finely carved lintels and consoles on the south side directed towards Jerusalem. Between the central door and the side doors the foundations of two structures have been found.

The sophisticated carving of the cornice includes motifs from both the Judaic repertoire (five- and seven-branched menorot, the shofar, the lulav, five- and six-pointed stars, pomegranates, palm leaves, palm trees) and the classical (shells, Greek fretwork, garlands, eagles, mythical crea-tures like the griffin and the sea-horse). The sculptor was not inhibited in the representation of animals, which cannot then have been considered inimical or offensive to Jewish belief, but subsequently the animal figures were attacked by iconoclasts. Of particular interest is a piece of the frieze sculpted with a shrine on wheels, apparently a mobile Ark.

Although Capharnaum was the most imposing, there were other hand-some synagogues of the basilical-hall type, similar to it in plan and pre-sumably of about the same period. In the hills north of Capharnaum the black basalt ruins of the synagogue of Chorazin may be seen. A ruined synagogue at Chorazin is mentioned in the fourth century by Eusebius[35] and again by Petrus Diaconus in the twelfth century. A rectangular basili-cal hall, 20 × 13 m, it had like the Capharnaum synagogue three rows of columns parallel to the east, west and north walls, masonry benches along the east and west walls and a tripartite entrance facing south towards Jeru-salem. The sculptured reliefs at Chorazin featured human figures includ-ing a Hercules and a scene of vintagers treading grapes, as well as animals, flowers, foliage, and a head of Medusa. There were even three-dimensional ornaments – lions, symbols of Judah, sculpted in black basalt. A cathedra, apparently the seat of honour of the archisynagogue, discovered at Chorazin bears an inscription in Aramaic[36] which reads in translation: 'REMEMBERED BE FOR GOOD YUDAN SON OF ISHMAEL WHO MADE THIS STOA AND ITS STAIRCASE. AS HIS REWARD MAY HE HAVE A SHARE WITH THE RIGHTEOUS.'

On a hill-top at Meiron in Galilee a synagogue of similar plan was built against an outcrop of rock. Two doorways of its tripartite entrance directed towards Jerusalem survive. An inscription records that the build-ing was erected by 'SHALOM SON OF LEVI'.[37] At Bar'am (K'far Birim)

OPPOSITE Meiron, Israel. The façade of the synagogue built on a hill-top in Galilee by Shalom son of Levi in the fourth century. The monumental doorway faces Jerusalem.

BELOW Basalt capital, part of the synagogue excavated at Katzrin.

Detail of the splendid polychrome mosaic floor of the synagogue at Hammath-by-Tiberias in Galilee. The Greek sun god Helios is depicted the centre of an animated zodiac.

Central entrance and ruins of the ancient synagogue discovered at Katzrin in the Golan Heights.

in north Galilee near the frontier of Lebanon are the substantial remains of another synagogue (18.1 × 13.95 m) of this type; it had a colonnaded portico in front of the tripartite entrance which faced towards Jerusalem.

A German engineer made the first archaeological survey of surface finds in the Golan in 1884–6 and listed twelve sites with Jewish symbols. Israeli archaeological surveys conducted since 1967 have explored over one hundred sites. Among the most interesting synagogue ruins are those at Dabbura, at Yahudiyya (where a Jewish community lived until the thirteenth century and was visited by travellers who saw the synagogue), at Fik, and at Katzrin. The Katzrin synagogue, a rectangular hall 18 × 15.4 m built on a north–south axis with the entrance in the north wall, had two tiers of benches made of smoothed basalt blocks 40 cm high along its walls. Because of the durability of the basalt the scroll carving of the capitals, the work of local artisans in the Semitic Aeolic idiom (ancestor of Ionic), has been remarkably preserved. The columns and capitals of the building have been excavated, and the doorway – 1.9 m in height, of hewn basalt with carved jambs and lintel – is *in situ*; it would not be difficult to achieve a reconstruction of this synagogue, which was only uncovered in 1967 and 1971.

Ruins of several apsidal basilicas have been found. In this type of synagogue, which was subsequent to the rectangular basilical-hall type, it was the apse rather than the entrance which was directed towards Jerusalem. An exception was the sixth-century synagogue of Beth Shean where the apse is on the north-west while Jerusalem is to the south. In the synagogue at Jerash (Gerasa) in Transjordan, found beneath the ruins of a Christian church which was built over it in CE 530, the square apse was separated from the body of the hall by a screen with columns, reminiscent of the chancel screen of a church. The ruins of another basilical synagogue with the apse pointed towards Jerusalem stand on a hill-top at Hammath Gader overlooking the valley of the Yarmuk, a place where Jewish leaders could meet without attracting attention on the pretext of taking the thermal waters. In this synagogue too a screen separated the apse from the nave; the floor was paved with mosaic. Another basilical synagogue with a Jerusalem-directed apse was found at Khirbet Kerak (Beth Yerah) on the shore of the Sea of Galilee and within the precincts of a Roman fort; its mosaic floor included a human figure, lions and a horse.

The synagogue of Hammath-by-Tiberias, originally a broadhouse building with a basalt flagstone floor, underwent several architectural modifications over the centuries, eventually being transformed into an apsidal basilica. On the evidence of pottery and coins found under the last of its marble floors, this synagogue remained in use until the tenth or the eleventh century.[38] In the course of modifications effected during the Islamic period the mosaic floor laid before the end of the Patriarchate was covered over; a wall of this period runs right across the brightly coloured figure of Helios the sun god in the centre of a splendid zodiac with the symbols of the twelve signs. This was one of three panels in the floor; another contains a Greek inscription between two lions and the third an Ark flanked by menorot and Judaic cult objects. An inscription names one Profuturos, who built part of the synagogue, and another, one Severus, an official of 'the most illustrious patriarchs'.[39]

Stone seats from the synagogue at Hammath Gader, Erez Israel, found when the hill-top site was excavated in 1932.

In the mosaic floor of the Jerash (Gerasa) synagogue, Noah is depicted with his family leaving the Ark, surrounded by animals and by the Judaic cult objects – menorah, etrog, lulav and shofar. One inscription in this floor appears to refer to the artists Pinehas, son of Baruch, Jose, son of Samuel, and Yudan, son of Hezekiah;[40] others name many donors of portions of the mosaic, such as Thaumasis with Hesychios his wife, their children and Eustathia his mother-in-law. Another biblical story, that of Daniel in the lions' den, is depicted in the mosaic floor of a synagogue near the ancient city of Jericho which was discovered when an Austrian shell fired against the British in 1917 exploded a hillock at Ain-Duk, the ancient settlement of Na'aran; it was excavated in 1921 by the Ecole Biblique et Archéologique Française, Jerusalem, of the Order of St Dominic. As well as the Daniel scene the mosaic contained Judaic emblems, zoomorphic motifs, foliage, and a zodiac with epigraphic designation of the signs. Subsequently iconoclasts deliberately defaced the human and animal figures. Aramaic inscriptions in archaic Hebrew characters set in various parts of the floor name some of the benefactors of the building, Pinehas the priest, son of Josiah who gave 'THE PRICE OF THE MOSAIC OF HIS OWN MONEY', Rebecca wife of Pinehas, Khalifou daughter of Rabbi Safrah, and Benjamin the parnas, son of Joseph.[41]

The mosaic floor of the Ma'on synagogue near Nirim in south-west Israel, which was excavated in 1957, has a border of interlacing flowers pointing alternately inwards and outwards. This resembles the border of the Ain-Duk (Na'aran) mosaic, but at Ma'on the field is a panel of fifty-five medallions in eleven rows of five which form a sort of vine-trellis issuing from a vase flanked by peacocks in the first row and rising to a menorah flanked by lions and palm trees in the tenth and eleventh. The vine is a symbol of Israel and also of Jesus. Similar vine-trellis designs appear in the mosaic pavements of Christian churches; one example may be seen in a small chamber off the main hall of the Monastery of Lady Mary at Beth Shean, where the vine-trellis of medallions issuing from an amphora has been dated to the sixth century. At Ma'on the vertical axial row of medallions contains objects such as a basket of pomegranates, a bowl of fruit and a caged bird; the others contain beasts (elephant, bull, stag, eagle, ibex, buffalo, sheep) and birds (crane, goose, pheasant, flamingo, guinea-fowl, vulture, partridge and eagle). Although the ruined condition of the foundation of the Ma'on synagogue makes it difficult to determine its original plan with certitude, it appears that it was an apsidal basilica with the apse pointed north-east towards Jerusalem.[42] The mosaic pavement (10.2 × 5.4 m) was in the nave.

The fashion in synagogue mosaic, which in the earliest buildings contained only non-figurative geometric designs, changed; in the fourth, fifth and sixth centuries human and animal representation was not merely tolerated but favoured. The change in fashion is evident in particular in those synagogues where the early floor with a geometric design was later covered with a figurative one. An example of this can be seen at Ein Geddi where a rectangular bimah in front of the Torah niche was also constructed when the new floor was laid. It is clear that before the end of the Patriarchate figurative art was approved or at least tolerated in Erez Israel, as is testified by the floor of the Hammath-by-Tiberias synagogue and by the fourth-century Palestinian Talmudist, Rabbi Abun, who wrote that in his time figurative decoration was practised and allowed.[43] The fact that some floors with figurative decoration were later covered over (for example, Hammath-by-Tiberias) reflects a stricter attitude which coincided with the rise of gaonic (see p. 50) influence again under the Caliphate and the influence of the academy which again flourished at Tiberias in the eighth century. A basilical synagogue with an apse, discovered in the course of planting banana trees north-east of ancient Jericho in 1934, has a mosaic floor of the early period of Arab occupation. Here there is no human or animal representation: the artist limited himself to the Ark, Judaic cult objects, and geometric and floral designs.

The consistent representation of the Ark in the synagogue mosaics as a pedimented aedicule suggests that descriptions of the Shrine of the destroyed Temple were in circulation. In the modern synagogue at Peki'in in northern Galilee remnants salvaged from an ancient synagogue have been preserved and set in the walls. These include an Ark sculpted in relief, similar to those depicted in the synagogue mosaics.

Mosaic floors have also been found in synagogues of the early Diaspora. One was excavated on the Greek island of Aegina where a little synagogue was discovered, a rectangular chamber 13×7.6 m, with an apse in the east wall. Here the mosaic floor is entirely non-figurative: it is designed like a carpet with an all-over interlacing pattern within a central panel which is surrounded by a broad patterned border and a narrow terminal border, all in blue, red, grey and black. The building apparently remained standing until the seventh century.[44] The floor appears to have been laid in the fifth or sixth century: a Greek inscription at the entrance end records that '... THEODOROS THE ARCHISYNAGOGUE WHO FUNCTIONED FOR FOUR YEARS BUILT THIS SYNAGOGUE FROM ITS FOUNDATIONS. REVENUES AMOUNTED TO 85 PIECES OF GOLD AND OFFERINGS TO GOD TO 105 PIECES OF GOLD.'[45]

In North Africa, where the Emperor Justinian commanded in 533–4 that synagogues should be transformed into Christian churches, a mosaic synagogue floor was found in 1884 on the Hammam-Lif beach at Naro in Tunisia. This synagogue served one of the prosperous and cultured communities which existed in Tunisia where a large number of Jews had settled in the years immediately after the destruction of the Temple. Their numbers were augmented by their intensive proselytizing activity among the Punic and Berber populations. The Jewish communities had a well-organized administration. Women were admitted to the bosom of the community councils and a woman, Julia, was one of the principal benefactors of the Hammam-Lif synagogue. Fortunately the French officer who discovered the site made sketches of the floor – fragments have now been lost. The parts which were taken to Paris were acquired by the Brooklyn Museum, New York, where the original composition of the floor has been determined. The Hammam-Lif mosaic artists included an expert craftsman, skilled in working with tiny, irregularly shaped tesserae in a technique called *opus vermiculatum* which produces an excellent visual effect of shade and contour. This technique was employed for the human and animal heads in framed medallions which include a bust of a spear-carrying helmeted Amazon. Other sections of the floor which portray animals and plants, with a decorative panel showing a menorah between two Judaic cult objects in the centre, are in *opus tesselatum* – regularly shaped stone cubes of equal size: here the tints are subdued, since only natural coloured stone was used. At a more distant settlement of the Diaspora, Elche in Spain, the mosaic floor was found of a synagogue (10.9 × 7.55 m) with an eastern apse; it includes an inscription naming the leader of the community.[46]

Of the mosaic synagogue floors discovered in Erez Israel the best known are those of Beth Shean (which has been moved to the Israel Museum, Jerusalem) and of Beth Alpha, Hefzibah, about six kilometres apart and, according to inscriptions, the work of the same Jewish artists, Marianos and his son Hanina. The synagogue of Beth Alpha with its marvellous floor was discovered in 1928 when an irrigation ditch was being dug, and its excavation was financed by the congregation of the Temple Emanu-El, New York City.

Marianos and Hanina, like the designers of other mosaic synagogue floors of the period of the Byzantine rulers, belonged to a Judaic tradition which had absorbed much from the Greco-Christian world. The resemblance of some aspects of their work to the mosaics in the church of San Vitale at Ravenna in Italy (530–47) suggests that Ravenna-like mosaics

Detail of the scene depicting Abraham's sacrifice in the sixth-century mosaic floor of the synagogue at Beth Alpha, Hefzibah, Israel, the work of Jewish mosaicists named Marianos and Hanina.

may have existed in some Christian churches of the region, from which Marianos and Hanina, who worked in the sixth century, could have drawn inspiration. It is known that they worked in Beth Shean and their Hebrew zodiac in the Beth Alpha synagogue does recall the Greek zodiac in the monastery of Lady Mary at Beth Shean, founded about 567. However, even if it was subjected to these influences, the work of Marianos and Hanina at Beth Alpha does emerge as the work of original artists, Jews who belonged to a non-classical culture. Meyer Schapiro has aptly likened their brilliant work to that of a folk poet, the colours and shapes being deliberately shown not quite as they are, and he has pointed out their controlled fantasy of shapes, particularly noticeable in the scene of Abraham's sacrifice, where there is a peculiar liaison between the stripes of Abraham's robe, the lines of the altar and the flames, in a matching counterpoint of directions.[47] The floor is divided laterally into three panels. On entering, the worshipper was confronted by a religious idea – divine intervention by God in the life of man, shown in a representation of Abraham's sacrifice in which the hand of God directing the human drama is placed out of sequence in the top centre of the scene above a ram tied to a bush. It is of interest that this ram, which represents the ram which Abraham saw caught in a thicket by its horns, is depicted with only one horn, as is the ram in the zodiac panel – a reference by the Jewish artist to the shofar, the ram's horn of the priesthood. Abraham, although crudely drawn without regard to anatomical structure, is a bold, captivating, corpulent figure in a colobium, wearing shoes, and armed with a lethal-looking knife, his head cocked alertly. The theme of the central panel of the floor is the divine government of the universe, the heavenly order of nature, God's rule, shown by a zodiac circle with the symbols of the twelve months. Surrounding the zodiac are figures of women symbolizing the four seasons and drawn from the repertoire of pagan art. In the centre of the zodiac a youth riding a horse-drawn chariot symbolizes the sun; the moon and stars are in the background. The panel before the apse shows the sacredness of the shrine, the depository of the scrolls which contain God's word. In a carefully symmetrical composition the artists depict the Ark in the middle with a bird above the outer top corners of the decorated door panels. On each side is a lion below a giant menorah; disposed around them are the customary Judaic cult objects.

While the status and conditions of the Jews who remained in Palestine were slowly deteriorating under the rule of the Christian Byzantine Emperors, the Jews in Babylonia continued to enjoy a privileged measure of autonomy presided over by the Jewish government of the state-sanctioned Exilarch, who was the recipient of honours and prerogatives under the Persian Sassanid kings. The first Exilarch, who claimed Davidic descent, had been appointed by the Parthians about CE 100. The office endured until the eleventh century with the Exilarch in the role of a quasi-prince living surrounded by semi-royal pomp, wielding considerable power in his authority over a vast population of Jews who enjoyed full civil rights. These favourable political, social and economic conditions in Babylonia were, of course, conducive to the development of the Jewish academies there which grew and prospered, so the network of Jewish communal institutions remained intact.

The Babylonian Jews were active missionaries and their dissemination of a monotheistic ethos over a wide area as far as the Yemen was a factor, together with the missionary work of Christians in Arabia, in bringing about an indigenous Arabic monotheistic religion – Islam – which grew with amazing rapidity. The Moslems, whose armies rapidly overran not only the Middle East but also North Africa and the Iberian peninsula by the eighth century, respected the Jews as 'people of the Book' (the Bible) and they did not dismantle the Jewish administrative structure which had developed under the Sassanid kings, or interfere with internal Jewish affairs. The Caliphs recognized the authority and jurisdiction of the Exilarch and through him that of the Babylonian *gaonim*, the chiefs of the Jewish academies of Sura and Pumbeditha, to whom the Exilarch assigned the contributions which flowed in from the communities of the Diaspora for their support. Therefore, although the Palestinian *gaonim* at Tiberias were able to exert their influence and gain recognition in Syria, Egypt and Spain in the ninth century, between the tenth and twelfth centuries the Babylonian rabbinate became the official mediators of Jewish legal and theological matters for the Jewish communities of the Diaspora in all the lands under Moslem sway, and Babylonian Judaism became generally adopted as authentic Judaism.

The Babylonian *gaonim* opposed with severity any deviation and combated the Karaite heresy which challenged rabbinical law and authority in the ninth century, but they were unable to halt the dissemination among Jews of Greek philosophy, and of science in Arabic translation. In Persia there were sporadic revolts against exilarchic taxation and administration, while with the development of local schools and talent among the wealthy Jewish communities living in North Africa and Spain lay the grounds for dissidence and open questioning of gaonic absolutism. The translation of the Bible and of scriptural commentaries into Arabic in the tenth century by the Egyptian-born Gaon of Sura, Sa'adia ben Joseph al-Fayyumi, made the scriptures accessible to a very large number of Jews who spoke only Arabic, and contributed to the spread of spiritual, intellectual and theological self-sufficiency throughout Egypt, Tunisia and Spain.

Little is known of the architecture or appearance of the synagogues of Babylonia. The discovery of the synagogue at Dura Europos in eastern Syria in the present century leaves hope that further east the remains of other synagogues may be found of the many that must have flourished there under the Sassanids and the Caliphate in a thousand years and more of Jewish autonomy after the destruction of the Temple.

It is in Spain in the Middle Ages, in Egypt and in Iran that synagogue buildings and parts of synagogue buildings have been found which reflect that Golden Age of Judaeo-Arabic culture which reached its highest point under the Western Caliphate in Andalusia. This was to provide the source for the Moorish Revival style in synagogue architecture in Europe and North America in the nineteenth century.

The Jews in Italy and those who had settled in central and western Europe by the Middle Ages derived their cultural orientation from a different source, the Latin-Christian civilization of Italy and Palestine, and they were to follow this tradition when they built their houses of worship.

3 *The Middle Ages*

The Jewish merchant-traveller Benjamin of Tudela, in the account of his travels[1] of several years' duration from his home-town of Navarre to at least as far as Mesopotamia, whence he returned in 1173, left a lively record of the Jewish communities which he visited as he crossed southern Europe. Italy at that time had a sizeable Jewish population, mostly living in the southern part of the peninsula and in Sicily. Despite times of serious difficulty (such as when the Byzantine Emperor Basil I, involved in the struggle between Christians and Moslems, in 873–4 forbade the Jewish cult in his Italian dominions and ordered the conversion of all Jews) the Jewish communities in southern Italy contrived to prosper until the end of the fifteenth century when, under Spanish domination, they were all banished. After the death of Basil I in 886 his severe measures were no longer implemented, and usually when decrees were pronounced against them by the sovereign or the ecclesiastical authorities, the Jewish communities were able to buy off their enforcement. The wealth of the Jews, who were widely engaged in silk-weaving and cloth-dyeing as well as other lucrative trades, was considerable. Robert Guiscard, the Norman adventurer who drove the Byzantines from the south of Italy and laid the groundwork for the Norman kingdom in Sicily, gave the taxes of the Jews of Bari to his wife as her dowry. After his death in 1085, she gave them to the Archdiocese of Bari and those of the Jews of Palermo to the Archbishop of that city in 1089. Frequently Jews ceded to the pressure exerted by the Church and converted to Christianity. In the Apulian port-town of Trani, where Benjamin of Tudela had found 200 Jewish families in the 1160s, there were as many as 870 families of neophyte Christians in 1443, still living ambiguously in the Jewish quarter. There were also a few conversions in the other direction: the most prominent was at Bari, a centre of Jewish scholarship, where in about 1072 the Archbishop became a Jew. He was obliged, in consequence, to quit the country, as was a Norman noble who accepted Judaism in the south of Italy in 1102.

In Sicily, which was invaded by the Saracens and governed from 827 to 1061 by Moslem emirs dependent on Tunisia and Egypt, the Jews fared better than on the Italian mainland. The Arab–Moslem culture in Sicily outlasted the Emirate. Arabic was still widely used under the subsequent rule of the Christian Norman kings; many of the Normans even became proficient in the language, among them King William II, who read, wrote and spoke Arabic fluently. The Sicilian Christian women continued to go about veiled in the Moslem fashion and stained their fingers with henna. When the Capella Palatina, the royal chapel of the Norman monarchs, was built at Palermo in 1140, Arab–Moslem painters were engaged with others to decorate its interior. In this hybrid cultural environment, Italic, Byzantine, Arab–Moslem and Norman, the Jews seemed less alien than in the north and under the Norman rulers in Sicily they enjoyed full rights of citizenship.

Palermo had the largest Jewish population in the island, larger also than that of any town on the Italian mainland. Benjamin of Tudela found about 1500 Jewish families living there in the 1170s, so there must have been about 8000 Jews out of a total urban population of around 100,000. Strange as it may seem now, the synagogues in Sicily were usually called mosques. In 1403, long after the Arabs had been vanquished, the

PREVIOUS PAGE The harmonio
interior of the synagogue built at Tole
about 1200 and later turned int
church dedicated to Santa Maria
Blanca. The plan and workmanship is
the tradition of Islamic architectu
in Spai

OPPOSITE The magnificent hill-top si
of this Galilean broadhouse-typ
synagogue at Khirbet Shema w
revered as the burial place of the firs
century sage Rabbi Shemai. On this hil
according to tradition, the Messiah w
stand on a rock, 'The Throne of t
Messiah', and blow a shofar
announce the redemption of the worl

FOLLOWING PAG
LEFT Page from a biblical text dat
1301, illuminated in Provence, southe
France. (Now in the Royal Librar
Copenhagen
RIGHT Detail of the Ark doors of th
German synagogue, Venice, donated b
Rabbi Menahem Cividale in th
seventeenth centur

כל אלה בהיות הכל על מכונו ומקום שדקרש

תקון וחבורתו ואשר יהכהו יגיע ראותיה

registers of the royal chancellery referred to the synagogues at Trapani as '*moschee ovvero sinagoghe*'[2] (mosques, or alternatively synagogues), and employed the same term for the new synagogue built at Palermo in 1467. In 1343 the synagogue at Marsala was described in the registers of the royal chancellery as '*una piccola Timisia ovvero Sinagoga*'.[3] The meaning and etymology of '*Timisia*' are uncertain.

Under the Angevin kings who came to power in Sicily in 1265, restrictions were imposed on the construction of new synagogue buildings or the enlargement of existing ones. In 1366 the monk Fra Nicola of Palermo was instructed by the monarch, Frederick III, to survey all the synagogues in Sicily; three years later the Dominican Inquisitor, Fra Simone del Pozzo, was ordered to have any new synagogue buildings pulled down. In 1347, at Messina, as a result of a blood libel in which the Jews were accused of murdering a boy, their synagogue was transformed into a chapel dedicated to the Beata Vergine della Candelaja[4] (Blessed Virgin of the Candelabra), apparently a reference to the menorah of the synagogue building (see also p. 86). Permission was sometimes granted for a new building or an enlargement; frequently the authorities exacted a payment in return for the permit. The Jews of Marsala, who comprised one-tenth of the population, pleaded in 1373 that their number had increased and that they could not all fit into their little building; they were granted permission to enlarge it in 1375.[5] After the expulsion of 1492 this synagogue was converted into a church dedicated to the Beata Vergine Sedes Sapientiae[6] (Blessed Virgin, Seat of Wisdom), perhaps a reference to the former use of the synagogue also as a place of instruction. In 1361 the Jews of Castrogiovanni were allowed to build a new synagogue within the city walls in place of their old one. In 1486 a new Jewish colony at Militello was authorized to build a synagogue for its use and in the same year the Viceroy permitted the Jews of Santa Lucia to enlarge their synagogue as long as it was not made to look better than a church. Only four months before the order of expulsion from Sicily in August 1492 the Viceroy issued a permit for a synagogue at Termini near Palermo.[7]

The ecclesiastical authorities were quick to complain about any infringement of the regulations. In 1455, at the express request of Pope Calixtus III, King Alfonso had the synagogue at Taormina closed because the chanting there disturbed the Dominicans in their convent nearby.[8]

A serious survey of the medieval synagogues of Italy and Sicily has yet to be made. In 1977 the remains of a synagogue and *mikveh* with Hebrew inscriptions were discovered underneath a baroque church at Syracuse in the course of repairs to the church. Undoubtedly the remnants of many synagogues could be discovered under, or incorporated into, later buildings, or transformed into churches. At Trani in Apulia, where four synagogues are said to have been converted into churches, there is a Hebrew synagogue inscription in one, now named Sant' Anna; another was given the name Santa Maria Scolanova (New School), apparently the actual former name of the synagogue itself – the term *scola, scuola* (school) being commonly used in Italy for the synagogue, just as *schul* was used in German. A *sinagoga hebraeorum*[9] of Naples was mentioned in 1097 and a second synagogue was completed in 1165, at which time, according to Benjamin of Tudela, 500 Jewish families were

OPPOSITE Silk paroketh embroidered for a Venetian synagogue by Stella Cohenet, wife of Izchak da Perugia, who died in 1673. It was possibly inspired by El Greco's triptych of Mount Sinai.

living there. After the expulsion of the Jews the principal synagogue of Naples was converted into a church, Santa Caterina Spinacorona, later renamed Santa Maria della Purificazione. At Salerno, south of Naples, Benjamin of Tudela encountered the largest Jewish community on the Italian mainland – 600 families; at Capua near Naples he found 300 Jewish families, the same number in the southern port-city of Taranto, and at Otranto, where he embarked, 500.

Unfortunately, descriptions of the medieval synagogues of Sicily and the mainland of Italy are scant, although it is known from documentary evidence that there were many, not only in towns but also in villages. In Sicily it appears that the synagogue architecture was a blend of Byzantine and Saracen styles. Rabbi Obadiah da Bertinoro, from Forlì in northern central Italy, visited Palermo in 1487 and described the synagogue there as the most grandiose in Sicily and more sumptuous than any on the Italian mainland; in fact he considered that it 'had not its equal in the whole world'.[10] When 'La Moschita', as it was known, was built in 1467 the Jews had been fined for exceeding the permitted dimensions. A hostel-hospital, a community house and a *mikveh* were included in the synagogue complex, which was situated close to where the convent church of San Nicola da Tolentino of the Discalced Augustinians later stood, and near to the Palazzo Senatorio. According to Rabbi Obadiah the synagogue was surrounded by two courtyards, the outer one enclosed by a vineclad colonnade, the inner one sunken, with a fountain in the middle and marble seats. The synagogue building, at the back of the three-sided inner colonnade, was a square edifice, forty cubits square (about 22.5 m square) decorated with marble revetment, marquetry, tapestries and silver ornaments. The bimah was a wooden platform in the centre of the room, and the Ark was a domed structure at the eastern end. Rabbi Obadiah remarked on the custom there on Yom Kippur and Hoshan Rabbah of reopening the doors of the Ark after the service when the women entered on one side, prostrated themselves before the Ark, kissed the Torah scrolls, and went out on the opposite side. Rabbi Obadiah also visited a similar synagogue at Messina which was 'not as large ... but very beautiful'. Although he does not state that these square buildings were covered by a dome it is likely that they were archaic in style when built, cubes with Saracenic domes, resembling the Cuba of King William II at Palermo built in 1180, the geometry of the exterior contrasting with the decorative richness of the interior.

When the Jews were expelled from Sicily in 1492 many of the synagogues were expropriated without compensation, although in some cases, such as at Palermo, the property was sold and the community received the payment. The émigrés had to obtain a permit to take with them the furnishings of the synagogues, described as Torah mantles of brocade or silk, copper candelabra and silk drapes or curtains; if permission was granted, the value of the articles had to be paid to the authorities.

Two domed Arks with finely carved panels exist which are possibly similar to the one that was in the Palermo synagogue in the latter half of the fifteenth century. According to tradition they were brought to Livorno in the sixteenth century by refugees from North Africa and Spain or Portugal. One is still preserved at Livorno in the basement of the

modern synagogue; the other was sent to Israel where it was repaired and is now in the Eliyahu Hanavi synagogue in the old city, Jerusalem.

An Ark dated 1505 from the synagogue of Modena in northern Italy is now in the Musée de Cluny, Paris. This handsome piece of furniture with exquisitely carved panels in marquetry frames was certainly purpose-made by an expert craftsman for use in the synagogue; it has a draw-out flap on which to rest the scrolls and a marquetry reader's stand. This Ark is a product of the sober, elegant taste of northern Italy during the transition from the Gothic style to that of the early Renaissance. The exquisitely carved decoration is in the earlier style; the cresting, the geometric tracery in lancets and the reticulated tracery enclosing quatrefoils are all from the Gothic repertory. The twisted columns to which the Jews were partial because of their traditional association with the columns of Solomon's Temple, and their capitals, belong to the repertory of the Renaissance. An illuminated codex from the north of Italy, Rabbi Jacob ben Asher's *Arba'ah Turim*, according to its colophon the work of a Jewish scribe at Mantua, Isaac Sofer ben Obadiah, and made for Rabbi Morde-chai ben Avigdor in 1435, includes a scene of the reading of the Law in a synagogue. Here the decoration is Gothic, the bimah is a small, simple lectern in the centre of the room; the Ark is elaborate, with an ogee-shaped dome and crocketing.

While the synagogues of central and northern Italy in the medieval period may have contained such fine furnishings, outwardly, in order not to attract attention or criticism, they were unobtrusive vernacular buildings. The Jewish quarter of a number of towns is still remembered, sometimes by its original name, but the synagogue buildings have rarely been identified. One exception is at Sermoneta, a small town in the former Papal States, about sixty kilometres from Rome. Here the medieval synagogue, abandoned when the Jews were expelled by papal order in 1555, dates from the thirteenth or fourteenth century. A two-storey stone edifice with an entrance on both levels, it is distinguished from the surrounding buildings by a small rectangular turret, undoubtedly added to conform with the Halakhic requirement that the synagogue should rise above the other buildings of the place. The Sermoneta synagogue is now used as a leisure residence by an Italian orchestral conductor. In Rome there are vestiges of a synagogue in the Vicolo dell'Atleta, formerly the Vicolo delle Palme, in Trastevere, where most of the Roman Jews lived in the Middle Ages; this was probably the synagogue founded in 1101 by the lexicographer Nathan ben Jechiel. The synagogue mentioned in the fourteenth century near the church of San Tommaso across the Tiber, where the Jews settled subsequently, has vanished.

Adventurous Jews from Italy crossed the Alps into Germany in the wake of the Roman legions and settled in towns founded along the Rhine. As early as the fourth century CE a community of Jews is mentioned at Cologne. Under the Carolingian monarchs they formed an accepted and respected urban minority in towns of the Rhineland. Their presence is recorded in the tenth century in the episcopal cities of Mainz and Worms in the Rhineland and Regensburg in Bavaria, a former Roman stronghold on the Danube, and also at Prague in Bohemia. Jews were invited by the Bishop to settle at Speyer in 1084;[11] he granted them trading rights

OPPOSITE ABOVE A product of the period of transition from the Gothic style of the Middle Ages to that of the early Renaissance in northern Italy, this Ark from a synagogue at Modena, Italy, is dated 1505. It is now in the Musée de Cluny, Paris.

OPPOSITE BELOW The synagogue building at Sermoneta, south of Rome, in the former Papal States, abandoned by the community when the Jews were expelled by papal order in 1555.

Jmpator redit dans Judeis legē moysi ī rotulo.

Miniature on parchment of about 1330 from a register book of Baldwin of Luxembourg, Archbishop of Trier in the Rhineland and Elector of the Holy Roman Empire. It shows the Emperor Henry VII bestowing a charter with privileges on the Jews of Rome during his visit to Italy 1310–13.

as well as permission to erect a wall for their convenience and protection around the quarter where they lived.

In the eleventh century the legal and social status of the Jews was regulated by Imperial decrees, but with the First Crusade in the spring of 1096 their situation underwent an alarming turn for the worse. The crusaders, in their belligerent fervour to vanquish the enemies of Christianity in the Holy Land, saw no reason to spare the Jewish infidels they encountered nearer to home in the Rhineland, so they slaughtered Jews in brutal massacres which the bishops and the Emperor, Henry IV, were unable to prevent. The Emperor's order issued in their defence was not heeded; all he could do subsequently was to allow those Jews who had converted to Christianity in order to save their lives to revert to their own faith. The antagonism of the crusaders spread, however, and the Jews were eventually forced out of the city trade-guilds. As a result they turned to money-lending, which became the hallmark of Jewish life in Germany. This increased their unpopularity, nourishing the anti-Jewish sentiments which emanated from the Church and exacerbating popular attitudes of envy and jealousy.

At the time of the Second Crusade in 1146, a monk, Radulph, incited the populace to attack Jews. Such violence was condemned by the Cistercian Saint Bernard of Clairvaux, who intervened in favour of the Jews both orally and in writing and forbade attacks on them. However, their situation worsened when the Fourth Lateran Council ordered the clergy in 1215 to restrict business relations between Jews and Christians and cause Jews to wear distinctive clothing. As Jewish–Christian relations deteriorated, accusations of ritual murder and desecration of the Host proliferated. Jews were butchered at Frankfurt in 1241 when they attempted to prevent the conversion of a member of their community; at Munich in 1280, because of a blood libel, the community of 180 persons was put to death by burning.

In 1236 the Emperor Frederick II declared the Jews of Germany 'servi

age from the Codex Rossi, a
fteenth-century illuminated
anuscript, showing the interior of an
alian synagogue with a domed Ark.

camerae nostri'. Thus they and their possessions became the legal property of the Emperor, vassals of the Imperial treasury. While this afforded them the interested protection of the Emperor, it made them pawns in the power struggle between him on one side and the princes and city-governments of Germany on the other. The Emperor Henry VII is portrayed in 1312 as giving a charter to his Jewish bondsmen, but despite such privileges their situation worsened. During the awful epidemic of plague called the Black Death which raged during 1348–50 the Jews may have suffered less than the populace at large because of their superior standards of hygiene and knowledge of medicine. They were accused of poisoning the wells throughout Europe, and when a Jew at Chillon in Switzerland confessed under torture to such a genocidal plot, the rioting populace in Germany, gripped by hysterical fear, destroyed 300 Jewish communities.

Persecutions and orders of expulsion became increasingly frequent. With the expansion of commerce in Germany in the fifteenth century, the services of the Jewish capitalist, hitherto essential, became superfluous. The Jews were banished from Austria in 1420–1 and from the Tyrol in 1492; in the fifteenth century the cities of Cologne, Nuremberg and Breslau expelled their Jewish communities; Brandenburg followed suit in 1510. One of the worst periods of persecution was provoked by the arrival in Germany of a fanatic Italian Franciscan monk, Giovanni da Capistrano (1386–1456). He had incited attacks on Jews at Naples in 1427 and, after a visit to the Holy Land, served as Inquisitor of Sicily before coming to Germany to stir up anti-Jewish hatred. For this heroic work he was canonized in 1690. Nor were the wretched Jews in Germany to fare better in the sixteenth century under the Protestant reformers. Martin Luther, who was vehemently opposed to the Jews, called on the German secular rulers to sequestrate their homes and either banish them or put them to forced labour – an advice which a German government was to implement without mercy 400 years later.

The well-organized structure of German Jewry weakened; order in the community and in the synagogue consequently disintegrated under the increasingly adverse conditions, which stimulated an eastward migration of German Jews into Poland. Administration of community affairs was in the hands of its leaders, who referred to themselves in a petition at Cologne in 1301 as '*Nos Episcopus, magistratus Judeorum ac universi Judei civitatis Coloniensis*',[12] borrowing the title of 'Episcopus' (bishop) from the Church. The uses of the synagogue building were strictly regulated. Rabbi Meir of Rothenburg (died 1293), for instance, forbade the use of the garret of the synagogue building for 'profane, degrading or indecent acts'.[13] Not infrequently a private house had to serve as the synagogue, with a cupboard for the Ark and a lectern for the bimah, and it was not easy for the worshippers to attach a sacred value to such a place. Wronged members of the community were permitted to interrupt prayer during the services until they received redress:[14] apparently the officers of the synagogue were able to control this faculty so that the service did not degenerate into pandemonium. Business dealings between the community and government officials were also often conducted in the synagogue, and legal actions were sometimes heard there because the communities were closed legal bodies subject to their own laws and judges.

OPPOSITE This view of the portico of the medieval synagogue at Regensburg in Bavaria was etched by the artist Albrecht Altdorfer (1480–1538), a member of the town council which decreed the demolition of the building in 1519.

LEFT The exterior of the medieval synagogue at Worms, Germany, from the north-west, after restoration.

Within this closed community life of their choice which was the source of their spiritual strength, the Jews remained extraneous to the prevailing culture, removed from their environment as much by their own isolationist and conservative tendencies as by the hostility of non-Jews. They remained attached to obsolete cultural levels and medieval forms. When they migrated to countries to the east they continued to cling to the Franconian dialect in their speech; Judaeo–German or Yiddish which derived from it became the colloquial language of the Ashkenazim as far off as Lithuania, the Ukraine and Romania for centuries to come.

The Jews in Germany sought in the repertory of medieval architecture of the eleventh and twelfth centuries forms that were not used by Christians for sacred buildings. This was not only to differentiate the Jewish places of worship from the Christian churches but also because the longitudinal plan did not suit Jewish liturgical requirements. The choice of the Jews fell upon the single-nave hall, and the twin-nave hall – a type employed in the Middle Ages for civic council chambers, for audience halls and for refectories. One or other of these plans was used predominantly for synagogues in Germany until the sixteenth century and sometimes later. The single-nave plan was used, for example, for the synagogues of Speyer, Fürth and Frankfurt, the twin-nave at Worms, Regensburg and Erfurt, and with the eastward migration it spread to Bohemia, Hungary and Poland. In both types of building the Ark was on the east wall, frequently in an apsidal niche about two metres above the floor level, and the bimah was in the centre of the room.

There are indications that the medieval synagogues in Germany were decorated with wall-paintings. A rabbi at Regensburg in the second half of the twelfth century expressed the opinion that a synagogue wall-painting depicting horses and birds was acceptable; however, opinions varied, and at about the same time a rabbi at Mainz objected to the representation

of foliage with birds which he had seen in a synagogue at Meissen.[15]

The earliest known mention of a synagogue belonging to the community formed in 1084 at Speyer dates from 1096. This building was damaged by fire in the course of anti-Jewish demonstrations in 1196. It was rebuilt in the same style when the community was readmitted in the fourteenth century and at that time a women's prayer-hall with narrow Gothic windows and a small forecourt was added on the south side, parallel to the original building. The north side of the building was on the Judenbadgasse where there was a subterranean *mikveh* – the main entrance to the synagogue being at the middle of the long north wall. In the fourteenth century another annexe was built at the east end of the Judenbadgasse, a small, square, vaulted chamber, probably for use as an administrative office. Of the early single-nave synagogue which measured about 17.4×10.85 m, and which was still intact in the eighteenth century, only a pair of simple Romanesque west windows with a sturdy dividing pillar have survived; this remnant is in the Historisches Museum der Pfalz. The original building had an apsidal niche 2.63 m wide cut in the east wall; an oculus above it and the two pointed side windows were fourteenth-century additions.

The medieval synagogue of Worms survived until it was razed by the Nazi authorities in 1938 and 1942; after World War II it was rebuilt with the maximum accuracy by the German government. The date of the building, 4035 (or CE 1175), can be construed from an addition of the numerical value of the letters of a Hebrew inscription based on 1 Kings 7:40–9, carved on the capital of one column of the twin-nave hall. This agrees with the dating on stylistic grounds by Professor Richard Krautheimer,[16] who made a comparison between the decorative carving in the synagogue and on the portal and capitals of the cathedrals of Worms and Fritzlar. A subterranean *mikveh*, very similar to the one at Speyer, was built to the south-west of the synagogue in 1186; in 1213 the separately roofed *Frauenschul* with a central supporting pillar was added. This work coincided with a spate of church building in the Rhineland. Another separately roofed annexe, a *yeshiva* known as the Rashi chapel, was added to the complex in 1624. It appears that the twin-nave hall of 1175 (which took the place of a synagogue founded in 1034), had round-headed Romanesque windows. The *Frauenschul*, whose building date (1213) is known from an inscription, revealed signs of the transition to Gothic forms; its east windows had Romanesque arches, the west ones Gothic moulding. About the same time the windows of the original synagogue were altered and given pointed Gothic arches; the south windows, pointed inside, remained rounded outside. The whole building was extensively restored following an Imperial decree of 1616: the bimah was reconstructed in 1620, the central column of the *Frauenschul* was replaced, a door was opened between the *Frauenschul* and the main prayer-hall, and a vestibule was built at the north end of the *Frauenschul* with a community room above it. The complex was re-roofed with a hipped roof and a beautiful courtyard entrance with blind arcading was created in front of the main entrance. The synagogue was again repaired in 1697. In the course of alterations in 1843 two large openings with Gothic arches were made in the wall between the main hall and the *Frauenschul*, the west win-

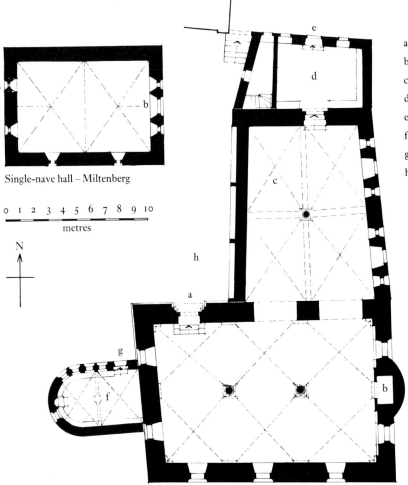

a – Entrance
b – Ark
c – *Frauenschul* (women's prayer-hall), added 12
d – Women's vestibule, added later
e – Women's entrance
f – Rashi Chapel, added 1624
g – Entrance to Chapel
h – Courtyard

Single-nave hall – Miltenberg

0 1 2 3 4 5 6 7 8 9 10
metres

N

Twin-nave hall – Worms, 1175

Medieval German synagogue types
(after Krautheimer).

dows of the *Frauenschul* were bricked up, and the old rectangular, kiosk-type bimah – a wrought-iron cage over a podium – was demolished.

The twin-nave synagogue at Regensburg was built on a newly acquired site, in the Gothic style, shortly before 1227. It was destroyed in 1519, but a record of its appearance has survived in the etchings of Albrecht Altdorfer (1480–1538), a member of the city council which banished the Jewish community in that year and decreed the demolition of their place of worship. Altdorfer, who was named city architect of Regensburg in 1526, was a painter of merit, the principal master of the Danube school, and considered an equal of Dürer in some of his landscape work. He was also an accomplished engraver. In his view of the Regensburg synagogue it can be seen that the two naves were divided by three columns on steep plinths into eight equal bays covered by cross-vaulting; the rectangular bimah in the style of the early Renaissance stood between the second and third columns.

In his work on medieval synagogues Professor Krautheimer reported on other early German synagogues: a small one at Miltenberg (late thirteenth-century), one at Bamberg (pre-1350) which was transformed into a Christian chapel, several at Frankfurt (including one built for the community in the fifteenth century with a *mikveh*, a community hall and a dance hall, all paid for by the city authorities), Nuremberg (1352), Erfurt (1353), a later one at Schnaittach (1570), and one at Fürth (1617) which amalgamated Gothic and Baroque forms, as well as synagogues at Metz in Lorraine and Rufach in Alsace. The Rufach synagogue, apparently built in the last years of the thirteenth century, became the property of the Bishop of Strasbourg when the Jewish community was expelled in 1338. It was a rectangular building, almost square, 11.35 × 10 m with a small apse 2.3 m above the floor level on the east wall and a ledge for books on the walls.

Jews moving eastward from Germany took with them their synagogue styles. At Eger in northern Hungary, where the synagogue was built before 1350 and transformed into a church in 1468, the prayer-hall was a single-nave chamber with a central pillar like the Worms *Frauenschul*; the bimah was, perhaps, a platform surrounding this pillar. Remains of a late medieval synagogue at Buda were discovered in the course of building research in the Hungarian capital in 1964 and the general development of the old castle area. The Jews of Hungary, who, under an edict of King Bela IV in 1251, had enjoyed freedom of worship, the right to elect their own administration and to build synagogues, were expelled by King Lajos the Great in 1360. When they returned four years later they settled in Buda in a new quarter, now M. Tàncsics utca, where the synagogue has been found. An inscription recording that the building was eighty years old in 1541 indicates the building date – 1461; this coincides with the stylistic evidence of the late Gothic flamboyant decoration of the fragments of stonework. It was a vaulted twin-nave building, about 19 × 9 m. The vaults collapsed under the bombardment during the siege of Buda in 1541 and a new synagogue, 26.5 × 10.7 m, with a prominent tower was built over it. During the excavations charred skeletons were found, remains of many members of the Jewish community who perished in the synagogue in 1686 when the Imperial army liberated Buda from the Turks. At Sopron in Hungary a fourteenth-century synagogue building has survived: it is a lofty, single-nave, cross-vaulted hall with a niche above steps on the east wall and pairs of pointed windows high up in the east and west walls. At Pozsony in Hungary, where the existence of several medieval synagogues is documented, the demolition of one, newly built in 1335, was ordered by Pope Benedict XII if the complaint proved true that the noise issuing from it disturbed the neighbouring Ursuline monks at their devotions.[17] A *bet midrash* which survives at Pozsony, probably built as late as the seventeenth century but in medieval style, is a twin-nave building with five ribs to the cross-vaults of each of its six bays. This unusual use of a fifth transverse rib is found also in the medieval synagogue at Miltenberg and in the Altneuschul at Prague. A not wholly convincing explanation that has been offered for it is that the builders wished to avoid the form of a cross. It is more likely that it was used as a device to strengthen the vault, and that six ribs, more usual in such a case, could not be used because a sixth rib would have necessitated the addition of a central pier at Miltenberg or three supporting piers along the east–west axis at Prague and Pozsony. The piers would have occupied too much floor space, and in the Altneuschul would also have interfered with the central position of the bimah and as a result would have obstructed the passage to the Ark.

The Altneuschul (Old-new-school) at Prague in Czechoslovakia

The Altneuschul, Prague. Detail of the handsome inner door, the main door to the prayer-hall. The decorative tympanum is finely carved with stylized vine leaves.

appears to have got its name because, when it was built at the end of the thirteenth or beginning of the fourteenth century, it was a new synagogue building (synagogues are mentioned at Prague in the twelfth century), but later it could no longer be referred to as 'the new' when another newer synagogue was erected – so it became the 'old-new'. It has a twin-nave prayer-hall, 15 × 9 m, in the tradition of the Worms synagogue. Two octagonal columns on plinths divide the space into six equal bays, which are covered by cross-vaults with five ribs. The bimah, enclosed by a wrought-iron grille, is placed centrally between the two pillars; the Ark is on the east wall above a short flight of steps. Like the Worms synagogue the Altneuschul is surrounded by annexes; the earliest is a low, tunnel-like vestibule on the south side. This appears to have been added in the fourteenth century, together with the distinctive red-brick gables of the synagogue. The low annexe, part of which was used for a women's section behind the west wall with splayed openings into the main hall, was added late in the seventeenth century, at which time a new Ark was installed incorporating the pediment of the original one. The rich vine-leaf carving on this pediment, on the corbels of the vaulting and the bosses, and in the tympanum of the splendid Gothic entrance door on the south wall, recalls the leaf-carving on the pediment of the medieval Miltenberg Ark. The use of the fifth transverse rib in both synagogues also suggests a definite association between the two buildings. A further low annexe for women was added on the north side in the eighteenth century with the same funnel-shaped apertures as in the west annexe which it joined; another low annexe behind the east wall was an even later addition. A late Gothic vaulted synagogue survived also at Lipnik in Moravia.

Further east, in Poland, the German twin-nave synagogue plan was used in the fourteenth century for the Stara synagogue at Cracow, which is larger than either Worms or the Altneuschul, Prague. The Stara, now a Jewish Historical Museum in the care of the state, is discussed in Chapter 5. The group of old synagogue buildings at Poznan in Poland surveyed by Grotte prior to their destruction in 1908 included a single-nave Gothic hall with the vaulting directed towards the Ark.

In France, where there is evidence of Jewish life in the south before the destruction of the Second Temple, the Jews flourished particularly from the eighth to the tenth century. French Jewish merchants were successful slave-traders engaged in the lucrative transportation of slaves acquired in the Slavic lands for sale to the Moslem caliphs in Spain for their harems and bodyguards. In the fifth and sixth centuries the Jews had proselytized actively in France among the poor and the slaves. In the reign of Charlemagne a Jew, Isaac, held the rank of ambassador, and under the Carolingian monarchs, when the Jews enjoyed complete judicial equality, employed Christians, and owned pagan slaves, they extended their proselytizing to the upper classes. Bodo, a Frank, deacon of Louis the Pious (the son of Charlemagne), was converted to Judaism in 839 and married a Jewish woman in Spain.

When the Church formulated anti-Jewish edicts in the ninth century Charles the Bald, son of Louis the Pious, refused to ratify them. In his reign great Jewish schools flourished at Narbonne and at Troyes.

Synagogues are mentioned as early as 582 at Paris and prior to 585

ABOVE Interior of the synagogue with Gothic vaulting at Lipnik in Moravia, Czechoslovakia, from an old photograph

OPPOSITE Interior of the medieval Stara synagogue, Cracow, Poland, a fine example of the twin-nave hall with central bimah. The building was restored after the ravages of World War II.

at Orleans,[18] but practically all traces of the medieval synagogue build-ings of France have vanished although Hebrew synagogal inscriptions have been preserved. The conditions of the Jews began to deteriorate in 1007, when the Church instigated attacks against them on the pretext of their supposed complicity in a plot with the Egyptian Caliph, Hakim the Mad, to desecrate and destroy the basilica of the Holy Sepulchre at Jerusalem. During the crusades the situation became even worse, although it was in Germany that the Jews bore the brunt of the crusaders' zeal. Eventually, after sporadic orders of banishment, the Jews were expelled by a general order of 1498, enforced in 1501, from all the territory of France at that time except Alsace, Lorraine, the county of Nice, and the Comtat Venaissin, a papal enclave. The synagogue buildings were then put to other use or demolished. One medieval synagogue building at Sens, south of Paris, survived until its demolition in 1750. Vestiges remain of medieval synagogues at Draguignan, Trets, Provins, Mende and Rouen. The recent authoritative *Histoire des Juifs en France*[19] dis-misses the supposed medieval synagogue at Chablis as a fraud and those of Lunel and Peyrousse-le-Roc as the products of imagination, devoid of authenticity.

At Carpentras, one of the towns of the papal enclave in Provence where Jews remained, the present synagogue stands on the site of one built in 1367 which was a small two-storey edifice. The women sat in the base-ment, the men on the floor above where the Ark was placed. There was a similar arrangement in the medieval synagogue of Avignon, where a visitor described the women's room in 1599 as 'a true cellar, receiving light from the room above through a vent'.[20] The present synagogue at Cavaillon, built on the foundations of one of the fourteenth century, had the same arrangement. The street-level, cellar-like prayer-hall of the women also contained the oven for baking unleavened bread; above was the men's prayer-hall. In these synagogues a women's rabbi or cantor conducted their services. A description of the medieval synagogue of Rouen in Normandy, in the north of France, tallies with what is known of those in Provence. It was described as '*un vieil édifice carré à deux étages*'[21] (an old square building of two storeys).

It was from Rouen, where there was a Jewish colony living under the Norman rulers, that Jews crossed to England following William the Con-queror's successful invasion in 1066. Jews remained in England, at first treated tolerantly by the Norman kings, by whom their services as financiers were appreciated. In 1290 they were banished entirely by Edward I unless they accepted conversion, as the community at Dun-stable did.

In London the Jews were living around the *vicus Judaeorum*, first mentioned in 1128 and still known as Old Jewry; their synagogue was sequestrated in 1232 because the chanting could be heard in a nearby church. At Lincoln, the home of the great Jewish capitalist Aaron of Lin-coln (died 1186) who financed the building of abbeys and monasteries, the Jewry was around the street now known as Steep Hill; the Lincoln synagogue, sacked in 1266, may have been a building in that street, or a building still remembered as the Jew's House. At Oxford, the Jewry was in St Aldate's Street; the synagogue was situated between Jewry Lane

This medieval building at Lincoln where the synagogue was sacked in 1266 is still remembered as the Jew's House. It is a reminder of the prosperity of English Jewry before they were obliged to accept conversion or leave the country in 1290. It may also have been associated with the famous blood libel charge over the death in 1255 of the child known as Little Saint Hugh of Lincoln.

and Saint Frideswide's Lane. The medieval synagogue of Canterbury, at the corner of High Street and Stour Street, survived until the seventeenth century. There appears to be no evidence to substantiate the claim that Moyse's Hall at Bury St Edmunds was the synagogue of the Jewish community there, massacred in 1190.

The first accusation of ritual murder against Jews in Europe occurred at Norwich in 1144, when the community was accused of acquiring a Christian child named William, inflicting on him the tortures of Jesus' passion, and hanging him on Good Friday. A more publicized blood libel in 1255 concerned the child known as Little Saint Hugh of Lincoln, remembered by Chaucer's Prioress in her *Tale*:

> O yonge Hugh of Lincoln slayn also
> With cursed Jewes, as it is notable
> For it nis but a litel whyle ago;
> Preye eek for us.

The English Benedictine chronicler Matthew Paris recorded the accusation made that in this instance the child was first fattened with bread and milk and then that 'all the Jews of England were invited to the crucifixion'.[22] The truth of Hugh's case is impossible to ascertain but reputed miracles which followed the exhumation of his body certainly aggravated anti-Jewish sentiments.

Allegations of desecration of the Host, engendered by mistrust of the Jews and by the emotional and superstitious attitude to the Eucharist which was prevalent, became frequent in Europe in the Middle Ages. In the thirteenth century blood libel accusations were also common, especially in Germany; from England accusations had quickly spread to the continent. Instances are on record at Paris and Blois in France as early as the twelfth century, as far away as Prague, and at Saragossa in Spain by 1182.

Jews settled in Spain when it was a part of the Roman Empire; their presence there was significant enough to attract the attention of the Christian Council of Elvira in CE 305. Under the rule of the Visigoths, who took Spain in the fifth century, the situation of the Jews varied from reign to reign according to the attitude of the king after Christianity had been declared the religion of the state in 589. Policies of enforced baptism and expulsion, accompanied by conversion and emigration, alternated with more tolerant policies accompanied by recantations. Finally in 694 King Egica, fearing that the Jews would side with the Moslem invaders, had them all declared slaves: some were reduced to servitude, some fled. When Tariq ben Ziyad arrived with the Moslem armies in Spain in 711 there were no openly professing Jewish communities in the country.

Under the new, tolerant rule of the Moors a marvellous period dawned for Jews in Spain. Crypto-Jews returned to their ancestral faith, many Jews who had fled to North Africa to escape the degradation of the Visigothic circumscriptions returned to the country, and more Jews from Egypt and Tunisia followed the invaders to Spain and settled there. Spain became both numerically and culturally the most important land of Jewry. In the independent state established in 755–6 by Abd-ur-Rahmen I, with its capital at Cordoba, and especially in the Caliphate which followed in the tenth century, the Jews, who assumed Arab names and spoke and wrote Arabic perfectly, reached a dazzling peak of scholarship, prosperity and political power. Hasdai ibn Shaprut, the head of Spanish Jewry in the tenth century, was the Caliph's Inspector-General of Customs and in charge of foreign trade and affairs. Jews were active in agriculture and the crafts as well as in trade, and attained fame in poetry, philology, geography, astrology, philosophy and medicine. In the eleventh century the head of the Jewish community, Samuel ibn Nagdela (ha-Nagid), a scholar of distinction, patron of the arts, lexicographer and prolific poet, was chief adviser to the king and commander of the army at Granada. At Seville the Chief Rabbi, Isaac ibn Albalia, was the court astrologer. The foremost intellectual figure of all, Moses Maimonides, was born at Cordoba in 1135; his works have influenced both Jewish and non-Jewish scholars. The Jewish literati and upper classes in particular contrived to harmonize their own religion with the brilliant Arabic secular culture and with neoplatonic philosophical concepts.

In the twelfth century fanatic Berbers and then the conquering Almohad dynasty turned against the Jews. Judaism was forbidden, the synagogues and *yeshivot* were closed and the Jews obliged to embrace Islam or flee. Some remained as crypto-Jews, many crossed to North Africa or moved into the Spanish Christian kingdoms of Aragon and Castile. In the thirteenth century the rulers of those kingdoms eventually captured all of Moorish Spain except the kingdom of Granada, which included Almeria and Malaga.

Under the kings of Castile the rights of the Jews were defined in the *Siete Partidas*, a code formulated in 1263 which confirmed their complete religious liberty but limited the number and size of synagogues; a royal official was appointed to supervise Jewish affairs. In Castile, Jews rose to high positions: those in court circles were frequently influenced by their Christian environment. In Aragon the rights of the Jews were guaranteed by the Charter of Valencia of 1239, which placed them and their property under royal protection, prohibited harassment of Jews, and recognized the judicial authority of the rabbinical courts to judge all cases involving Jews except trials for murder. By the fourteenth century the Jews were governed by their own elected councils, which formed part of a complex administrative body with written constitutions. An elite group, the *judios francos* (free Jews) were not subject to the community authority or to the Jewish fisc, although most of them adhered to the tenets of Judaism. Among the *conversos* – Jews who had become Christians, often for convenience – there were also many who clung to Judaic beliefs.

Towards the end of the fourteenth century a wave of anti-Jewish feeling provoked harassment and acts of violence. Some Jews who were converted to Christianity, like Solomon ha-Levi who became Bishop of Burgos, made efforts to convert their erstwhile co-religionists, exercising more heavy persuasion and coercion than tact. In their missionary zeal Christian preachers like the Dominican friar Vicente Ferrer (Saint Vincent Ferrer, 1350–1419), preached inflammatory sermons which provoked antipathy to the Jewish population and outbreaks of violence against them. The Archdeacon of Ecija claimed in 1388, perhaps with exaggeration, to have destroyed twenty-three synagogues in the town of Seville '*edificadas contra Dios e contra derecho*'[23] (built against God and against the law).

Through the marriage of Ferdinand of Aragon to Isabella of Castile in 1469, the two kingdoms were united in 1479. Although Jews still held important posts like that of Abraham Señeor, the Chief Rabbi of Castile, who was Chief Collector of Taxes for the united kingdoms, Ferdinand and Isabella, who were granted by the Pope the title of *los Reyes Catolicos* (the Catholic Kings), instigated a relentless campaign to root out the pseudo-Christians among the *conversos*. Ferdinand and Isabella invited the Holy Office to extend the activities of the Inquisition to Spain, to pursue and eliminate the crypto-Jews and crypto-Moslems. In 1483 the Queen's redoubtable confessor, an intransigent Dominican, Tomàs de Torquemada, was appointed Grand Inquisitor of Spain. Local tribunals of the Inquisition were established throughout the country. Torquemada's cruelty was so outrageous that in 1494, even though he was supported in his abominable bigotry and fanaticism by the bulk of public opinion and sentiment, the Pope appointed four assistants to restrain him. During his term of office *conversos* were apprehended and tortured; about 13,000 were punished and about 2000 who were not brought to reconciliation with the Church were burned at the stake. The discovery of the strong influence of Judaism which became manifest during the interrogation of *conversos* suspected of Judaizing led to radical measures against the Jews, whose very presence was considered nefarious. In 1492, Queen Isabella gave approval for the momentous expedition of Columbus to the New World, on which he took astronomical charts prepared by Abraham Zacuto, a Jew. In the same year the Moslem kingdom of Granada, where 20,000 Jews lived in the capital, fell to the 'Catholic Kings' and the triumphant monarchs signed an edict for the expulsion of the Jews from the whole of Spain. All Jews who were unwilling to accept baptism had to leave the national territory. The last professing Jew left Spain on 31 July; about 100,000 went to Portugal, whence too they were expelled shortly afterwards. Many went to North Africa and to the lands of the Ottoman Empire in the eastern Mediterranean, Turkey and the Balkans; some settled in the states of Italy, a few reached Poland and a few went to Erez Israel. Many Jews, like the Chief Rabbi, Abraham Señeor, reluctantly opted for baptism rather than exile. While there were no racial motives behind the edict of the expulsion, the new Christians who remained and their descendants were hectored and examined by the vigilant Inquisition in its implacable intent to eradicate Judaic beliefs.

Professor Francisco Cantera Burgos, in his comprehensive work *Sinagogas Españolas*,[24] records 118 towns in Spain where there was at least one synagogue in the Middle Ages. In many towns there were several; for example, as many as five synagogues are mentioned at Saragossa in a notarial act of 1485.[25]

The notarial archives in Spain contain many acts relating to synagogues and there are many interesting decrees concerning them in the ecclesiastical and state archives. In 1263, for instance, King James I of Aragon licensed a Jew, Bonanasco Salomón, to build a synagogue in his own house or in any other place he wished in the Jewish quarter of Barcelona in which the 'Books of the Law of Moses called Scrolls' and other Jewish books could be kept, and for prayer. In 1267 the same monarch authorized the Jews of Barcelona to enlarge their old synagogue and increase its height.[26] In 1490 a suit was heard at Valladolid between the Jewish community of Bembibre and the parish priest of the parish of San Pedro in that town, who had seized their synagogue. He pleaded that the Jews merited the sequestration because their synagogue was '*mas ricca e mas sunptuosa que la que antes tenían*'[27] (richer and more sumptuous than the one they used to have). The ecclesiastical judge decided that the sequestrated synagogue should continue in use as a church but that because the priest had not acted legally he should provide the Jews within six months with an alternative place of worship of specified dimensions but without any painting or moulding on its timber surfaces.

Many synagogues were converted into churches even before the order of expulsion of 1492 and some synagogues themselves were former Moslem mosques. In 1252 King Alfonso x gave to the Church all the mosques of Seville which existed under the Moors '*fueras tres mezquitas que son en la judería que son agora sinogas de los judios*'[28] (except three mosques which are in the Jewish quarter which are now synagogues of the Jews). Of the four Seville synagogues which are known to have been subsequently transformed into churches, one was dedicated to Santa Maria la Blanca, a favourite name for ex-synagogues; the ancient door with fine Visigothic capitals survives, although the building has undergone changes. Another, a single-nave hall with a richly ornamented ceiling in the Mudejar style, survives in the chapel of the Dominican convent of Madre de Dios. It was first occupied in 1487 by the congregation which was founded in 1472. Other known examples of synagogues which became churches are one of the synagogues of Avila, which became the church of Todos los Santos before 1476, and the principal synagogue of Ciudad Real, the Sinagoga Mayor, which became the church of San Juan Bautista before 1407. It is most probable, but not absolutely certain, that the chapel of Espiritu Santo at Caceres was once a synagogue. The interior is in the Mudejar style of the fifteenth century, the painted horseshoe central arches of the two arcades of the nave being higher than the pointed side-arches. The triple naves run latitudinally rather than, as usual in a church, longitudinally.

Actual remains of the many medieval synagogues are scant – a few inscriptions, a doorway at Bejar, the ruins of a building destroyed by fire at Segovia. Three synagogue buildings have, however, survived as reminders of the once splendid life of medieval Spanish Jewry. The one at Cordoba was used as a quarantine hospital for victims of rabies and then as an oratory for the guild of shoemakers and dedicated to Saints Crispin and Crispinian. The two at Toledo were both used as churches, Santa Maria la Blanca and Nuestra Señora del Transito.

The important medieval Jewish community of Cordoba must have had several places of worship. The erection of one synagogue in 1250 caused the ecclesiastical authorities to complain to the Pope about its '*superflue altitudinis*'[29] (excessive height). In reply, Innocent IV issued a bull directing the bishop to deal with what he termed a scandal to faithful Christians and a detriment to the Cordoban church.[30]

Interior of the medieval synagogue at Cordoba, Spain, near the birthplace of Maimonides. Although it was later used as a quarantine ward for rabies victims, and as an oratory of a trade guild for centuries, much of the superb Mudejar decoration and the Hebrew inscriptions have survived.

One synagogue which has survived is a small building, 6.95×6.37 m internally, standing behind a patio in the Calle de los Judíos, known for some years as the Calle Maimonides to commemorate the birthplace of the philosopher in the vicinity. The almost square plan with the entrance in the middle of the south wall, a deep niche for the Ark in the middle of the east wall and a recess for the bimah in the middle of the west wall, has been compared by Otto Czekelius[31] to that of the medieval synagogue at Rufach in Alsace. However, in Professor Krautheimer's opinion the eastern recess at Rufach was the blocked-up former main entrance.[32] Father Mariano Párrafa brought the Cordoba synagogue building to the attention of the public in 1884 and in consequence the diocesan authorities consented to its deconsecration and it was declared a National Monument in 1885. The interior was thus saved from further deterioration but some of the splendid Mudejar-style stucco decoration had already been spoiled and some of the inscriptions partially obliterated, and the lower part of the walls, up to 2.26 m from the floor level, had already lost its ornamental facing; this surface was probably embellished with tile mosaic or with tile sgraffito, in which the glaze is cut from the tile in patterns. Scholars have made slightly different readings of a commemorative inscription on the east wall but there can be no doubt that it names one Ishaq Moheb, the donor or founder of the מִקְדָשׁ מְעַט (the lesser sanctuary of Ezekiel 2:16) and gives a date which corresponds to CE 1314–15.

The deep, angular apse in the middle of the east wall, 2.8 m in width, beginning just 18 cm above the floor level, must have contained the Ark. It has two round-headed ambries in its back wall: one measuring 1.5×0.43 m begins 1.12 m above the floor level, the other, 2×0.65 m, begins 0.76 m above the floor level. Above the opening of this apse is a panel with intricate ornamentation, and a cresting of merlons which betrays the Gothic influence in the Mudejar work. On either side of the apse are large panels with a stellar decoration in stucco. Five round-headed windows high in the north wall light the room; below them, between bands with verses from the psalms in Hebrew, is an ornamental stucco frieze, decorated panels and a dado. The west wall attracts the most attention; it recalls the *qibla* wall in mosques. The shallow central recess, 43 cm in depth, is framed by a lobate arch in a panel richly decorated with intricate stucco work; on each side are stucco panels, also richly carved, between a frieze and a dado. The bimah was apparently a timber structure in the central recess. The graceful arcade on the south side of the room is a later addition; it creates a vestibule in front of the entrance and supports a gallery with three windows overlooking the room. These are surrounded by stucco panels carved with a pattern of minute palmettos and acanthus leaves in five-, six- and eight-pointed stars.

At its zenith the Jewish community of Toledo numbered about 15,000 persons engaged in textile manufacture, cloth-dyeing, tanning and agriculture, as well as banking; the number and the unrivalled beauty of its synagogues are mentioned by Yehuda al-Harizin in the twelfth century in his *Tahkemoni*. The poet Ya'agol Albeneh evoked them in his elegy on the martyrs of an anti-Jewish rampage at Toledo in 1391, lamenting in one strophe: 'Alas for the synagogues turned into ruins where vultures have made their nests.'[33] Besides five Midrashim the poet names nine synagogues in Toledo: the Sinagoga Mayor (Great Synagogue) which the Crown gave to the knights of Calatrava as a church for their order soon after the expulsion of 1492; the Templo Viejo (Old Temple), where the poet says that strangers had set up 'an idol'; the Templo Nuevo (New Temple) built at the end of the twelfth century by Yosef ibn Susan (died *c.* 1203–5), *almojarife* of King Alfonso VIII; the Sinagoga del príncipe Sĕmuel ha-Levi (of the prince Samuel ha-Levi) – this magnificent synagogue, which is still standing, was built about 1357 by Samuel Ben Meir ha-Levi Abulafia; the Sinagoga del Cordobès (of the Cordoban); the Sinagoga de Ben Zizá; the Sinagoga de Ben Aryeh; the Sinagoga de Algi'ada; and the Sinagoga de Ben Abidarham. This last-named was not built, as David Kauffman has claimed,[34] by the David Abu Darham who was collector of the Jewish taxes under Sancho IV (1284–95), but in the twelfth century by an earlier David ben Sĕlomó ben Abu Darham, as proved by a document of 1271 in which it is mentioned specifically.[35] It was also known as the Sinagoga de Almaliquin.

A Toledan synagogue mentioned in documents of 1397, 1402 and 1403 as the '*sinagoga del sofer*'[36] (presumably 'of the shofar'), may be one of the nine of Albeneh's elegy under another name. It has not been possible to determine which of the synagogues of the elegy is the one which became the church of Santa Maria la Blanca and is still standing. Professor Cantera Burgos, while pointing out that there is absolutely no shred of historical evidence for the often-repeated story that it was turned into a church in 1411 by Saint Vincent Ferrer, suggests that it was the Templo Nuevo (New Temple), built about 1200 by Yosef ibn Susan, to which the story alluded.[37] This fits with a stylistic dating. The building is without distinction externally and its harmonious white interior is an exquisite surprise. The internal space is divided longitudinally by four parallel arcades with octagonal piers and horseshoe arches into a nave 12.5 m in height and four aisles, the inner ones 10 m high, the outer ones only 7 m. These arcades, which differ in length owing to the irregular shape of the building, are in the tradition of early Islamic building in Spain like those of the eighth- and ninth-century parts of the Great Mosque at Cordoba. The mural decoration above the arches and on the upper tier of blind arcading with lobate arches, however, is geometric interlacing, originally a Seljuk Persian motif and found also in the later buildings of the Almoravid dynasty in Morocco, such as the Friday Mosque at Tinmal (completed 1153–4) and the second Kutubiyya Mosque at Marrakesh (1162, completed about 1190). The carved woodwork of the doors is an intricate stellar interlace in the Mudejar tradition. The capitals of the columns of the arcades are sculpted with curiously elongated pine cones found also on the capitals of the former synagogue of Segovia, now in ruins. Not only the capitals but also the octagonal piers and the horseshoe arches of the arcades of both synagogues are so similar that it must be assumed that there was some association in their construction. The Segovia synagogue was smaller than 'La Blanca' with only two parallel arcades, and one aisle on each side of the nave; it became a church in 1410. According to an account written forty or fifty years later, this was because of the attempted desecration of a consecrated Host which some Jews had received as a pawn.[38]

The Ark wall with intricate polychrome Mudejar stucco work and an ornamental niche for the Torah scrolls in the synagogue at Toledo built by the financier Samuel b. Meir ha-Levi Albulafia. The building was later used as a church dedicated to Nuestra Señora del Transito.

The plan of the 'La Blanca' synagogue with its nave and four aisles is not well suited to the synagogue service. It would have been impossible to place the Ark in a position where all the congregation could see it. It seems that its place was the recess in the east wall at the end of the inner south aisle. Presumably the bimah was a timber structure in the centre of the nave but it would have been hidden from view for some worshippers by the pillars of the arcades. In Hebrew illuminated manuscripts of the fourteenth century from Spain the bimah is shown as an elevated structure. In one, a Haggadah from Barcelona, the cantor is depicted holding up a Torah scroll in its cylindrical domed case; he stands under a baldachin with twisted columns raised on a masonry structure of pillars joined by trefoil arches.[39] In another Haggadah, probably also from Barcelona, the hazzan is depicted reading the Haggadah;[40] he is above the heads of the congregation in a free-standing pulpit of gilded wood with finials, raised on four columns with carved capitals, and reached by a stair. A Haggadah of the same period from Castile also contains an illustration of a synagogue interior with a bimah raised above a stair.[41] One of the Hebrew inscriptions in the 'Transito' synagogue of Toledo actually refers to the bimah as the 'wooden tower for the Reading of the Law in the centre [of the building]'.

The 'Transito' synagogue has kept this name from the centuries after its sequestration when it was a church dedicated to Nuestra Señora del Transito (Our Lady of the Dormition). It was built about 1357 by the financier and philanthropist Samuel ben Meir ha-Levi Abulafia, as witnessed by some of the Hebrew inscriptions. Inscriptions on the Ark wall commemorate Samuel in grandiloquent terms as 'prince of the princes of the Levites'[42] and also extol King Pedro I. Samuel was chief treasurer to this King, remembered as Pedro the Cruel. He helped to consolidate the power of the monarchy by supporting the King in his struggle against the grandees in 1354 but the King turned against him and had him arrested in 1360. Samuel died in prison after torture in 1361 and his colossal fortune was confiscated.

The exterior of the synagogue is simple (the bell-tower is a much later addition) but the interior, a masterpiece of Toledan craftsmanship, befits the endowment of a magnate. It was declared a National Monument in 1877 and has since been repaired and restored. It consists of a rectangular single-nave hall 23.12 × 9.5 m with annexes to the north and south. The entrance is at the extreme west end of the south wall through the vestibule in the southern annexe. Above this annexe is a gallery divided into five compartments and apparently used by the women; it had a separate external entrance and stair and also communicated with an adjacent building which may have been a part of the donor's residence. The walls are richly decorated with intricate multi-coloured Mudejar stucco ornamentation in panels and with bands containing biblical verses in Hebrew. The east wall has a central niche for the Torah scrolls with three windows with lobate arches and slender transoms in a lofty panel of Mudejar stucco work. Above the panels a decorated frieze, 1.6 m in depth, runs round the room; on the east wall it is exquisitely carved with a delicate pattern of stalactites. Above the frieze is a tier of arcading with lobate arches and paired columns with foliate capitals; there are nineteen bays on the north and south walls where windows with perforated alabaster screens alternate with blind arches, and eight bays on the west and east walls. On the west wall the four windows are in the centre, flanked by two blind bays on each side; at the east end the arcade is blind except for the two windows high above the Ark which may symbolize the Tables of the Law. Three windows below the arcade in the west wall also have alabaster screens perforated in a beautiful lace-like pattern of rosettes with elongated petals. The perforated screen, or *mushrabiyya*, is a popular element of Islamic architecture found in both windows and blind arcades in Mozarabic and Mudejar buildings in Spain. The sumptuous interior of the synagogue was completed by a polychrome mosaic floor with a pattern of geometric interlacing and a beamed ceiling of inlaid larch.

One synagogue survives in Portugal from the period prior to the expulsion of the Jews from that country in 1496. Portuguese architecture in the fifteenth century was late Gothic in style, including the full-blown Flamboyant introduced from abroad; by the end of the fifteenth century it reached its climax in the lavish over-decoration and structural extravagances of the Manueline style. The late-fifteenth-century synagogue at Tomar, now a museum, is, however, a sober building, small but dignified. It is basically Gothic with four slender Gothic columns supporting groin vaults, but the corbels of the vaults have Ionic volutes. The synagogue chamber, 9.5 × 8.25 m, has an annexe which was a later addition.

For the European Jews the end of the Middle Ages coincided with a period of migration: from Germany eastward to Poland and beyond, from France eastward to Alsace and to Italy, from Sicily and southern Italy to the north, and from Spain and Portugal to North Africa, Italy, the Balkans and the Levant. The Grand synagogue of the Hara of Tunis dates from the Middle Ages. A number of Jews reached Erez Israel, which became part of the Ottoman Empire in 1517. They took with them to their settlements at Hebron, Safed and Jerusalem the architectural traditions of the Middle Ages in Europe and they encountered in Palestine the Byzantine and Islamic building traditions of the Near East. Those who reached Jerusalem found the Ramban synagogue, built by Rabbi Moses ben Nahman in the thirteenth century. When it was sequestrated by the Ottoman governor in 1586 the community built new synagogues. The Ashkenazim erected the Hurva synagogue and the Sephardim the Eliyahu Hanavi, to which was added the Yochanan ben Zakkai and later the Emtzai (Middle) and the Istambuli synagogues, the four forming one complex. The buildings fell into disrepair owing to the poverty of the community but were repaired in 1835; in 1870 they were visited by the Emperor Franz Josef II of Austria. When the old city of Jerusalem was in Jordanian hands between 1948 and 1967 the complex of Sephardic synagogues was badly damaged and filled with garbage. The priceless antique furnishings were stolen but the walls, roofs and domes were found intact in 1967 and the synagogues have since been entirely repaired. All four have sunken floors. The Yochanan ben Zakkai and the Emtzai synagogues have Gothic cross-vaulting and the former has twin Arks and Gothic arches, but both buildings have Moorish features too – the windows of the Yochanan ben Zakkai and the perforated stone fanlights of the Emtzai. The Eliyahu Hanavi and the Istambuli synagogues are irregu-

The Ha'ari synagogue, one of the surviving houses of worship at Safed built during the period of Ottoman rule when this historic city of Upper Galilee, a centre of mystical Jewish teaching, was the home of many celebrated rabbis.

Interior of the Yochanan ben Zakkai synagogue, Jerusalem, part of a complex of synagogues erected by the Sephardim after the sequestration of the Ramban synagogue by the Ottoman governor in 1586. It was repaired and restored after being desecrated, ransacked and damaged during the period of Jordanian occupation of the city, 1948–67.

Decoration over the entrance to the Eliyahu Hanavi synagogue, Jerusalem. Similar work is to be found on synagogues at Safed erected by communities formed in Erez Israel in the sixteenth century after the expulsion of the Jews from the Spanish dominions.

larly shaped buildings with a central dome with windows in the cupola, supported by four broad, pointed arches in a local building style which adapted Byzantine and Islamic forms.

One synagogue at Fostat (old Cairo) already appeared to be ancient to the traveller Benjamin of Tudela when he visited Egypt in the twelfth century.[43] In the ninth century the Jews had acquired from the Patriarch an early Coptic Christian basilica and rebuilt it as a synagogue. Maimonides taught in this synagogue in the twelfth century. Benjamin of Tudela visited other synagogues but most of these were reported to be in ruins in the seventeenth century by the Egyptian Jewish chronicler, Joseph ben Isaac Simbari (1640–1703) in his *Divrei Yosef*. The ancient synagogue, however, survived. According to Jacob Safir[44] it had been rebuilt three years before his visit in 1864 but the attic was left intact. It was from this hiding-place, the now famous Cairo *genizah*, that in 1896 Solomon Schechter extracted 100,000 pages including invaluable ancient Hebrew texts and brought them to Cambridge University. A further 100,000 pages from the same source, procured by other scholars and by dealers, have been assembled.

Benjamin of Tudela's journey took him as far as Baghdad, where he described the principal synagogue, a columned hall opening on to a courtyard. He mentioned too that the synagogue was magnificently adorned with ornamental lettering; his description[45] calls to mind the bands with biblical inscriptions in the synagogues of Cordoba and Toledo, where the communities had contact with those of Egypt and Mesopotamia. The medieval synagogue at Damascus was a vaulted three-bay hall; that of Aleppo in Syria resembled on a smaller scale the Mosque of Ibn Tulun at Cairo built on to the old Amr Mosque between 877 and 879 because that one was too small. The bimah was a roofed pavilion which stood in the middle of a spacious square *sahn*, an open interior court, enclosed by a *ziyadah* under whose porticoes the congregation could shelter in inclement weather. The Ark was placed in a wall niche corresponding to the *mihrab* in the *qibla* wall of the mosque. This was also the plan of later synagogues in western Asia, including the New Synagogue of Baghdad.

Early in the seventeenth century an Italian Jesuit missionary in China came to know that there were Jewish communities of long standing in that country – where they had arrived, probably from Persia, by the beginning of the twelfth century. The synagogue of Kai-Feng, the capital of Honan Province in central China, was constructed in 1163 and restored in 1279. In 1653 the synagogue was rebuilt with the financial help of a Chinese Jewish mandarin, Chao Ying Ch'en. The synagogue complex consisted of four courts pointed west towards Jerusalem, covering an area 92–123 m in length and about 46 m wide; the prayer-hall (about 18.5 × 12.3 m) was in the innermost court. Drawings of the synagogue made by Jesuit missionaries are in the Archives of the Society of Jesus in Paris. In 1870 it was reported that the community had disintegrated and the building was in ruins.

In Europe, in the countries of settlement after the dispersals at the end of the Middle Ages, synagogue building continued, subject to the prevailing conditions. The search for an ideal arrangement in a period of new awareness of architectural themes led to different solutions – variations of a latitudinal plan in Italy and of a concentric plan in Poland.

4 *The Renaissance in Italy*

In Italy the period from about 1450 to 1650 was characterized by a dazzling intellectual and cultural reawakening and a metamorphosis which sprang from a rebirth of classical forms and ideas in the arts and the development of secular culture. The agrarian, feudal and monastic patterns of the Middle Ages were overwhelmed by an urban mercantile civilization in the fourteenth and fifteenth centuries, most remarkable in the city-states of Florence, Milan, Venice and Ferrara. The Renaissance was born in the northern half of the peninsula and flourished in an area roughly bounded by Rome, Milan and Venice. With the possible exception of the lively Neapolitan court, the south, under the rule of the Spanish house of Aragon, was barely affected by these events in the north. The individual thinker, characteristic of the Renaissance, first appeared in Florence, where the Medici family had established their control of an elegant, developing mercantile and domestic civilization. Already by the end of the fifteenth century the revival of classical learning dominated intellectual life and this provoked a new freedom of thought in morals and theology. The classical ruins, especially those of Rome, were eagerly examined with new attention. Architects sought to rediscover the secrets of mathematical proportion, the harmony of elements, the relation of the human figure to the circle – all principles that had been established by the Greeks.

The Renaissance intellectual sought a perfection based on order, an order in which the dignity and importance of man himself was adequately expressed. The research of the architects and their contemplation of antiquity resulted in an immense change in architectural forms in which the shapes related to the intellect, and the juxtaposition and connection of defined spaces were subject to the requirements of harmony. As the fifteenth century drew on, this relentless striving for the finite resulted in a purism which some artists found restrictive. By the middle of the century their efforts to break away and seek a new concept of space gave birth to an architectural approach now called Mannerism. In the latter half of the century a metamorphosis in thinking took place: the classical finite, characterized by factual expression, gave way to the infinite, characterized by imaginative expression. This resulted in the baroque style which reached its zenith in the seventeenth century under Bernini and Longhena. In architecture the component parts were arranged in spatially complex compositions; the architect delighted in expansive forms where curve chased curve, and in expansive vistas where space volumes followed one another in exuberant progression. The decorative details of the style were in the same vein.

At the end of the fifteenth century Italy was divided into a number of independent states, in all of which Jewish families were residing. Some had ancient roots in Italy where the Jewish presence had been continuous for 1500 years or more, because despite intermittent persecutions there had never been a general order of expulsion. Over the centuries the first settlers had been joined by immigrants from Palestine, North Africa, the Levant and northern Europe. At the dawn of the sixteenth century a wave of refugees fleeing from the expulsion order in Spain in 1492 sought new homes in Italy; they were followed by others expelled from Portugal. The anti-Jewish decrees in Spain were also implemented in Sicily and Sardinia, ruled by the house of Aragon, and in the Kingdom of Naples, which

PREVIOUS PAGE The lavishly carved bimah with sweeping double-stair in the Levantine synagogue, Venice, attributed to the sculptor Andrea Brustolon (1662–1732).

came to include all the south of the peninsula after union with Sicily under the Spanish crown in 1504. By 1541 the Jewish population had been expelled from the whole of the south, where there had been a number of long-established communities including thirty in Sicily. Only at Benevento, which was a papal enclave, were Jews able to remain. The unfortunate Jews who lived in the southern part of the country were obliged to go abroad or seek new homes in the states of central and northern Italy where their own language, Italian, was spoken.

The Italian Jews were a heterogeneous group, representing many social strata and varying degrees of culture, economic stability, integration and religious orthodoxy. Rabbi Obadiah di Bertinoro passed through Sicily in 1488 on his way to Jerusalem and noted in his journal the low state of morality that prevailed among the Jews there because they were forced to live in the worst areas along with beggars, prostitutes and petty criminals. The Rabbi reported that most of the Jewish brides were already pregnant when they stepped under the wedding canopy.[1] Such moral lapses were not confined to the communities in Sicily. In 1526-7 when the population of Rome numbered 55,000, of whom 1750 were Jews, there were 1500 prostitutes including thirty Jewish women.[2] Nor did the young Jewish men confine their proclivities to their future brides or to harlots. In the sixteenth century instances of homosexual acts are reported,[3] behaviour which was practically unheard of elsewhere in Jewry until recent times and apparently so alien to the Jewish nature that the sages held that Rabbi Judah's forbidding two bachelors to sleep together under one blanket[4] was quite unnecessary, it being so unlikely that anything untoward might occur.[5]

The most influential Jews were the pawnbroker-bankers, not only because some of them had amassed great wealth which they administered with a consummate skill far in advance of their time, but also because their services were invaluable to the rulers. The practice of usury was still forbidden to Christians but as it was recognized to be a necessary social evil it was permitted to Jews, who were considered to be past redemption anyway. Consequently they were frequently invited to open pawnbroking and moneylending establishments. Jewish banks had flourished in surprising numbers even in small towns and villages for many years before the Renaissance. Many immigrant refugees who were experienced bankers and pawnbroker-moneylenders were able to continue their business and became financiers of importance. Communities grew up and flourished internally around these wealthy families. The conditions of the communities and the attitude of the authorities towards them varied periodically and from state to state.

Rome was the capital of the Papal States, which extended across the middle of the peninsula, stretching north to include Bologna (taken by Pope Julius II in 1506 and annexed in 1513) and east to the important Adriatic port of Ancona (annexed in 1532). During the Renaissance, both abroad and in Italy, the political and spiritual dominion of the Church was on the wane but the popes kept extravagant court in Rome and lived like lay sovereigns. Alexander VI (Borgia), one of the most memorable Renaissance pontiffs, reigned in sumptuous style; he died at a banquet by drinking the poison he had prepared for a guest. Several Renaissance

popes were enthusiastic students of the humanities and classical antiquity, and great patrons of the arts. The revival of classical learning was
not considered incompatible with the glorification of the Church.

The position of the Jews in Rome and the Papal States was unique
because the Pope was at the same time their temporal ruler and the head
of the Christian Church. Consequently the papal attitude to the Jewish
subjects was ambiguous. The Jews were ridiculed and ceremonially
rebuked, made the object of public scorn and the butt of scathing anti-
Jewish sermons, yet able Jewish physicians like Bonet de Lattès were
appointed to the person of the pontiff. The services of the Jewish bankers
were sought after and later, even after severe restrictions had been
imposed on the Jews and Jewish physicians forbidden to treat Christians,
Pope Sixtus v did not disdain business dealings with Meir Magino, the
Jewish inventor and silk manufacturer in whose favour he issued a papal
bull in 1587 granting special privileges in the silk industry; Meir in return
promised to pay half his profits to the Pope's sister. Pope Leo x (Medici),
who incurred the protests of Luther by his sale of indulgences, was a
great patron of the arts. He bestowed the title of count on the musician
Giovan Maria, a converted Jew, and also gave him a castle. During the
reign of this pope (1513–21) the Rabbi of Rome was a frequent visitor
to the Vatican. Anna, a Jewish cosmetician, and Jewish fortune-tellers
were patronized by ladies of the Roman aristocracy.

In 1524 a fantastic Jewish adventurer, David Reubeni, appeared in
Rome, presenting himself as the envoy of his brother Joseph, the king
of an Arabian realm whose subjects were all Jews, descendants of the
lost tribes of Israel. Reubeni's glamour was enhanced by his ostentatious
progress from place to place on a white horse and by his exotic clothes
and impressive mien – at times devoutly ascetic, at times boastful and
belligerent. Reubeni promised that King Joseph's army would, if
equipped with arms by the Pope and the Christian sovereigns, defeat the
Turks and sweep the Moslems out of Palestine. This prospect appealed
to Christians, and also to Jews, to whom Reubeni explained his mission
as one which would terminate the Diaspora and lead to their return to
Erez Israel, the Land of Promise. He contrived to be received by Pope
Clement vii with great pomp; the Christians of Rome thronged about
Reubeni and his escort, a retinue of ten Jews. The Pope was totally hood-
winked by this extraordinary person and furnished him with letters of
introduction to other sovereigns. The euphoric Roman Jews placed their
resources at his command.

Another curious person, Salomon Molco, a Portuguese Marrano who
had returned to the Jewish faith through the influence of Reubeni, after
spending some time in Palestine where he developed mystical and mes-
sianic pretensions, also managed to reach the presence of Pope Clement
vii, to whom he prophesied a great flood of the Tiber, an earthquake
in Portugal and the appearance of a comet. When these three events duly
occurred in 1530 and 1531 and Molco's prestige soared, he proclaimed
his pretension to be the Messiah more openly. Consequently the Inquisition condemned him to be burned but the Pope helped him to escape
abroad. However, he was captured in Germany, sent back to Italy and
burned at the stake at Mantua in 1532.

...ws from the Rome ghetto may have ...en models for Michelangelo's ...ophets painted on the ceiling of the ...stine Chapel in the Vatican, ...mpleted in 1512. This is the ...gnified head of the prophet Ezekiel.

Despite the cruelty of the Inquisition, merciless to Marranos suspected of reverting to Judaism, the broader intellectual and cultural horizons · of the time coincided in Rome with an unaccustomed magnanimity towards the Jews, which was partly due to academic curiosity. The new interest of the Renaissance scholars in the Pentateuch led to the establishment of a Chair of Hebrew at the University of Rome in 1514 and contacts between Jewish and Christian scholars of Hebrew. Michelangelo's statue of Moses interested and delighted the Jews of Rome who flocked to inspect and admire it.[6] He probably used models from the Roman Jewish community for his biblical prophets painted in the Sistine Chapel of the Vatican Palace (1508–12). The general *détente* in Jewish–Christian relations in Rome during the papacy of Pope Leo X so overwhelmed the Roman Jews that the community wrote to the sages in Jerusalem to enquire whether any premonitory signs had been noted there of the coming redemption of the Jewish people.[7]

It was customary for the Jewish community to present the Books of the Law to a new pontiff during his coronation procession. For Leo X's coronation the Jews erected at the door of the Castel Sant'Angelo a dais on scaffolding all covered in cloth of gold, from which to make their presentation. 'We confirm but we do not approve,'[8] said the Pope, taking the book and dropping it.

By 1554 there were nine synagogues in Rome; these included old buildings like the medieval synagogue of Quattro Capi, adjacent to the bridge of that name across the Tiber, a synagogue in the Arenula quarter, the French synagogue (for whose foundation in 1504 by his personal physician Samuel Zarfati, Pope Julius II issued a bull), the Castilian synagogue which shared the same building, and the synagogue of the Catalans who had come from the region of Barcelona and the Balearic Islands, for which Pope Leo X granted papal approval in 1519.[9]

Each foreign language group and liturgical rite had its own synagogue while the Italian Jews had four, segregated according to the length of time of their family's residence in Rome. The influx of refugees provoked serious rifts in the community: these squabbles were resolved on the administrative level by an influential banker from Tuscany, Daniele di Isaac Pisa, who in 1524 persuaded the various factions to agree regarding the distribution of offices in the community.

Throughout the sixteenth century the Jewish community resident in Rome had increased in numbers; 1750 Jews were recorded in 1526–7 and 3500 in 1592,[10] but around 1550 the number was much larger because many left for states where better conditions prevailed and others resorted to conversion after the promulgation of the infamous edict, *Cum nimis absurdam*, by Pope Paul IV in 1555. This edict began with a reminder that through their own fault God had condemned the Jews to eternal slavery and that therefore it was intolerable that they should live among Christians, in the best streets and squares of the city and close to churches, without any distinguishing mark in their dress, and employing Christian maidservants and wet-nurses. The papal bull introduced fourteen restrictive measures which included the enclosure of all Jews in towns of the Papal States in a walled-in quarter with only one entrance gate; each such ghetto was allowed only one synagogue – all others were to be demolished.

All property owned by Jews was to be sold immediately to Christians. All male Jews were to wear a yellow beret, and the females a yellow shawl or veil. Jews were forbidden to employ Christian servants or even maintain familiar or intimate relationships with Christians. Jews were banned from all trading except in old clothes and junk, while those who had banking licences had limitations placed on their business activity. All previous concessions whatsoever made to Jews individually or collectively were abrogated.

The Roman community attempted to buy off the implementation of these crushing laws by offering the Pope a huge sum of money, but their offer was rejected. The ghetto was enclosed, and Jews' property was sold at far below its value under the watchful and partisan eye of the Apostolic Chamber. Special commissioners were dispatched to other towns and villages of the Papal States to supervise the strict application of the edict. In Rome a few Jews opted for baptism to preserve their property and social dignity. In one village in the Marches seventeen Jews accepted baptism; at Benevento, a papal enclave south of Rome, it appears that many of the community resorted to baptism, since the church of the neighbourhood where they lived was renamed Santo Stefano dei Neofiti (St Stephen of the Neophytes). Many affluent Jews emigrated to Turkey and Palestine, but the plan of one entire Jewish community of about 200 persons in the little town of Cori, south of Rome, to reach the Jewish settlement at Tiberias in Galilee in 1556, never came to fruition.

In 1561 Pius IV mitigated some of the harsh decrees of 1555, permitting Jews to engage in other trades, have shops outside the ghetto, make small loans charging up to eighteen per cent interest, purchase property up to a value of 1500 gold scudi, and travel without wearing the distinctive cap. In 1566 Pius V revoked these concessions and again implemented the earlier restrictions, so that those unfortunate Jews who had purchased property in the interim were once more obliged to sell to Christians at a loss. Another harsh edict followed in 1569 – Pius V's bull *Hebraeorum gens sola quondam a Deo Dilecta*, which expelled Jews from all places in the Papal States except the ghettos of the cities of Rome and Ancona. More than fifty communities were totally eliminated; their synagogues were abandoned at the dispersal of 1569 and put to secular use or converted into churches, as implied by the name of San Gregorio della Sinagoga at Spoleto. In 1554 there had been no fewer than 106 taxed synagogues in the Papal States[11] excluding those in Rome.

Rabbi Josef Zarfati, a native of Fez in Morocco who was converted to Christianity in 1552 and took the name of Andrea de' Monti, induced Pope Gregory XIII to issue the bulls of 1557 and 1584 which ordered that, wherever the Jews had a synagogue, members of the community above the age of twelve must attend a weekly service preached by a priest in a nearby oratory, preferably on the Jewish Sabbath and geared to confute the text read that day in the synagogue. A college was founded to train theological students for this task and among the most zealous preachers were a number of converted Jews. In 1581 Montaigne, on a visit to Rome, saw about sixty Jews attending an obligatory sermon. The practice continued to be enforced until it was abrogated by Pope Pius IX in 1847. Another initiative of Gregory XIII was a decree of 1581 by

An old photograph showing a street in the Rome ghetto before the urban re-planning at the beginning of the present century. Several thousand Jews lived within the walls of this confine of just under one hectare (two-and-a-half acres).

To cater for the ethnic, linguistic and social differences of the Roman Jewish community the synagogues of five congregations, the Cinque Scuole, were accommodated in two buildings at the corner of the central square of the ghetto. One main entrance was maintained to satisfy the papal rule allowing only one synagogue. An old photograph taken before the complex was demolished in 1910.

which Jewish physicians were forbidden to treat Christians. This suffocated many of the best practitioners in Europe, whose science and skill had been appreciated by earlier popes, and rendered a disservice to civilization in impeding the progress of medicine. This decree also empowered the officers of the Inquisition to search inside the ghetto for prohibited books or any signs of infractions of the law.

Several thousand Jews were crowded into the Rome ghetto, an area of only one hectare. Because of ethnic, linguistic and social differences they were unwilling to worship together in the one synagogue permitted, so for a while six, and subsequently five, separate synagogues were accommodated in two adjoining buildings at the corner of a square called the 'Jews' Market', the only open space in the ghetto. The date of this edifice, the Cinque Scuole, can be accurately established as between 1573 and 1581. The ruinous church of Santa Maria a Capite Molarum, otherwise known as Santa Maria a, de, or iuxta, Flumen and also called Santa Maria in Candelabro (perhaps because of a menorah sculpted in the vicinity) was deconsecrated by *motu proprio* of Pope Gregory XIII, 1 February 1573,[12] and on its site the Cinque Scuole buildings were erected some time before 1581 when the Pope ordered the community to maintain the appearance of a single synagogue by eliminating all but one entrance.[13] A few years later the Vatican Archivist, Michele Lonigo, reported that the church of Santa Maria a Capite Molarum had been demolished and that it stood in the Jewish quarter 'where their *scuola* is'.[14]

The architect was challenged by spatial problems which did not arise in churches or civic buildings. The Ark and the bimah, the two focal points, had to be carefully balanced. At the same time the twin functions of the building, one sacred, the other social and didactic, had to be considered. The restrictions of space made the problem more acute in the towns with an overcrowded ghetto but it is not surprising that in Renaissance Italy a rational and agreeable solution was devised in a bifocal arrangement of the prayer-hall on a latitudinal plan. The Ark and bimah were placed to face one another against the two short walls and an ample aisle was created between them by aligning the stools or benches in two sections facing one another and parallel to the two long walls. The entrance door was usually in one of the long walls. It has not been determined when and where this layout was first employed; possibly it was in the Cinque Scuole building in Rome at the end of the sixteenth century. By the end of the seventeenth century this plan was in widespread use in Italy. There is nothing in the scant iconographical and descriptive evidence of the arrangement of the medieval Italian synagogues to indicate that the bifocal latitudinal plan was in use there before the Renaissance. While it appears that the Ark and bimah were placed on opposite walls in the small synagogue at Cordoba, and it is possible that refugees from Cordoba who had seen this experiment of the decentralization of the bimah brought the idea to Italy, it is difficult to give much weight to this theory. The architect David Cassuto, who has devoted study and thought to the question, suggests that the Christian architects in Renaissance Italy, considering the needs of the community to use the prayer-halls also as Midrashim for study, were inspired by the arrangement of the contemporary universities in Italy to devise the latitudinal plan for the synagogue.

It is frustrating that no accurate description has been found of the layout of two synagogues in the papal enclave in the south of France, the Comtat Venaissin. The first synagogues built at Carpentras (1367) and Cavaillon (1499) have undergone several changes over the centuries: however, it does appear that from an early date their plan did not include a central bimah and that something close to the bifocal arrangement may have been employed.

In Rome, the Scuola Tempio of the Italian congregation had the choicest location in the Cinque Scuole complex. It occupied the first floor and was reached by the main stair. On the floor above was the Talmudic Academy (Talmud Torah). The plan of the synagogue, which measured 20×12.5 m,[15] was latitudinal. The architect took pains to achieve equilibrium between the Ark and bimah by dividing the short walls into three bays by means of twisted columns. The Ark stood on a raised platform reached by four steps in the larger central bay at one end, flanked by a pair of smaller Arks to complete the symmetry in the adjacent bays. The central bay opposite the Ark contained the bimah, raised on columns with gilded Corinthian capitals. Four gilded Corinthian columns decorated with a design of palm leaves and branches supported the triangular pediment of the elegant Ark, which was in the form of a classical prostyle temple-front with the Tables of the Law in the tympanum. Three rows of benches were aligned parallel to the long walls. The handsome decoration was completed by a fine carved frieze and a deeply coffered ceiling of the type found in Roman Renaissance palaces.[16]

Of the same dimensions as the Scuola Tempio, and situated on the floor beneath it, was the Catalan synagogue, also arranged on the latitudinal plan with the same disposition of the Ark, bimah and seating. Across one short wall over the bimah the women's gallery was fitted. Between 1622 and 1628 the officers of this congregation had their premises refurbished. To do this they employed the Roman architect Girolamo Rainaldi[17] (1570–1655) – an ambitious choice, for he had been trained by the famous papal architect Domenico Fontana. Among Rainaldi's achievements were the Colonna Chapel in the Basilica of St John in Lateran, the design for the ornate altar of the Pauline Chapel in the Vatican, and the execution of designs by Michelangelo for Roman palaces. He also began the church of St Agnes in Agone in Piazza Navona for Pope Innocent, but after his death it was altered and completed by Borromini. It is interesting not only that such a distinguished architect was picked to work on a synagogue, but also that he accepted the commission. The revetment of the walls in polychrome marble was probably part of his redecoration, as well as the frieze sculpted with swags, winged heads of cherubim and urns in the manner of contemporary church altar-pieces, and the classical Ark whose pediment was supported by fluted Corinthian columns with gilded capitals and crowned with a menorah reminiscent of the one sculpted on the Arch of Titus. Instead of smaller Arks, the Catalan synagogue Ark was flanked by handsome marble seats for the Parnassim, apparently part of Rainaldi's decoration.[18] A covered balcony in the form of a classical temple protruding from the façade of the building on the first floor over a portico possibly also dates from the time of Rainaldi's work.

The rest of the Cinque Scuole complex adjoined the taller building at right angles; its pleasant Renaissance façade had five-bay loggias on the first and second floors. The Castilian, Sicilian and New (Nova) synagogues were housed in this part as well as the united congregations of the Quattro Capi and Portaleone synagogues (whose old building had been outside the ghetto) until they ceased to worship separately in 1667. The Castilian synagogue had marble revetment on the walls and marble seats for the Parnassim flanking an elaborate, heavily carved Ark with a gilded Hebrew inscription in the tympanum of its open segmental pediment[19] and ornate bronze rails and fittings. The modest Sicilian synagogue was also arranged on the latitudinal plan. The carving on the bimah included a Judaic symbol – six pomegranates – and the triangular pediment of the Ark was crowned with the Tables of the Law.[20] The intricacies of condominium in the Cinque Scuole frequently caused friction and fierce arguments flared up over the joint use of the internal corridors and stairs by which each congregation reached its own synagogue from the one main entrance. Over the centuries superb gifts were donated to the synagogues: candelabra, ritual objects in silver, and tapestries. Some of these are now in the museum of the community in the present synagogue. The Cinque Scuole complex itself was damaged by fire in 1893 and eventually demolished in 1910 as part of the replanning scheme for the ghetto area.

In the Adriatic port-city of Ancona the Jewish community was herded into an enclosed ghetto subject to the changing attitudes and humours of the reigning pontiffs until 1848, when the liberal Pope Pius IX had the walls and gates thrown down. Ancona, an important trading port for the Middle East, attracted Jews and Marranos from the Levant. When twenty-six wretched Marranos, who included Turkish citizens, were suspected of reverting to Judaism and burned at the stake, the energetic Gracia Nasi procured the interest of the Sultan and attempted a boycott of the port in retaliation.

The Levantine synagogue survives: it is arranged on the latitudinal plan with rows of double benches on the long walls, but the Ark is much more important than the bimah and dominates the room. It stands between two windows under which are the chairs of the Parnassim and is enclosed by an imposing wrought-iron grille crowned with a cupola.

The small Italian synagogue of 1635 which was demolished in the course of urban replanning in 1932 was a barrel-vaulted chamber measuring only 12.2 × 6.4 m.[21] Its plan was the latitudinal one with the entrance in the middle of one long wall and double benches in rows, but the short walls were entirely occupied by the Ark and the bimah which together took up one-third of the total floor space. The Ark, with fine silver doors, was surrounded by a wrought-iron grille and flanked by windows, as in the Levantine synagogue; beneath them the sumptuous baroque armchairs for the Parnassim were of the type found in princely Italian palaces of the seventeenth century. The arch over the Ark continued on each side to form a three-bay screen reminiscent of the iconostasis of eastern churches. The bimah was raised on columns and reached by twin flights of steps placed against the walls and curving round the corners on each side. The entrance was placed on the west wall underneath the bimah

...th Jews and Christians in the ...venteenth century were interested in ...e appearance of the Temple. This ...ded carving on the bimah made for ...e Italian synagogue in Pesaro, Italy, ...picts the Temple according to the ...agination of an artist influenced by ...ssicism.

and facing the Ark, an arrangement used also at Pesaro and in the synagogues of the Comtat Venaissin in France.

Immediately to the north-east of the Papal States lay the Duchy of Urbino ruled by the Montefeltro family. Until its annexation by the Papal States in 1631 this Duchy was a haven for many Jews, although Duke Guidobaldo II instituted a ghetto system in 1570 because of the influx of refugees fleeing from the papal restrictions. Duke Federigo, who reigned from 1444 to 1482, employed the greatest painters, artisans and architects in Italy to embellish his hill-top citadel. A predella in the Ducal Palace, painted by Paolo Uccello for the Urbino Confraternity of Corpus Christi in 1467–8, depicts in three scenes a Jew in a banking establishment purchasing a Host from a poor woman, the desecration of the Host, and the execution of the Jew with all his family. In *Il Cortegiano* Baldassare Castiglione described the refined court of the next Duke, Guidobaldo I, when Urbino was a dazzling centre of Renaissance activity which included the painter Raphael (Raffaele Sanzio) who was born in a house near the palace in 1483. Perhaps the bearded officiant in his painting *The Marriage of the Virgin*, painted in 1504 and now in the Brera Gallery, Milan, may have been inspired by a rabbi he saw in his native Urbino. In the reign of Duke Francesco Maria I, a Jewish wedding was solemnized in 1511 in a room of the palace by formal consummation before witnesses,[22] a practice permitted but not encouraged by rabbinical law.

After the annexation of the Duchy by the Pope in 1631, the Jewish population dwindled. In a Hebrew manuscript of 1704, the *Sefer Ha-Maftid* of Urbino, published in facsimile at Jerusalem in 1964, there is a bird's-eye view of the interior of the Urbino synagogue which certainly had a centrally placed octagonal bimah. The manuscript also includes a drawing of the Ark made in 1551 and shows that this handsome Renaissance piece, now in the Jewish Museum, New York, was originally crowned by a balustrade and three domes. The domes are similar to those of the early Ark preserved at Livorno and of an Ark brought from Livorno to the Eliahu synagogue at Jerusalem. Without the top the Ark resembles the breakfront cabinets made for domestic use in the sixteenth century; according to tradition it was a gift from Duke Guidobaldo II to the Jewish community. After the community disintegrated the synagogue fell into disuse and in the eighteenth century was partly owned by Christians.

At Pesaro, a port-city of the Duchy, a Jewish community existed from the thirteenth century onwards. The two synagogues, one Italian, one Spanish, which once served a thriving mercantile community, are no longer in use. The ghetto was established and enclosed with 500 inhabitants at the papal annexation of 1634.

Both synagogues, which appear to date from the late sixteenth century with signs of later renovation, are built on the latitudinal plan. The architect of the Italian synagogue achieved a fine symmetry and a felicitous balance between the Ark and bimah, which stand on the short walls set in pavilions beneath little cupolas. Each has six columns: those of the Ark, fluted Corinthian, those of the bimah, smooth Ionic. Only the arm-rests differentiate the chairs of the Parnassim from the benches. The modesty of these chairs was intentional, in order not to detract from the Ark. In one long wall are twin entrances to the room. The Spanish synagogue employed the imaginative solution to the problem of spatial relationships used at Ancona and in the Comtat Venaissin. The handsome vaulted ceiling decorated with classical rosettes in high relief descends without interruption to the crowns of triple arches above the bimah and the flights of the curving twin-stair which flank it; the bimah is raised up on columns and the entrance door is beneath it on the west wall so that, on entering, worshippers immediately faced the splendid gilded Ark surmounted by a crown on the short east wall opposite. Despite the grandeur of this Ark, a signed and dated work of the early eighteenth century now set up in the Livorno synagogue, it was overshadowed by the importance of the bimah complex which recalls the church layout of a high altar set up above the crypt.

A third Jewish community was permitted in the Duchy of Urbino after 1631, at Senigallia, where there were then forty Jewish families. A century later 600 people were living in the ghetto. The Spanish synagogue, now no longer in use, had affinities with those of Pesaro and Ancona in both style and arrangement.

Further north the Duchy of Ferrara, ruled by the Este family, was another haven for refugee Jews from abroad and from the Papal States until 1598 when the Pope obtained the sovereignty of this Duchy also. However, an illegitimate branch of the Estes continued to rule a part of the Este dominions, the Duchy of Modena, and many Jews settled there to continue to enjoy Este protection, swelling the community founded in Modena by bankers in the fourteenth century. A Christian musician at Modena, Orazio Vecchi (1550–1605), fascinated by the alien sound of Jews at worship in the synagogue, made it the subject of his polyphonic work *Amphiparnasso*. The old synagogue of the Sephardic rite was demolished when a new one was built in 1882; the beautiful and unusual Ark, a work of the fifteenth or early sixteenth century, is in the Musée de Cluny in Paris. There were 2000 Jews in Modena when the ghetto was eventually instituted in 1669–71, another thousand were scattered among smaller towns such as Carpi, Correggio, Guastalla and Mirandola, and there was a community at Reggio.[23]

When the powerful Estes ruled Renaissance Ferrara they conducted progressive economic policies, patronized and practised the arts and planned matrimonial alliances with other Italian dynasties as part of a policy of peaceful coexistence. Duke Ercole I's brilliant daughter Isabella married the Gonzaga ruler of Mantua, another daughter, Beatrice, married Lodovico Sforza ('Il Moro'), Duke of Milan, while his son and successor, Duke Alfonso I, married Lucrezia, daughter of the Borgia Pope, Alexander VI, herself a patroness of letters, arts and science.

On hearing that twenty-one Jewish refugee families had landed at Genoa from Spain in 1492, Duke Ercole I invited them to settle at Ferrara where there was already a prosperous Jewish community, founded at the end of the thirteenth century. The first refugees were joined by others, including a number of Marranos. The astute Duke was not disappointed in his hope that these versatile immigrants would stimulate the economic development of the Duchy and contribute to its intellectual life. He granted the settlers permission to open and administer their own synagogue. In 1532, Duke Ercole II welcomed refugee Jews from Bohemia and permitted them to establish an Ashkenazi synagogue, and in 1540, when the Duchy of Milan was annexed to the Spanish crown, the Duke encouraged the Milanese Jews to settle in Ferrara. The community thus increased so rapidly that by the middle of the sixteenth century there were ten synagogues in the city, some of which must have reflected the wealth of the leading families in their splendid ornamentation. With the papal takeover in 1598 the Jews were allowed to retain only one synagogue for each rite, Italian, Spanish-Portuguese (Sephardic) and German (Ashkenazi). All three were installed on the upper floors of unobtrusive buildings. Fascist gangs desecrated and ransacked them in 1941 and again in November 1944 when the regime was in its death throes, pillaging and devastating also the archives, library and asylums.

The Spanish synagogue, rebuilt in the seventeenth century, was designed on the latitudinal plan, 20×6.8 m; an opening without doors in one of the long walls communicated with a spacious vestibule which had fitted benches against its walls. The Ark and bimah, as usual, faced one another on the short walls but when later a women's gallery was inserted at the bimah end, the bimah was moved to a new position at the crossing of the main axis of the synagogue room and the vestibule. The seventeenth-century decoration was reminiscent of that of contemporary Catholic churches; the vault was decorated above the cornice with stucco swags and festoons of fruit. The Ark, with its imposing, ornate polychrome marble surrounded by bronze grille and gates, is like a baroque altar. A persistent tradition would have it that the black marble spiral columns of the Ark were brought to Ferrara from Spain by the first refugees, but this is most unlikely. There are examples of twisted columns in secular Spanish Gothic buildings but it was not until about 150 years after the great Jewish exodus that barley-sugar columns became a popular feature of baroque in Spain, where they were known as *Salomónica* because of the current belief that this style was used in Solomon's Temple. In Italy in the seventeenth century, when the Ferrara synagogue was redecorated, the so-called Solomonic order had been made fashionable by Bernini, whose marvellous *baldacchino* in St Peter's, Rome, with its twisted columns recalled the Colonna Santa in the basilica which, according to tradition, came from Solomon's Temple. In the light of this association it is not surprising that the style found favour among the Jews also. The Ark and bimah, which were salvaged and repaired after the sacking of 1944, were installed in the Lampronti Oratory beneath the Livorno synagogue.

The Italian and German synagogues were rebuilt in the eighteenth century so nothing remains to reflect the splendour of the synagogues of Ferrara Jewry in its heyday under the Este dukes when the community included outstanding personalities like the Abravanels and Gracia Nasi.

The Abravanels came to Ferrara in 1541 from Naples, where they had lived since the expulsion from Spain. After Samuel's death in 1547 his widow, Benvenida, a woman who possessed outstanding intellectual and cultural gifts, administered his financial affairs with great ability. Through the marriage of her former ward, Eleanora de Toledo, to Cosimo de' Medici, Grand Duke of Tuscany, Benvenida was able to maintain relations with their court in Florence and negotiate important commercial concessions; her son Jacob acted as trustee for Cosimo de' Medici in banking matters. A letter of 22 July 1557 from Cosimo to '*Mᵒ Giacob, hebreo in Ferrara*' survives; in it he asks Abravanel to settle a debt of 5000 scudi to the Duke of Ferrara, on his behalf.[24] The Abravanels lived in high Renaissance grandeur in Ferrara, welcoming in their circle both Christian and Jewish scholars and extending generous help to the needy Jewish refugees who arrived there. Poets and chroniclers extolled Benvenida's virtues. Immanuel Aboab described her as the most noble and high-spirited Jewish woman since the dispersal,[25] but Benvenida failed to display her usual astuteness when the adventurer Reubeni reached Ferrara; she espoused his cause enthusiastically and embroidered for him a gorgeous banner depicting the Ten Commandments.

Gracia Nasi left her native Portugal as a young widow in 1537. She had been brought up as a Christian because her rich Jewish parents had become Marranos. After a sojourn in the Netherlands she came to Venice, where she was denounced as a Judaizer by her own sister and only escaped the Inquisition because her nephew procured the diplomatic intervention of the Sultan on her behalf. She moved to Ferrara, where she was able to discard all pretence of being a Christian and laboured energetically to help Marranos flee from Portugal. Gracia's political, academic and commercial acumen made her a valued member of the Jewish community during her residence at Ferrara. The Ferrara Spanish Bible, printed in 1553, was dedicated to her. In that year she left for Constantinople where she joined her nephew Joseph Nasi, later Duke of Naxos, who married her only child Reyna. There, Gracia established schools and synagogues and obtained from the Sultan a lease of Tiberias in Palestine in order to found a Jewish settlement, to which Jews from Italy were invited to come and to engage in the wool and silk industries.

The Republic of Venice was ruled by a Doge and Great Council. Venice itself was an opulent maritime centre specializing in trade with its own colonies, Crete and Cyprus, as well as the rest of the Levant. This commerce helped to maintain Venice's centuries-old cultural links with Byzantium. The Republic also included a large area of the fertile hinterland with several important towns and many prosperous villages. Venice's position in the network of Italian states was a peculiar one. It was relatively immune from ecclesiastical control. The entire city was excommunicated in 1483 and in 1606 it was placed under an interdict by Pope Paul v but this was contemptuously disregarded.

The Gothic style in architecture lingered longer in Venice than elsewhere in Italy, perhaps because its practitioners produced examples of extraordinary grace and charm. When Renaissance ideas took root the great Venetian school of painting was born, beginning in the fifteenth century with Jacopo Bellini and his sons Gentile and Giovanni and continued by Carpaccio, Titian, Tintoretto, Veronese and Tiepolo. The erudite architect Palladio (1508–80), who published his influential *Quattro Libri dell' Architettura* (Four Books of Architecture) in 1570, worked principally in Venice and the territory of the Republic, where he designed urban palaces, splendid villas, superb churches such as San Giorgio Maggiore (begun in 1566) and Il Redentore (1576) in Venice, and the famous theatre at Vicenza (1580).

The sermons of Rabbi Leone Modena, one of the most eloquent of the Venetian rabbis, attracted Catholic clerics, foreign intellectuals and Venetian nobles to the synagogue where he preached. This portrait is from the frontispiece of his book *Historia de' Riti Hebraici*, an apology of Jewish life and customs published in 1637.

The Venetian Jewish community was not an ancient one. The Jews of the sporadic pre-Renaissance settlements were originally obliged to reside on an island, the Giudecca. At the beginning of the sixteenth century the community, which was greatly enlarged by the arrival of refugees from Spain, Portugal and the Spanish territories, was fortunate in having as its leader the richest Jew of the day, Asher Meshullam, better known as Anselmo del Banco. By arguing with the Venetian Senate that if the Jews were expelled they would lose the benefit of his substantial loans to the government as well as the taxes they collected on his colossal fortune, he was able to overcome the opposition of an unhealthy alliance between firebrand Christian preachers and a superstitious populace. The Senate negotiated terms for the permanent residence of the Jews but confined them to a quarter (chosen in March 1516) which could be closed and have its gates locked at night. It has been widely held that the Venetian name of this quarter, the *geto nuovo* (new foundry) gave rise to the word 'ghetto', later used universally to describe a restricted Jewish quarter. Eventually the meaning of the word was extended to denote any poor Jewish neighbourhood and more recently it has been applied to the residential areas of other underprivileged minority groups. It seems more likely that in fact the term 'ghetto' originates from the practice of forcibly disembarking the refugees from Spain on the jetty at Genoa and confining them there in a sort of quarantine. This is mentioned in an account of a refugee in the 1490s included in the *Responsa* of Rabbi David Ha-Cohen of Corfu, published at Constantinople in 1536, in which the Genoese are called 'Ghenovesi' and the *getto* or *gettata* 'ghetto' because of the customary guttural pronunciation of the soft 'g' in Spanish.[26]

The Venetian ghetto was the most extreme form of segregation yet imposed on a Jewish community, but it was tolerable because the rules were mild compared with those of most of the other Italian states. When expulsion orders were issued in 1527 and 1571 the community negotiated their suspension, and apart from the residential confinement the Jews were not deprived of other civil rights. As Shakespeare knew, while the Venetian authorities exacted a lot of money from the Jews, they afforded them the protective arm of the law. Shakespeare's Venetian merchant Antonio says,

> The duke cannot deny the course of law;
> For the commodity that strangers have
> With us in Venice if it be denied,
> Will much impeach the justice of this state;
> Since that the trade and profit of this city
> Consisteth of all nations.

Christians and Jews associated in commercial dealings. The merchant Antonio and the moneylender Shylock in *The Merchant of Venice* indicate how well known these types were even in other countries. A tour of the ghetto was considered *de rigueur* for visitors to see the exotic demeanour and costume of the turbaned Levantine Jews; it also attracted artists. The populace flocked to see the plays and revelries of the Purim feast. Thomas Coryat, an English traveller who visited the Venetian ghetto in 1608, remarked on the wonderful appearance of the Jewish women he saw there, 'as beautiful as I ever saw ... so gorgeous in their apparel, jewels, chains of gold, and rings adorned with precious stones, that some of our English countesses do scarce exceed them, having marvailous long trains like Princesses that are borne up by waiting women serving for the same purpose.'[27]

Venice gained fame for its Hebrew printing presses and the reputation of the Venetian rabbis was widespread. King Henry VIII of England sought their opinion in his case for divorce from Catherine of Aragon. Later the eloquent rabbis of Venice attracted a learned Christian audience. The Duke of Orleans, brother of the King of France, attended the Spanish synagogue to listen to a rabbi's sermon, when he made a state visit to the ghetto in 1629. Rabbi Leone Modena was one of the most eloquent and certainly the most eccentric of these preachers. The elegant synagogues must have seemed more like smart *salons* when the intellectuals of the ghetto rubbed shoulders with Catholic priests and Venetian aristocrats who crowded in to hear his sermons. He was born in Venice in 1571 and spent most of his life in the colourful precincts of the ghetto. A child prodigy, he attained fame as an orator at an early age; when he was twenty-one, in 1592, a large audience assembled to hear him preach in the German synagogue in Venice. He served variously as schoolteacher, synagogue official and proof-reader for Hebrew printers. He also wrote nuptial hymns and epitaphs for fees, which were his main source of income. He was the author of a Midrash which bears his name, of introductory verse in Hebrew for Christian works including a volume of Catholic theology, and of a clandestinely published apology for Jewish life and customs, *Historia de' Riti Hebraici* (1637), which was prompted by the English Ambassador, Sir Henry Wooten, who had urged him to write an explanation of Jewish customs on commission for King James I. Rabbi Leone was a paradoxical figure. He frequently denounced gambling and published a pamphlet vigorously decrying the vice, yet he lost heavily at the gaming tables himself. His spirited autobiography reveals him as a true product of the Renaissance, albeit in its decline.[28]

The Venetian Jews wanted their synagogues to be dignified expressions of their own wealth, culture and refined taste and to reflect the sumptuous life of the city. They could hardly follow Palladio's recommendation that a house of worship should be built on a beautiful square high above the houses of the city although it agreed with the Talmudic recommendation that a synagogue should stand on an elevated site. The best they could do was to use an upper storey. However, there was no lack of luxurious furnishings in the ghetto. Foreign ambassadors to Venice rented the furnishings for a palace from Jewish dealers, who would supply damask hangings, tapestries, canopied beds, chairs, tables, cabinets, silver, opulent gondola trappings, and even a painting by Titian or Veronese purchased from an impoverished nobleman or held in pawn against a loan. There were five synagogues as well as oratories in the ghetto to satisfy the requirements of the heterogeneous community, which recognized three major divisions: Ponentini (Westerners) from Italy, Spain and Portugal; Levantini (Easterners) from Turkey and the Near East; and Tedeschi (Germans) from the German states, Austria and Bohemia, and Ashkenazim generally. The Italian rite had one synagogue, the Spanish

The Canton synagogue in Venice was built in 1531 and re-planned about 1672. This view shows the interior which was modified and redecorated in 1736.

one, the Levantine one, and the Ashkenazi two – the Great and the Canton. The bifocal latitudinal plan was eventually adopted in the Ashkenazi synagogues, and in all five synagogues the Ark and bimah are on the short walls and the entrance in a long one, except in the Spanish synagogue where it was not possible to make an entrance in one of the long walls. Late in the seventeenth century modifications were made to the Italian, Levantine and Canton synagogues, where an apse was built protruding externally from a short wall to accommodate the bimah better. In the seventeenth century two smaller synagogues were founded, the Coanim and the Mesullamim, and in the eighteenth century another, the Luzzatto.

The enclosing boundary of the ghetto, where space as usual was at a premium, precluded lateral expansion so edifices grew vertically, storey perched upon storey. In the synagogue buildings the ground floor, which was liable to flooding, usually contained the administrative offices, schoolrooms, students' lodgings and a vestibule. The synagogues all have distinguished interiors only impaired in some instances by over-elaborate decoration; with their carved and gilded ornamentation and embroidered silk hangings they resembled the crimson and gold reception rooms of palaces on the Grand Canal in the seventeenth century. The Arks were like the lavish altars of fashionable chapels. Further improvements were made by the congregations in the eighteenth century.

An inscription on the modest front portal of the Great Synagogue at the south end of the *geto nuovo* square records that the 'Great Temple of the Ashkenazi rite, gift of Josef and Samuele Matatiah' was founded in 1528. Another inscription under the cornice of the façade reads (in translation), 'Great School of the Holy Community of Germans with the protection of God, Amen.'

The irregular plan of the synagogue on the top floor of the building was dictated by the lie of the adjacent buildings and the course of the canal which runs along the back of the edifice. The Renaissance-style walnut panelling on the lower part of the walls and the delightful walnut benches and seats may date from the time of the foundation, but the general appearance is due to extensive renovation and decoration in the latter half of the seventeenth century, when with considerable skill an architectural remedy was found to lessen the defect of the trapezoidal floor-plan. The women's gallery was fitted all round the hall behind a beautiful elliptical balustrade, thus masking the irregular angles of the upper part of the room. Concentric ovals on the ceiling and a circular motif in the terrazzo floor heighten the effect of the elliptical sweep of the balcony. The Ark was then deliberately positioned off-centre but both the Ark and the bimah are on the axis of the oval of the balcony.

The richly gilded pedimented Ark and the flanking seats of the Parnassim form a tripartite complex crowned by decorative gilded vases and cornucopias in the baroque style. A Hebrew inscription on the steps of the Ark attesting that the donor was 'the oldest of the Zemal brothers, Rabbi Menachem Cividale' (who lived in Venice in the second half of the seventeenth century), shows that the Ark complex is a work of the period of modification and decoration. Inside the doors of the Ark are other Hebrew inscriptions in mother-of-pearl inlay. The bimah, an unusual double *baldacchino* enclosed by a balustrade matching that of the gallery, dates from the same time. Its cornice, crowned at the corners by baroque urns, is supported by eight slender columns with Corinthian capitals. The frieze around the room beneath the gallery is inscribed with the Ten Commandments in gilded Hebrew characters. The synagogue, now no longer in regular use, looked even more ornate when it was hung with red, blue, violet and gold embroideries and adorned with handsome silver *rimmonim* and silver candelabra. The Jewish Museum which is housed in this building preserves some of the treasures of the congregations of the Venice ghetto. Among them is a lovely blue silk paroketh, the work of Stella Kohenet, wife of Izchak da Perugia;[29] she died at Venice in 1673.[30] Her embroidery may have been inspired by El Greco's triptych of Sinai which he painted at Venice about 1565–70; on the peaks in the paroketh Stella depicted the Tables of the Law and the Temple in Jerusalem.

It is usually stated that the Canton synagogue, in a building at the corner of the square washed on two sides by the canal, was named after a rich German banking family called Canton who built it as a private oratory in 1531. *Canton* means corner in Venetian dialect and it seems probable that both the surname of the family and the name of the synagogue derive from the situation. The date of the foundation is recorded on the portal, which opens into a ground-floor vestibule fitted with benches for use as a classroom and for assemblies; the synagogue above measures 12.8×7 m. Nothing here has impeded the perfect use of the latitudinal arrangement although it may not have been the original plan. The Ark and bimah on the short walls are separated by an ample aisle between the two sections of benches. The delicate symmetry is enhanced by matching pairs of windows in both the short walls on either side of the Ark and the bimah, and by the sequence of five tall windows on the long west wall overlooking the canal, balanced by two panels on each side of the door which is in the middle of the opposite long wall. Above the door and these panels and flush with the wall is the grille of the women's gallery, built above the corridor which runs the length of the wall behind the entrance. The synagogue was redecorated around the same time as most of the others in the Venetian ghetto, in this case more precisely about 1672, the date which appears on the present Ark. At that time or in 1736, when further improvements were carried out, a curvilinear five-bay apse, 2 m in depth and projecting externally from the building, was constructed to contain the new bimah; it is lit by a quaint lantern above and windows in the bays flanking the central one, which is a panelled niche. The lower part of the walls of the apse is panelled, the upper part exquisitely stuccoed and gilded with the same pattern of convoluted swirls and whorls which covers the external surface of the Ark and bimah. The bimah is on a raised platform above decorated steps. The Ark, whose doors are decorated internally with the Ten Commandments beneath a Torah crown, forms the central part of a beautifully carved and gilded tripartite complex between the seats of the Parnassim.

The Italian synagogue is on the top floor of a building in the *geto nuovo* square. Above the central window of the five in the façade is a shield beneath a coronet like those used on patrician palaces. It is inscribed 'Holy Italian Community in the year 1575'. The appearance of the interior,

The interior of the Spanish synagogue, the most opulent of the places of worship in Venice attributed to the Venetian architect Baldassare Longhena (1598–1682).

BELOW An example of the Italian bi-polar plan (after Pinkerfeld). The Spanish synagogue, Venice, after seventeenth-century modifications.

a – Ark

b – Bimah

c – Entrance

d – Men's benches

e – Benches of the Parnassim (wardens)

f – Line of women's gallery above

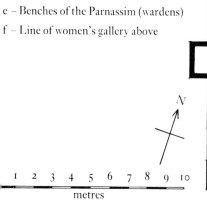

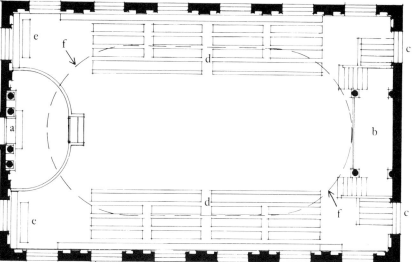

however, indicates that it was revamped at a later date, the last restoration being in 1740 by the Parnassim Coen, Nizza and Osimo, as recorded on a plaque. The synagogue is almost square, 10×9.5 m. The idea of an apse to accommodate the bimah was also employed here. The pentagonal apse, lit from above by windows in the drum of its baroque umbrella dome, was built out on to the roof of the adjacent building.

The harmonious composition of the façade of the Levantine synagogue gives it an air of distinction; its original symmetry was spoiled by the addition of the little cupolaed apse of the bimah, which juts out incongruously above the portal. The handsome building is situated in the quarter first settled by the eastern Jews, the *geto vecchio*, reached from the *geto nuovo* by a bridge over the canal. The ample ground-floor vestibule was adapted to house the Luzzatto *yeshiva*, at which time the front portal was blocked and a new entrance created at the side, leading to the marble stair to the synagogue on the first floor. The plan is the latitudinal one with two entrances in one long wall and the Ark and bimah on the short walls. The glory and eloquence of Venetian rabbinical preaching was intentionally expressed in the magnificence of the baroque bimah, an ornate *baldacchino* with 'Solomonic' spiral columns above a sweeping double stair; it overwhelms the room. The superb workmanship of the bimah and of the carved ceiling panels is attributed to an expert wood sculptor, Andrea Brustolon (1662–1732), who created wonderful baroque furniture such as his monumental suite for the Palazzo Venier, as well as the altar for the church of S. Pietro in his native town of Belluno. Despite its obelisks and urns the Ark is very sober and restrained compared with the bimah. The brass gates of the marble rail which surrounds the Ark, like the sanctuary rail in Christian churches, are later – the gift, according to the inscription, of Rabbi Menachem di Maimon Vivante in 1786.

The Spanish synagogue, near the Levantine, is the largest of the five in Venice. It is still in use, now serving the whole community, and has functioned in the same quarters for over four centuries; it was established in 1555. A variant of the usual latitudinal plan had to be devised here. The Ark is positioned on the wall directed towards Jerusalem but here it is flanked by the twin entrance doors because the long walls with enfilades of six windows are both external. With the possible exception of the panelled wainscot, the decoration dates from about a century after the foundation, the period when most of the other synagogues were renovated. There is a persistent but undocumented tradition that the renowned Venetian architect Baldassare Longhena (1598–1682) worked on the Spanish synagogue. Semenzato has pointed out in his monograph on Longhena that this attribution first appeared only in 1856 in a guidebook, which is, however, considered reliable.[31] On stylistic grounds Semenzato supports the attribution of the interior of this synagogue to Longhena and dates it 1655.[32] It is more probably ten or fifteen years later. Longhena worked for over fifty years – from 1631 – on his marvellous church of Santa Maria della Salute and began his secular masterpiece, the Palazzo Pesaro, in 1679, when he was over eighty. The synagogue has a sophisticated beauty, at once Judaic, Venetian and baroque, part *salon* and part house of prayer, worldly yet mysterious, especially when the full red curtains are drawn and the numerous chandeliers and candelabra are lit, enhancing the mellow glow of the polished benches, the glistening gilt and the streaked black marble columns of the Ark. The room is best seen from the women's gallery above. This elliptical gallery was created, presumably by Longhena, out of what was the attic floor of the building by cutting a great imperfect oval in the ceiling of the synagogue to unite it with the upper storey which became the women's section. The pediment of the Ark is crowned with the Tables of the Law, a feature used about the same time in London (1674) and Amsterdam (1675).

The most populous Jewish settlement of the Venetian Republic outside the capital was Padua, where the lucrative silk industry was introduced by Mosè Mantica in the fifteenth century and became the principal commercial activity of the Jews in the seventeenth, due to the initiative of the Trieste family. The ghetto was established in 1616 with 650 inhabitants and three synagogues: the Italian which now serves the whole community, the Spanish which was damaged by aerial bombardment in 1943[33] and the German, which was destroyed in the same air-raid.

The arcaded gallery at street level of the two-storey edifice in the Via S. Martino e Solferino which houses the Italian synagogue antedates the known date of its foundation, 1548. Possibly the upper floor (with three large windows overlooking the street) which houses the synagogue may have been built at that time. As the synagogue is long and narrow, 18.4×6.8 m, the Ark and bimah were placed at the middle of the two long walls; the niches over them are linked by a barrel vault with a window in each tympanum occupying the centre bay of the five-bay ceiling. The wooden Ark and bimah were similarly placed with benches on each side in the smaller Spanish synagogue of 1617, also long and narrow, 14×4.9 m, situated on the top floor of an unobtrusive building. The attractive rococo bimah and the baroque Ark were sent to Israel and set up in the Hechal Shlomo synagogue at Jerusalem after World War II.

The transitional style, between Gothic and Renaissance, of the chamber on the ground floor of the German synagogue indicates that this building, like the Italian synagogues, antedates the foundation in 1525.

Prosperous Jewish communities with synagogues flourished in Verona and Rovigo and in smaller towns and villages of the Venetian Republic. Those of Montagnana, Conselve, Cittadella, Monselice, Spilimbergo, Gonars and San Daniele del Friuli were suppressed in 1799 and the inhabitants dispersed. At Conselve the synagogue building is still identifiable; it is remembered by the inhabitants as the 'Palace of the Hebrews'. The San Daniele del Friuli community was a particularly successful one where the Jews were engaged in agricultural pursuits, cattle-dealing and the wool trade, in all of which the Luzzatto family was prominent. The communities at Conegliano and Ceneda (renamed Vittorio Veneto) survived into the present century. When the little Conegliano synagogue, founded in 1701 and measuring only 7.25×5.25 m, was closed, its delightful Venetian baroque interior was carefully dismantled and shipped to Israel in 1951 at the instigation of Federico Luzzatto and reassembled in the Italian synagogue at Jerusalem. While this move preserved the fine interior, the building in which it is now installed detracts considerably from its charm, being stylistically incongruous and of the wrong dimensions. The intimacy and the gilded opulence of the Vittorio Veneto

(Ceneda) synagogue, as well as the sensitivity and practicality of the original layout, have been preserved in the re-erection of the interior in a room specially built to house it in the Israel Museum, Jerusalem. The latticed women's gallery is particularly graceful (see p. 124). The Vittorio Veneto and Conegliano interiors are of about the same date and may be the work of the same architect. At Conegliano he designed the balustraded and screened women's gallery to continue along the short wall above the bimah, thus lending visual importance to the Ark.

In the Duchy of Mantua to the west of the Venetian Republic, the Renaissance spirit reached a high point of swashbuckling ardour in art, architecture and literature under the Gonzaga dukes, whose enormous palace included a splendid suite of apartments for the court dwarfs, designed to their scale. The reputation of the capital, which like Venice and Padua reverberated in the plays of Shakespeare, was that of a sixteenth-century city *par excellence*, famed for its magnificence and grandeur. A number of brilliant Jews were attached to the ostentatious ducal court where a Jewish dramatist had his plays performed with a Jewish cast and the Jewish composer Salomon de' Rossi presented his own madrigals and string compositions performed by his sister Europa and other Jewish musicians.[34] For several generations Jewish physicians, members of the Portaleone family, attended the reigning dukes, one of whom was obliged to intervene in a violent quarrel between an eminent Talmudist, the prickly Rabbi Joseph Cohen, and the author of *Nofet Zufim* (The Flow of the Honeycombs), a versatile philosopher-physician named Judah Messer Leon. Leon's book had been published at Mantua by one of the earliest and most important Hebrew printing presses in Italy, established in 1476. The Duke banished both the contentious wranglers from his state. The Gonzaga rulers rarely oppressed their Jewish subjects, indeed they were occasionally benevolent to them, but usually exacted as much as possible in return for their favour.

In 1495 Daniele Norsa, the head of a prominent Mantuan Jewish banking family, purchased a mansion in the centre of the city for a residence. He was permitted by the Bishop, in return for the payment of a fee, to remove an image of the Madonna from the façade of this building. The people of Mantua were outraged by this action, so the Duke placated them by ordering the demolition of Norsa's mansion. This was also convenient to him, as he was able to place on its site the church which he wished to erect as a monument to commemorate his questionable victory over the French at Fornovo. For this church, dedicated to Our Lady of Victory, the court artist Andrea Mantegna was commissioned by the Duke to paint a Madonna of Victory protecting the Gonzaga family under her mantle. The unfortunate Norsa was obliged to pay for this masterpiece, which is now in the Louvre. A student of Mantegna commemorated the whole incident in a painting which depicts the Virgin and Child being presented with a model of the new church; beneath them Daniele Norsa and three members of his family appear wearing the yellow badge recently introduced by the Duchess, and looking suitably distressed.

By 1603 as many as 3000 Jews were living in Mantua and there were besides about fifty communities in small towns in the Duchy such as Bozzolo, Luzzara, Sermide and Sabbioneta, which had a fine Hebrew print-

his finely sculpted and gilded Ark
d seats of the Parnassim, made in
43 for the synagogue of the small
wn of Sermide in the Duchy of
antua, are examples of the superb
rnishings of the synagogues in
naissance Italy.

ing press established by Tobia Foa. Each of these communities had its own synagogue. The Ark from Bozzolo was among those sent to Israel (it is now in the Ohel Izchak synagogue at Revacha); and the Ark from Sabbioneta is in the Beth Strauss synagogue, Jerusalem. Of exceptional quality are the Ark and accompanying seats of honour of the Parnassim from the synagogue at Sermide, now conserved in the Museum of the Italian Synagogue, Jerusalem: splendid examples of Italian Renaissance craftsmanship and design, they are dated 1543. The carved floral decoration was once gilded but now has a bronze-tinted patina. The *incipit* of the Ten Commandments are in gold letters on the inside of the doors. Small cupboards to store the ritual vessels are cleverly integrated with the bases of the columns and beneath them are drawers. The urns above the Ark are a later addition. In general the furnishings of these synagogues were equal in quality to the best contemporary furnishings of the provincial churches and secular mansions. A list of the many fine Arks and ritual ornaments transferred from Italian synagogues to Israel may be found in *Aronot Kodesh e Arredi Rituali d'Italia in Israele* by Umberto Nahon, published at Tel Aviv in 1970.

Spain annexed the Duchy of Milan in 1540 and expelled the Jewish population from the capital in the following year. No vestige has been traced of the places of worship of the Jewish community which had flourished there at the end of the fifteenth century, the time when Leonardo da Vinci, with a host of pupils and disciples, was promoting exciting new artistic and humanistic ventures.

The Duchy of Savoy extended beyond the Alps to include parts of what is now France and in the fifteenth and sixteenth centuries it had closer cultural links with France than with the rest of Italy. In 1560, when Duke Emanuele Filiberto decreed the expulsion of Jews from the Duchy, there were 600–700 living in Turin alone, representing about three per cent of the city's population which then numbered about 20,000. The decree was not implemented and only a few years later the Duke decided to incorporate his Jewish subjects in his programme of economic regeneration for the Duchy by forming an extensive chain of banks managed exclusively by Jews. Consequently by the end of the sixteenth century there were flourishing Jewish communities at Turin, Biella, Ivrea, Vercelli, Santhia, Mondovi, Cuneo and Chieri as well as nuclei in many smaller places. In 1601 the Jewish communities of Saluzzo and Carmagnola came under Savoy rule with the conquest of the Marquessate of Saluzzo. In 1708, when the Duchy of Monferrato was engulfed, the Jews of Casale also came under Savoy jurisdiction, like those of Alessandria which was transferred to Savoy in 1707. The humiliation of the ghetto came late. It was not imposed at Turin until 1679 and in the smaller towns only in the eighteenth century. The Jewish inhabitants of the Duchy lived mostly unmolested by the authorities through a period when the Protestant Waldensian subjects of the dukes were continuously harassed as heretics.

The Casale Monferrato synagogue, built in 1595 and enlarged in 1662, survives with an eighteenth-century interior. Eighteenth-century synagogue buildings survive at Carmagnola and Chieri. All the other earlier Piedmontese synagogues have been demolished, replaced by new ones in the nineteenth century or rebuilt, like that of Saluzzo in 1832. The sensational interior of the Casale synagogue, executed in 1765, is described in Chapter 6. Cross-vaulted passages lead from the synagogue to an arcaded courtyard which was used for classes.

The power and influence of the Medici family grew in the Republic of Florence as their great private mercantile empire expanded. From serving the city as mayors in the fourteenth and fifteenth centuries, they rose to be its lords and eventually attained royal rank in 1569 when Cosimo de' Medici became the first sovereign of the newly created Grand Duchy of Tuscany with Florence as its capital. The Medici firm had a network of agents as far afield as London, Bruges, Ghent, Lyons, Avignon, Milan and Venice, and through dealings with Jewish merchants and bankers they learnt to appreciate their financial acumen and the advantages of their international connections. At the end of the fifteenth century a number of rich and cultured Jews lived in Florence, then in its prime with princely palaces and villas which were treasuries of marvellous sculpture, paintings, jewellery and books. The prominent Jews lived in luxurious villas and several were connected with the humanistic circles where Plato's supposed birthday was commemorated and where brilliant philosophers expounded the belief that Christ's love was one with platonic love – the divine love which yearns for physical and spiritual beauty in the human being. Almost every genius in Italy came to Florence, the well-spring of the Renaissance spirit in that extraordinary era: their names are now world-famous – Leonardo da Vinci, Donatello, Brunelleschi, Verrocchio, Michelangelo, Botticelli, Ghirlandaio, Andrea del Sarto, Benvenuto Cellini and Machiavelli, to name but a few among the galaxy of sculptors, painters, architects, philosophers and writers who were associated with the city.

Cosimo I actively encouraged Jewish businessmen to settle in the Florentine Republic by his 'privilege' published in 1551 and addressed to Greek, Turkish, Moorish, Hebrew, Armenian and Persian merchants, who were promised that they would be 'received, caressed and favoured', safeguarded from molestation, never forced to baptism, and granted the opportunity to build mosques and synagogues.[35] Cosimo's wife, Eleonora de Toledo, had been educated in Naples by Benvenida Abravanel at the express request of her father, the Spanish Viceroy, because he admired the integrity and the intellectual capacities of this Jewish woman. Eleonora (who called Benvenida 'mamma',[36] and treated her with filial affection and respect) and the Abravanel family in Ferrara remained on intimate terms with the circle of Cosimo I where Benvenida was a frequent guest. There was one synagogue close to the Pitti Palace, a vast vaulted chamber which comprised the ground floor of the Belfredelli Palace.[37] However, the favourable conditions of the Jews in Florence changed drastically when Cosimo, who wanted the Pope to raise his status to that of a ruling sovereign, found it necessary to ingratiate himself with the ruling pontiff, the rabidly anti-Jewish Pius V.

Ultimately the Jews paid the price of Cosimo's grand-ducal crown. To gratify the Pope, Cosimo had first to impose the wearing of a distinctive mark upon his Jewish subjects in 1567, then in 1569 to refuse entry to Jewish refugees, and finally in 1571, having become Grand Duke, he

...simo I granted privileges and ...ours to Jews to encourage them to ...tle in Florence, and allowed them to ...ild synagogues. His wife, Eleonora ...Toledo, introduced to the intimacy ...the Medici court her beloved ...mer governess, Benvenida ...ravanel, an erudite Jewish lady who ...d been a second mother to her. ...wever, in 1569, in order to secure ...e grand-ducal crown of Tuscany, ...simo was obliged to please the Pope ...revoking the privileges and ...nfining the Jews to the ghettos, but ...1593 Ferdinand I, son of Cosimo ...d Eleonora, created a haven for the ...ws at Leghorn (Livorno) where they ...uld live freely, protected from ...assment and entitled to Tuscan ...izenship.

ordered the Jews to leave all places in his dominions except Florence or Siena where ghettos were established and enclosed. The palmy days were over for the Jews of Florence. At first they formed two communities in the ghetto, Western and Levantine, but these merged into one community in 1688, retaining their individual synagogues and rites. Eventually a synagogue of the Ashkenazi rite was established, situated in the same building as the Italian synagogue on the Via delle Oche. The building survives but it has been radically altered; the community sold it after World War II and sent the Arks of the synagogues to Israel. The enclosure of the ghetto was not ended until 1848 but as the anti-Jewish prohibitions were not always implemented in Tuscany, Jewish communities quietly sprouted up again, like the one at Pitigliano, a hill-top village near the frontier of the Papal States. The tall, narrow buildings of the Siena ghetto are only a few steps from the cathedral and the monumental piazza. The synagogue, whose present form dates from 1786, replaces an earlier one.

Livorno (Leghorn) became a veritable sanctuary for the Jews for no ghetto was ever instituted there. Ferdinand I, who succeeded as Grand Duke of Tuscany in 1587, was determined to develop a port on the west coast of his state. He chose Livorno and to launch its maritime and mercantile growth he published letters patent, entitled the *Livornina*, in 1593. This decree, which was a boon to the harassed Jews in Italy and to refugees from abroad, invited Jewish merchants, especially those suffering from persecution, to settle in Pisa and Livorno. The immigrants were granted a wide amnesty including pardon for apostasy committed in another state, a provision which was particularly attractive to the

Marranos. Forced baptism of Jewish infants was prohibited and the settlers were granted the right to build synagogues. As well as enjoying tax benefits and commercial concessions, the Jews were allowed to administer their own civil and penal legislation in cases involving only their own community. Most important of all, Jews entering Livorno and Pisa automatically received Tuscan citizenship. About 100 Jews immediately accepted the Grand Duke's offer. Within only thirty years the community had grown to 700. Before the end of the seventeenth century the community numbered 3000 and a hundred years later there were 5000, mostly descendants of Jews from Spain and Portugal who had fled first to North Africa. Many of these families claimed noble ancestry and sported heraldic devices on their silverware and on their elaborate tombs. Spanish and Portuguese, the languages of the majority and of the influential families, remained the predominant languages of the community. Synagogues were built at Livorno and Pisa at the end of the sixteenth century soon after the publication of the *Livornina*. The one at Pisa lost its original appearance when it was extensively rebuilt in the nineteenth century. The Livorno synagogue was transformed in the eighteenth century and it is described, as it then appeared, in Chapter 6.

The Renaissance and baroque architectural concepts were exported to other countries by Italian builders and architects who worked abroad and by foreigners who visited Italy. The precise arrangement of the Italian synagogue was not, however, reproduced in other countries though its influence may be discerned in the plan still favoured by Sephardic communities in the West. While the bimah (tevah) is not actually placed against the west wall it is, by tradition, placed in a westerly position in the synagogue and the seats are arranged in two parallel sections facing each other across the aisle between the Ark and the bimah. The decoration and furnishings of the Italian synagogue have been widely appreciated; the pedimented altar-type Ark flanked by columns or pilasters has enjoyed widespread popularity in synagogues of both the Eastern and Western Sephardim and of the Ashkenazim in many countries.

5 *The Renaissance in Poland*

At the zenith of their power the Polish monarchs of the Jagiellon dynasty ruled a vast empire, a territory which extended far beyond the present boundaries of Poland to include Ducal Prussia, the densely populated Duchy of Mazovia, the Grand Duchy of Lithuania with the city of Vilna, Livonia, the virgin forests of Byelorussia and the cities of Minsk and Brest-Litovsk, as well as the great fertile but largely unreclaimed steppe-lands of Carpatho-Ukraine (Ruthenia) and the city of Lvov.

The capital of the Jagiellon kings was at Cracow, where they held court in the Wawel Castle. Cracow, called *Cracovia totius Poloniae urbs celeberrima*, was one of the foremost cultural centres of Europe and an early recipient of Renaissance ideas from Italy, largely due to the importance of the Jagiellonian University where the illustrious astronomer Copernicus (Nikolaj Kopernik) was a student from 1491 to 1495 and where the future King Sigismund I himself studied under a renowned Italian professor, Filippo Buonaccorsi.

Many Italian builders, craftsmen and architects were attracted to Cracow; as early as 1502 a Florentine architect known as Franciscus Italus was working in the city. In 1518 King Sigismund married Bona Sforza of the ruling dynasty of Milan. She arrived in Poland with a considerable retinue and some wonderful Italian furniture which included magnificent coffers and chests and an ornate canopied bed. The Gothic castle of Wawel was then converted into a magnificent Renaissance palace residence. In the adjoining cathedral King Sigismund commissioned a lavish chapel, which was begun in 1519 by an Italian, Bartolomeo Berecci, who worked and died in Cracow, and completed by 1533 with the help of other Italians including Antonio and Filippo da Fiesole, Giovanni Cini from Siena, and the Paduan architect, medallist and sculptor Zuan Maria Padovano, also known as Mosca, who worked in Cracow for several years with his son Andrea. He introduced architectural elements and motifs of the Italian Renaissance such as barrel vaults, arcading and blind arcades, and secured important commissions, such as the extensive remodelling of the Sukiennice, the Clothiers' Hall.[1] Gaspare Gucci, a Florentine master-builder who was in Cracow by 1537, served as a town councillor there in 1545; Santi Gucci worked in the Wawel Cathedral, and another of the family, Matteo Gucci, remodelled the medieval Stara synagogue in the Cracow suburb of Kazimierz in 1570.[2] Among the many Italian architects who worked in Poland, at least two others can actually be identified with synagogue building there. Paolo Romano, a master-builder who settled at Lvov, built the TaZ synagogue there in 1582.[3] In the next century another master-builder, Francesco Olivieri, built the Izak synagogue at Kazimierz, Cracow, before moving on to Ljubljana in what is now Yugoslavia where he built the fountain in the Old Market.[4] Italian master-masons worked also in Bohemia. The groin vault of the Pinkas synagogue in Prague, which was rebuilt for Aaron Meshulam Horovitz, and also its fine internal Renaissance portal are typical of their work. Czechoslovakian architectural historians have suggested that Italian masons may have worked on the synagogue under the direction of the Bohemian court architect Benedikt Rejt.[5]

The cultural contacts between Poland and Italy continued throughout the sixteenth century. As well as administrators like Prospero Provano

PREVIOUS PAGE Photograph taken, before its destruction by the Nazis in 1937, of a wooden wall of the synagogue at Bechhofen in the distric of Feuchtwangen, Germany. It was painted in 1733 by Eliezer Sussman, ar intinerant Jewish artist from Poland who also decorated synagogues at Horb (see page 121), Kirchheim and Unterlimpurg (see page 127).

and Sebastiano Montelupi, the first two postmasters of the Cracow–Rome mail service established in 1558, there were numerous Italian artisans and craftsmen in the Polish capital, such as the court goldsmith Gian Jacopo Caraglio and the court painters Giovanni del Monte from Venice and Giovanni Battista Ferro from Padua. Among the men who went to Italy from Poland to study were Jewish physicians who later attended the Polish royal family and Hebrew printers like Isaac ben Aaron, who brought an expert proof-reader back from Venice to work at the press which he established at Cracow by royal licence in 1569.

Between the last decades of the sixteenth century and the middle of the seventeenth, the Jewish population of Poland had increased from about 150,000 to 300,000, or even, according to some calculations, as many as half a million.[6] The burgeoning economy and the reasonable attitude of the government to the Jews attracted immigrants not only from Bohemia and Germany but also from Italy, the Balkans, and the Levant, until about one-half of all the Jews in Europe were concentrated in Poland and it had the largest population of Jewish residents of any state in the world. This influx was curtailed by the wars which devastated Poland during 1648–58, disrupting the country and interrupting economic development. Before that calamitous decade, during the palmy period remembered as the Golden Age of Jews in Poland, they enjoyed religious liberty, a measure of self-government, and the opportunity to participate in an expanding and diversified economy. Under the terms of a medieval *Privilegium* the Jewish communities in the royal towns of western and central Poland enjoyed immunity from the municipal authorities, and some individual Jews incurred royal favour to such a degree that the king relieved them even of their financial obligations to the Jewish community: this, however, caused such strife that King Sigismund II Augustus was obliged to end the practice in 1563. While the Jewish court bankers and physicians rose to positions of influence in the royal cities, a number of other Jews held key positions in the financial administration and economic structure of the hundreds of privately owned townships and villages which were being developed in eastern Poland, particularly in Lithuania and the Ukraine where, following a deliberation of the Diet of Piotrków (1539), the Jews had been placed under the jurisdiction of the landowning nobility.

The new towns were the property of nobles who promoted these developments on their estates, generally exploiting serf labour in their foundation. These magnates protected enterprising Jewish settlers and financiers, actively encouraging them to establish residence in their new townships in order to stimulate and accelerate the process of colonization, urban growth and commercial expansion, so that from having been purveyors to the nobles, the Jewish entrepreneurs became in time their valued partners as economic advisers and managers. The system of *Arenda* was then in force in Poland, by which not only customs duties, public revenues, monopolies and prerogatives were leased out to private individuals, but also fixed assets, land, mills, breweries and distilleries and even agricultural and dairy produce. These leases could be highly lucrative; many Jews who acquired them amassed fortunes but gained no popularity with the disadvantaged peasantry in the process. The autonomy of the Jews under the nobles eventually resulted in the rise of a Jewish oligarchy composed mostly of wealthy tax-farmers and lease-holders. They formed an elite plutocracy far removed socially and economically not only from the indigenous peasantry but also from the poor Jewish proletariat among whom they continued to reside but in houses whose style and appurtenances reflected their status.

At the same time Jewish scholarship flourished: Poland with Lithuania became the main centre of Ashkenazic culture. A number of the leading rabbis belonged to the wealthy families. One such was the illustrious Moses Isserles, whose father was a very rich banker and Talmudic scholar. Rabbi Moses, considered by his contemporaries as the Maimonides of Poland, was known as ReMuh, an acronym of his name. His fame is as a codifier and Halakhic authority; he gained a worldwide reputation as a *posek* (decisor), but he was also versed in philosophy, astronomy and history, aware of the humanist precepts of the Renaissance thinkers. In philosophy he followed the teachings of Aristotle as expounded by Maimonides. This brought him into frequent disputes with another renowned *posek*, Solomon Luria, who accused Moses Isserles of mixing Aristotle with the living God.

In this climate of scholarship, prosperity and comparative religious freedom it is not surprising that there was a flurry of synagogue building or that the buildings should reflect some of the contemporary architectural developments and novelties in form, structure and technique, combined with an attentive awareness of the Halakhic requirements as interpreted by sages like Moses Isserles. In the royal towns the permission of the king was required to build a synagogue; usually this was granted without difficulty but whenever and wherever possible the Church tried to impose restrictions. The episcopal synods issued decrees urging the king to observe ancient statutes which forbade new synagogues to be built, only to permit repairs to old ones, and to order the demolition of those newly erected (Synod of Piotrków, 1542),[7] and objecting strongly to the 'vast new synagogues in brick, more beautiful than in former times and comparable to churches'[8] (Synod of Gniezno, 1589). In the new towns owned by the magnates the Jews were less affected by episcopal proscriptions and interference. This enabled them to build with even more attention to the requisites of Halakah and practically the only interdict which was observed was that of not erecting a synagogue in the immediate vicinity of a church. Generally the new towns were laid out around a central square: the church and the synagogue, sometimes both founded by the landowning magnate, would be built in streets off opposite sides of the square. Wherever possible the Jews chose a site for the synagogue on rising ground and near to running water and, like the other important buildings of the town – the church and the town-hall – it rose prominently above the surrounding shops and dwellings, and was frequently crowned with a decorated parapet, a device also used on civic buildings and patrician mansions.

Timber was a widely used building material in Poland, where it was both cheap and plentiful. Until recent times many village houses and farms were constructed of wood and it was also used for churches and synagogues. Despite this affectionate attachment to a vernacular type

[w]ooden synagogue at Pjehski, since [de]stroyed, typical of the many Jewish [ho]uses of worship built in this [ve]rnacular style in Poland, Lithuania [an]d Russia.

which was a distinctive feature of their architecture, the Poles realized the vulnerability of timber structures and it seems that, where possible, sacred buildings of wood were replaced by more durable masonry edifices. Undoubtedly most of the earliest Polish synagogues were timber constructions which perished during the ravages of the wars in the seventeenth and eighteenth centuries or else were victims of accidental fires. They were not always replaced by masonry buildings, however, possibly owing to lack of funds, possibly because of sentimental attachment to the old synagogue and a desire to rebuild it as it was. The wooden synagogue at Przedbórz which was destroyed by a fire before 1638 was replaced by another in the same material; when that one was demolished in wartime it was replaced by yet another wooden one between 1745 and 1760.[9] Another example was at Pohrebyszce, where the wooden synagogue which had been almost totally demolished by Cossack marauders was replaced in 1690 by another timber edifice incorporating the remains of the earlier one.[10] Sometimes the decision not to build in masonry may have been made despite the desires of the persons involved. In 1628 the Jewish *Vlaad* (Council) of Lithuania issued this communiqué to the communities in Lithuania, Byelorussia and Zhmood: 'If a community does not have a permit to build a new synagogue, or to replace a wooden building by a masonry one, it should not start building, nor should it demolish the wooden structure to make a place for the masonry building, before consulting the head of its *bet din* and requesting his advice.'[11]

A number of the timber synagogues survived until World War II when they were wantonly razed by the Nazis in their demented passion to obliterate Jewish civilization in Poland. It is therefore fortunate that some of the reports and photographs made before 1939 by architects and art-historians were salvaged and have survived as a record of these fascinating buildings, the earliest of which dated from the mid-seventeenth century, having been built then to replace earlier, war-destroyed examples.

It is clear, however, that whenever and wherever possible the early timber synagogues were replaced by stone, or stone and brick, buildings, as at Grodno in Lithuania where a wooden synagogue of 1575–8 was rebuilt in stone and brick by royal licence in 1627,[12] and Wilno, also in Lithuania, where the wooden synagogue built in 1573 on land owned by Prince Slucki was destroyed by fire in 1592 and replaced by a stone and brick building in the following year.[13] The masonry synagogue at Przemysl begun in 1592, the largest in Lesser Poland at that time, also replaced a wooden one.[14]

It is likely that the Italian architects and builders who worked in Poland had never seen the interior of a synagogue in their own country and there is no evidence that any attempt was ever made to introduce the bifocal latitudinal plan favoured in Italy. Even if this plan had been mooted it would undoubtedly have been vetoed by the Polish Jews because the influential Moses Isserles had pronounced strongly in favour of a central location for the bimah. Instead a spatial solution was devised which was in harmony with indigenous tradition – a concentric plan which led eventually to the deliberate arrangement of a square, or almost square, hall into nine equal bays by means of vaults. This arrangement stressed the central position of the bimah, which became an integral part of the building both structurally and architecturally rather than merely a furnishing or fitting.

The earliest masonry synagogue of the sixteenth-century building phase which can be dated is the brick and stone ReMuh synagogue at Kazimierz, Cracow, built in 1557 to replace one on the site built in 1553 and destroyed by fire.[15] Possibly the first ReMuh synagogue was a timber or part-timber construction. The synagogue was built for the use of the illustrious Moses Isserles by his wealthy father Israel, a court banker to King Sigismund II Augustus, and donated to the community. It is said that its foundation was in memory of Moses' young wife who had died in 1552, aged twenty. She was a daughter of Moses Isserles' principal mentor, Shalom Shakhna, the founder of Talmudic scholarship in Poland, appointed Rabbi of Lublin by King Sigismund I in 1541 and Chief Rabbi of Lesser Poland. The synagogue, which is still in use, stands at one end of Szeroka Street adjoining the cemetery where, among the many finely sculpted Renaissance tombs, may be seen that of the Isserles family inscribed with an encomium of Moses Isserles: 'From Moses Maimonides to Moses Isserles there was no Moses to equal him.' The 700 tombstones were unearthed during the restoration of the cemetery after the Nazi depredations of World War II: the beautiful Renaissance monuments were discovered under a top layer of stone, the earliest dating from the time of the foundation of the ReMuh synagogue, the latest from 1700. Apparently these tombstones had been buried deliberately by the community to save them from destruction by the army of Charles XII during the second Swedish invasion, and never disinterred.

The ReMuh synagogue building has immensely thick walls strengthened externally by massive buttresses. The men's entrance is through a small vestibule built on to the north side of the building; here the synagogue ornaments were stored in a great coffer and the books and records were preserved, including the Haftor manuscript (Seder Haftarot) donated in 1666 on the occasion of 'the coming of the Messiah and the imminent redemption of Israel'.[16] The most beautiful accoutrement of the synagogue was a copper laver exquisitely decorated in bas-relief with scenes of Isaac preparing the fire for sacrifice, Moses with the Tables of the Law inscribed with Roman numerals, and Jacob's dream. This was probably the work of a Christian craftsman.[17] The small, rectangular synagogue is covered by a barrel vault. It is lit by high, round-headed windows in the north and south walls and large lunettes in the east and west walls, which may have been later additions to the original building. An alms box in the form of an aedicule in a niche at the entrance is in Renaissance style as is the Ark, also in the form of an aedicule, set on the east wall with flanking pilasters and decorated capitals beneath a florid entablature. The rectangular central bimah on a plinth occupies much of the floor space of the room; it is encased by an ornate wrought-iron cage with two entrances, to one of which at a later date doors have been fitted which appear to have belonged to a late seventeenth-century Ark. A deep niche in the east wall accommodated the seat of Moses Isserles. The synagogue was sensitively restored in 1933 by the architect Herman Gutman and again repaired after World War II.

The bas-relief on the copper laver in the ReMuh synagogue recalls a relief on bronze of Isaac's sacrifice executed by Zuan Maria Padovano for the baptistry of Padua Cathedral prior to his emigration to Cracow, and the Renaissance aedicules are in the style of the monuments made for Cracow churches by Padovano and his son and their colleague Paolo Stella. This suggests that if Padovano himself was not actually associated with work on the ReMuh synagogue, some of his Italian collaborators may well have been involved.

The parapet decorated with blind arcading, a device which became popular in Poland and came to be known as 'the Polish attic', seems first to have been employed on a secular building at Cracow by Padovano about 1559.[18] The parapet had two useful functions besides its decorative value. It could be useful for defence in wartime and also served as a precaution against fire. Matteo Gucci placed such a parapet on the Stara synagogue when he was retained by the community to remodel the medieval structure extensively in 1570. The Stara (Old) which stands at one end of Szeroka Street about 100 metres from the ReMuh, was the oldest synagogue of the community, the focal point of Jewish life in Kazimierz. Here the elections of the Kehilla, the community authority, were held, as well as theological assemblies and debates and trials. Apart from its daily use for worship and prayer, royal decrees, announcements and decisions of the Kehilla and sentences of condemnation or excommunication were proclaimed from the bimah of the Stara synagogue. During the struggle for Polish independence in the late eighteenth and nineteenth centuries patriotic speeches were made from the bimah not only by fervently nationalist rabbis but also by Polish Christian patriots like the statesman Tadeusz Kosciuszko, who urged the Jews to join the fight for liberation. Hassidism was also attacked from the bimah by the rabbis during that period. For centuries the synagogue building was hemmed in by dwellings and offices, clustered around it like infants clinging to their mother's skirts. Some of these buildings communicated with the

synagogue by means of labyrinthine corridors and stairs, but they have all been demolished and the synagogue now stands free, only abutting on one side the ruins of the old fortification walls of Kazimierz.

The medieval synagogue had been damaged by a fire in 1557 and when Gucci took over in 1570 he extensively rebuilt the exterior of stone and red brick, adding the fashionable parapet which masks the roof. He also revamped the antique twin-nave interior which had been built in the tradition of Worms, transforming the columns and vaults to their present appearance. The spacious cross-vaulted vestibule below the street level and the first women's gallery at first-floor level behind the west wall are also Gucci's work. Poor Jews who did not have seats in the synagogue proper sat on benches in this vestibule, which has a laver in one corner fed by living water from a spring. The alms-box set in the wall of the vestibule appears to be a medieval artefact. It seems likely that it was the original alms-box of the early synagogue, removed by Gucci during his work of rebuilding, since before being set in its present position it had been put aside for many years in the community offices. The vestibule communicates by a stair with the offices on an upper floor and with the synagogue room (17.7 × 12.4 m) which is on a lower level, reached by six steps, through a handsome Renaissance doorway of the Gucci period. In the synagogue the bimah remained midway between the two columns from which spring the vaults, as in the medieval plan. It is raised on a steep, octagonal stone plinth reached by twin flights of steps on the north and south sides and protected by a delicately-wrought iron grille and cage. The torus of each of the two columns rest on steep-stepped plinths which raise the bases of the columns to about the floor level of the raised bimah.

Above the city walls of the Cracow suburb of Kazimierz rise the brick walls of the Stara synagogue and the parapet added by the Italian Matteo Gucci when he rebuilt the medieval fabric in 1570.

The floor level of the medieval room enhances the majestic effect of the vaulting. The sunken floor for a place of prayer was approved, it seems, by rabbis who considered that it complied with a literal reading of the Psalmist's cry, 'Out of the depths have I called Thee, O Lord,'[19] but it was not a Halakhic requirement.

The women's annexe on the south side of the synagogue with two grilles, which has the remains of frescoes with Hebrew inscriptions in panels, geometric designs and branches of fruit, and another women's annexe on the north side with four grilles, are additions made after the time of Gucci's work: his women's gallery is on a higher floor behind two grilles in the west wall. Wall shafts which were part of the original vaulting had to be removed to allow for these grilles and the vaults were then terminated with corbels. Gucci must have removed the wall shaft in the middle of the east wall and replaced it by a corbel, too. In this case it was to allow for fitting the Ark, a Renaissance aedicule surmounted by a decorated pediment above an entablature sculpted with a crown. On the north wall near the entrance is the alms-box, also in the form of an aedicule but surmounted by an open segmental pediment and three urns. Despite the rather clumsy workmanship, this alms-box with its stout iron door and bolt is indeed a delightful fitting.

After World War II the synagogue was in a derelict state. At the initiative of a member of the Parliament, Dr Boleslaw Drobner, its restoration was undertaken by the Polish government and financed by the Social Fund for the Protection of Monuments. Entrances were pierced in the north, south and west walls of the synagogue so that the annexes communicated directly with the main room and could be used for the exhibits of the Museum of the History and Culture of the Jews – the use to which the building was put on the completion of the restoration in 1959. It now functions in this capacity as a section of the Historical Museum of Cracow and preserves curios, paintings, photographs and objects of interest of the Jewish past, painstakingly gathered with help from the survivors of the Jewish community. One room is devoted to the martyrology of Polish Jews and preserves, together with an urn of ashes of cremated victims of concentration camps, photographs and documents which authenticate and illustrate the extermination campaign and the suppression of the ghetto in March 1943. The former treasure of the synagogue, accumulated over the centuries and exhibited in the offices prior to World War II, was plundered by the Nazis, who wrecked the bimah and stole the great bronze chandeliers to embellish the residence of Hans Frank, the German Governor-General.[20] The treasury comprised a great collection of precious manuscripts and silver, and numerous textiles including parokethim from the seventeenth century, of which the earliest, woven in gold thread, was dated 5385 (CE 1625).[21]

The Wysoka (High) synagogue building, known to the community as the Hoyche, is situated in Jozefa Street only a few steps from the Stara. It was built towards the end of the sixteenth century not long after Gucci had finished his rebuilding of the oldest synagogue of the community. It is a tall, imposing building but its name derives from the fact that the ground floor used to be occupied by shops and the synagogue was on the first floor; its barrel-vaulted ceiling rose through the second-floor level to the top of the building. The vault was divided into bays laterally; clustered columns on the north and south walls supported the dividing ribs. Since the Hoyche ceased to function as a synagogue after World War II its interior, which included an interesting Ark with sculpted doors signed by Jewish artisans (Zelman and Chaim, sons of Aron), has been dismantled. The premises are now used by an artists' co-operative and the external fabric of the building, with windows set high in its massive buttressed walls, is in fair repair.

In 1567 a synagogue was built at the foot of the castle-hill in Lublin for the *posek* Solomon Luria, the theological adversary of Moses Isserles. It was named the MaHaRSHaL, Rabbi Solomon's acronym, standing for Morenu ha-Rav Shalomo Luria. With the small adjacent Majer synagogue or Maharamschul, added later in the century, the building was burnt, and rebuilt after 1656; it was again damaged, and restored in the nineteenth century.[22] If, as seems likely, the mid-seventeenth-century rebuilding followed the plan of the original building of 1567, then the MaHaRSHaL was the prototype of the concentric synagogue design; it had four pillars upholding a masonry canopy over the central bimah, and supporting four barrel vaults which intersected at the corners to form an ambulatory around the room and the bimah, creating a space within a space. Four clusters of three slender columns were used in the rebuilding of 1656; these may have replaced four massive columns in the original building. Twelve windows, set high in the walls, three on each side, lit the room. In the year following the building of the MaHaRSHaL synagogue at Lublin, a large and beautiful synagogue was built in 1568 at Brest-Litovsk by the architect Piotr Ronka of Poznan.[23] It was demolished in 1842 and unfortunately reports of its appearance do not seem to have survived. However, several synagogues built in the last decade of the sixteenth century, notably those of Opatow, Przeworsk and Lancut, and the town synagogue at Rzeszow, were constructed on the four-pillar concentric plan with a built-in central bimah, indicating that they followed a model which was most probably the original MaHaRSHaL building. At Lancut the barrel vaults were reduced to barrel arches with cross-vaulting spanning the corners. Many later synagogues adopted the concentric four-pillar arrangement, giving increasing attention to the appearance of the built-in bimah. In some cases a two-storey effect was created by window openings in the upper part of the *baldacchino* which inevitably dominated the synagogue and eclipsed the eminence of the Ark. This deliberate architectural emphasis of the bimah realized a definite desire to express and stress its importance as forcefully as possible.

At Lvov (now in the USSR), a Jewish oligarch, Isaac ben Nahman, founder of the Nachmanovich family, had a synagogue built in 1582[24] by the architect Paolo Romano. Isaac, who served as chief of the representatives of the Jewish communities of the 'Land of Russia', was an immensely rich spice merchant and tax-farmer who leased customs stations and state revenues and was important enough to have personal access to King Sigismund II Augustus. The architect chosen to build the synagogue was presumably an Italian although one source states that he came from Chiamut in the Grisons.[25] Romano worked with Pietro di Barbona

Jewish artisans, Zelman and Chaim, sons of Aron, sculpted and signed these fine doors for the Ark of the Wysoka (Hoyche) Synagogue in Cracow, Poland, an excellent example of metal-work ornamentation of the Polish Renaissance.

on the bell-tower of the Wallachian church at Lvov, completed in 1580, and began the construction of the church itself. He also built the Bernardine church and the church and cloister of the Benedictine nuns at Lvov, where he died in 1618.[26] Isaac ben Nahman received authorization in 1581 to acquire a plot of municipal land on which to build his synagogue, but after its completion the Jesuits claimed that it was built on their land. The Jewish community won the suit but they had to purchase another site for the Jesuits in the suburbs. In his efforts to prevent the building of the synagogue the Archbishop of Lvov, Dymitr Solikowski, had even addressed his complaint to Rome, but to no avail.[27] The synagogue was named the TaZ, acronym of Turei Zahav, or Golden Rose, in honour if Isaac's beautiful and accomplished wife Rose, known as 'Di Gildene Roiz'. She took charge of her late husband's business affairs for over forty years after his death in 1597. About 1610 their sons Nathan, a court banker, and Mordecai completed the TaZ building, adding a women's gallery and donating magnificent requisites. Romano's design for the synagogue was a square hall with a barrel vault and lunette windows, a plan copied in other synagogues built in the last decade of the sixteenth and first years of the seventeenth century, such as those of Zamosc and Szczebrzeszyn.

The masonry synagogue built at Przemysl in 1592 to replace a wooden one was one of the largest in Lesser Poland at the time. Although the height and area of the new building were defined by the episcopal authorities (10 × 15 m; height 10 m),[28] its erection caused popular uprisings in the town which were discussed by the assembly of the nobles in 1593.[29] The interesting episcopal licence makes it clear that in this case the level of the synagogue floor was lowered in order to enhance the stateliness of the vaulted interior without exceeding the permitted height of the edifice externally. The building licence also mentions the parapet, which was allowed as a precaution against fire. The Przemysl synagogue was constructed on a square plan with a central bimah and barrel vaulting. The bimah was not built-in and the plan seems to have followed the simpler concentric arrangement of the ReMuh at Kazimierz, Cracow, and of the TaZ at Lvov.

As a result of the growth and redistribution of the Jewish population, synagogue building proceeded at a fast pace during the first forty years of the seventeenth century. Among the many known to have been constructed in those years in timber or masonry were: Wronki (1607), Leszno (1626), Grodno, Jablonow and Luck (1627), Wilno (1630), the Vorstadt (suburban) synagogue at Lvov (1632), Vilna (1633), Checiny and the Hersz Doktorowicz synagogue at Lublin (1638), Chodorów, Gwozdziec, Ostropol, Zabludow, Pinczów, Przytyk near Radom, Rozpray near Piotrków, and three synagogues in Kazimierz, Cracow – one founded by Wolf Bocian Popper, built in 1620, one by Mojzesz Jakubowicz some years before 1633, and the third by his brother Izak Jakubowicz, built in 1640. During this period a proclamation of King Wladyslaw IV in 1633 confirmed the right of Jews to enjoy unhindered use of all their synagogues within the realm but added that they were to observe the rules of the Catholic Church regarding the height of the synagogue buildings and their distance from a church.[30] The royal licence issued by King

LEFT Cossacks, Tatars and Turks frequently attacked the eastern borders of Poland. This old photograph of the synagogue of Luck in the Ukraine, now in the USSR, taken before World War II, shows a fine example of the fortress-type synagogue built to be useful in case of enemy attack. The royal licence for its construction in 1626 specified that it should have gun loops in the parapet and that it should be garrisoned at the expense of the community.

Sigismund III in 1626 for the construction of the synagogue at Luck had specified that it was to have embrasures or loopholes in the parapet on all four sides and that the Jews were to see that it was ably garrisoned at their own expense.[31] The Bishop of Luck and the local clergy were dismayed by the size and importance of this fortress-synagogue. They raised objections during its construction in an attempt to stop it, despite its obvious usefulness in repulsing eventual attacks by Cossack or Tatar raiders or Turkish invaders.

The erection of Izak Jakubowicz's synagogue at Kazimierz, Cracow, in 1640 also met with ecclesiastical opposition. Since the impressive edifice loomed above the surrounding houses, the Bishop of Cracow, Jakób Zodzik, found it too conspicuous and tried to prevent it being finished and put to use.[32] The building was, however, finished in 1644, according to an inscription which ascribed the incentive for its foundation to the founder's wife, Brajndla. For Izak Jakubowicz – the richest member of the rich Jekeles family – the Italian architect Francesco Olivieri had created a ponderous rectangular building with thick walls and stout buttresses. The starkness of the exterior may, perhaps, be attributed to the necessity of not further provoking the irate Bishop. The architect partitioned the west end of the building to form a vestibule and a small prayer-room or office on the ground floor, with the women's gallery above them overlooking the main hall through arches. The main entrance to the synagogue is on the south side, in Izak Street, through a handsome doorway of the style used in seventeenth-century Cracow mansions; it opens on to the vestibule. The women's entrance in the west front, in Kupa Street, originally had a single external stairway. This was replaced by a double stairway and small external porch when the building was repaired in the early years of this century. The interior is barrel-vaulted and divided into four lateral bays with one window high up in each bay on each side. The three bays of the main hall used by the men, which measured 12×18.9 m internally, are equal in size; the fourth bay, over the women's gallery, is larger. The bimah, in the tradition of the ReMuh and Stara synagogues, stood on a twelve-sided plinth, 3.15 m square,

The Izak synagogue in the Kazimierz suburb of Cracow was completed in 1644 by the Italian architect Francesco Olivieri, in spite of the opposition of the Bishop of Cracow who found the building too impressive and conspicuous. The stylistic influence of the architect's native land is evident in his handsome doorway.

enclosed by an imposing wrought-iron cage. It was positioned off-centre in the central bay, a little nearer to the Ark and the east wall than to the west. A wrought-iron grille with gates also enclosed the Ark – a pedimented aedicule with iron doors set up on the east wall. Only a few years after its completion the Izak synagogue was ransacked by Swedish troops. Subsequently it was presented by King Jan Casimir to the parish priest of St Hedwig's, Stradom,[33] but it was recovered and served the Jewish community until the annihilation of Cracow Jewry in World War II. The building is still standing but in an abandoned state and its interior has been dismantled.

Mojzesz Jakubowicz, a less affluent brother of Izak, founded a school and a small synagogue on a site belonging to the family in Szeroka Street for his son-in-law, the cabbalist Natan Spira, who died in 1633. On the ground floor of the building was a small *mikveh*; on the floor above was the modest synagogue, a plain rectangular room with a little vestibule. It was known as the Synagogue on the Hill (*auf'n Bergel*).

Wolf Bocian Popper, the founder of a synagogue at Kazimierz, Cracow, which bore his name, was one of the richest Jews in Poland in his day. He was a banker and a merchant, involved in extensive financial and mercantile transactions, trading in saltpetre from Wroclaw where he maintained an agency, and in cloth, imported mainly from Cologne, Germany, for sale at fairs throughout Poland and in Schleswig. At his death in 1625 his fortune was assessed in hundreds of thousands of zlotys. He financed the construction of the Popper synagogue in Szeroka Street in 1620 and endowed it richly. The building, easily recognizable as once having been a synagogue because of its thick walls, stout buttresses, and enfilade of high windows, is now used as a youth club. The interior, a cross-vaulted hall with a women's gallery over the vestibule at one end, has been dismantled and there is no trace of Leon Schenker's twentieth-century mural of Moses with the Tables of the Law mentioned by Helen Rosenau.[34]

The rectangular plan as employed in the Popper synagogue, with a women's gallery over a vestibule at the west end, conceived as an organic part of the synagogue building, is one pattern which was established by the second quarter of the seventeenth century; another early example was the synagogue at Pińczów. In Cracow, undoubtedly through attachment to the beloved Stara, the free-standing bimah enclosed in a cage remained in favour while elsewhere other arrangements were experimented. The plan of the MaHaRSHaL in Lublin, with minor variants, was widely used. A further development of this concentric plan, with the four columns of the built-in bimah supporting the vault, emerged in the 1630s. The arrangement was the division of a square into nine equal bays spanned by cross-vaults; the bimah was not built-in, but free-standing under the vault of the central bay and between the four supporting pillars, either raised on a plinth and surrounded by a balustrade or in the form of a kiosk or pavilion. This plan has been described as a full answer to the problem of a centrally conceived liturgical function.[35] It appears to have been first employed for the Vorstadt (suburban) synagogue at Lvov (1632) and at Vilna (1633). This plan also allowed for the possibility of a women's section over a vestibule adjacent to one side of the square; more frequently a women's section was placed on the ground floor along

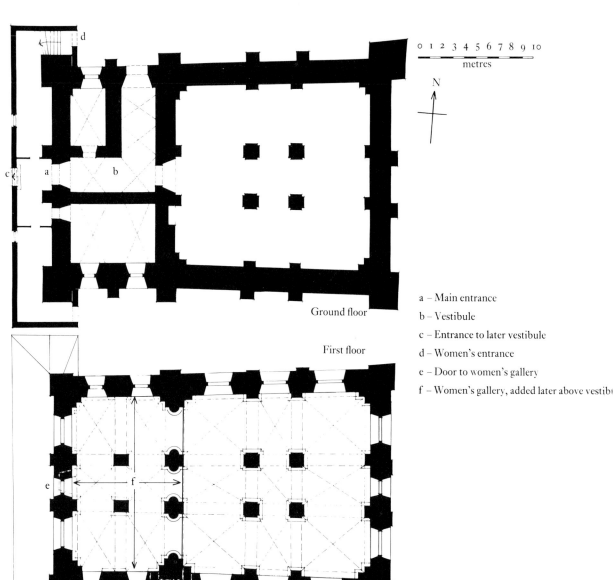

Ground floor

First floor

a – Main entrance
b – Vestibule
c – Entrance to later vestibule
d – Women's entrance
e – Door to women's gallery
f – Women's gallery, added later above vestibule

0 1 2 3 4 5 6 7 8 9 10
metres

N

Example of the Polish nine-bay
concentric plan – Rzeszow (based on
plans made in the Architectural
Institute of the Warsaw Polytechnic).

one or two sides (north and south) and the vestibule along the west side,
so that externally the building became an oblong. Sometimes these
annexes were an organic part of the original building, contemporary with
the main prayer-hall; frequently they were added later from time to time
as the need became apparent.

The almost square prayer-hall of the Lvov Vorstadt building, 19.28 ×
20 m internally, was flanked on the west side by a vestibule with two
entrances for the men, a place for a pillory used to punish miscreants,
and small meeting-rooms for the Jewish trade-guilds. Above the vestibule
was a gallery used for a choir-loft. Cross-vaulted women's sections with
external entrances flanked the prayer-hall on the north and south sides.
The Ark was above a stairway in the middle bay on the east wall. The
bimah stood in the centre of the room, free-standing on a dais between
the four octagonal piers and reached by two flights of stairs. At Vilna
the pavilion-type bimah stood on a dais well above the heads of the con-

gregation, its importance accentuated by the elongated stairway leading up to it and the four massive piers surrounding it like great sentinels.

Usually the interior decoration of the concentric synagogues stressed the unity of the layout. One decorative device was a frieze – sometimes blind arcading to match the parapet, sometimes an arched frieze around the walls below the windows. Pilasters were also used, placed to correspond with the division of the vaulting and so marking the bays vertically. In some synagogues a combination of vertical and horizontal decorative elements was tried, using both pilasters and a frieze. As variations of the basic plan were experimented, progressively more attention was paid to the middle bay of the east wall and to the Ark itself; the simple aedicule of the Renaissance was given increasingly elaborate additions, often with far from felicitous results.

Synagogue-building only picked up again slowly in the 1670s as the country and the Jewish communities recovered from the catastrophic years of bloodshed, famine, destruction and epidemics when Poland was invaded and ravaged by Swedes, Tatars and Cossacks, and the government was in disarray. In western Poland, although the Jews suffered along with others at the hands of the Swedish invaders, somehow they were blamed for aspects of the Swedes' success and accused of complicity with the enemy. Consequently Jewish property, including synagogues in many places, was confiscated and the Jews were victims of the backlash of popular discontent. In eastern Poland the Jews were hated by the subjugated Ukrainian proletariat as part of the oppressive Establishment, because of their role as tax-collectors and hatchet-men for the landowning nobles; consequently Jews were massacred by the furious peasants, as well as by the Tatar and Cossack hordes, in the course of the bloody Chmielnicki uprising which began in 1648 and only came to an official end with the treaty of Andrusovo in 1667. The Ukraine was then divided in two. The Jews were expelled from the part on the east of the Dnieper, which went to Russia. In western Ukraine, retained by Poland, the Jewish population trebled between 1640 and 1740.

The synagogues of Stryj (1677), Brody, Jaryczów, Jaroslaw, Jarmolince, Janow Trembowelski, Leszniów, Kamionka Strumilowa, Lanck-

fanciful attempt at the grandiose – the nah of the Isabjellin synagogue, the rk of local carpenters.

Wooden synagogue at Grodno, Byelorussia, USSR.

orona, Wysokie Mazowieckie, Buczacz, Tarnopol, and Husiatyn and Zol-kiew (both rebuilt in 1692), were constructed in the post-war building phase at the end of the century; a number of these were timber buildings. In style and plan these synagogues followed the pre-war edifices. The concentric pattern had become firmly entrenched; the nine-bay arrangement in particular endured throughout the eighteenth century.

The Archbishop of Lvov issued a licence for a brick synagogue at Zol-kiew in 1692[36] to replace a wooden one. Basically the new synagogue, almost a perfect cube, conformed in plan to the patterns in use for over a century. Zolkiew was on the private estate of King Jan Sobieski who had a residence there. In 1692 the president of the Kehilla was the King's tax administrator, Bezalel ben Nathan, a lordly court Jew in charge of leasing the regional taxes and tolls. Owing to his influence and the King's generally favourable disposition towards the Jewish inhabitants of the town it is likely that the court architect, Peter Beber of Wroclaw, was retained to work on the synagogue. Beber had built the Zolkiew town hall in 1687 and it is known that he was still working there in 1692. The exterior was not without a little pretentiousness: the customary parapet with uniform blind arcading on all four sides was surmounted by fancy curvilinear indentation and had domed lantern-like turrets at the angles. The similarity of appearance of the Zolkiew synagogue and the Stara at Kazimierz, Cracow, is so marked that it can hardly have been coinciden-tal. The low annexe with zigzag gables added to the west side and contain-ing the men's and the women's vestibules is particularly reminiscent of the annexe added to the north side of the Cracow Stara to accommodate an additional women's section. At Zolkiew the three round-headed door-ways with plain voussoirs were set in elaborate baroque surrounds.

The architectural development of the wooden synagogues ran parallel to that of the masonry synagogues in Poland, the simple concentric plan frequently evolving into a careful nine-bay arrangement. The use of piers was taken from the masonry constructions, but since they were not usually required as supporting columns for the vault in a timber building they were more frequently employed as supports for a baldachin over the bimah. The beautiful ceilings of many of the wooden synagogues were the work of the same carpenters who made the cradles for the vaults of the masonry buildings, and they managed to achieve the same sought-after monumental effect. A few masonry synagogues were built with wooden vaults, possibly for economy, but perhaps too because of the excellent illusory effects achieved in wood by the skilled carpenters, who lavished exquisite workmanship on the timber structures despite their perishable nature. Wood carving which simulated drapery was an especi-ally prized form of ornamentation: this included carved fringes, swags, lambrequins and even draped curtains. In the eighteenth century wooden synagogues were constructed with internal cupolas masked on the outside by a gabled roof. The synagogues of Grodno, Olkienniki, Sniadowo (1768), Targowica and Janów Sokólski, for example, were all built with an octagonal cupola. The wooden synagogue of Nowe Miasto (1779–80) had a two-tier octagonal cupola; the lower tier was crowned with a blind balustrade, the upper tier was elliptical. Cupolas were also added to beautify old buildings, often at the time of repairs to the roof. This

OPPOSITE Detail of the wooden ceilir of the small synagogue at Hor Germany, painted in 1733 by Eliez Sussman, an itinerant artist fro Polan

FOLLOWING PAG LEFT The 'Esnoga' of the Spanish ai Portuguese congregation Amsterdam, dedicated in 1675, becam the mother-synagogue of Weste Sephardim. The dignity and grande of the interior expresses the elegan and the cultural importance of tl seventeenth-century communi

RIGHT The English architect Pe Harrison built the synagogue Newport, Rhode Island in 1763 ir style which was suitable to a Ne England town, but the interi arrangement derives ultimately fro the Amsterdam Esnog

appears to have been the case at the early eighteenth-century synagogue of Wolpa in Lithuania, the roof of which was repaired in 1781. Invariably the transition from the square plan of the hall to the polygonal plan of the cupola was contrived by means of pendentives. Vestibules and women's sections were sometimes constructed as an organic part of the wooden synagogue from the outset, as in the masonry buildings, being placed laterally to the central square and covered by the same roof. Frequently annexes with separate roofs were added later to serve as vestibules, women's sections, council chambers and offices, clustered about the main body of the synagogue. There were also instances of the construction of corner pavilions, a feature found on secular buildings in Poland. In the case of the synagogues there were used as offices, or meeting-rooms for the trade-guilds.

Jewish artists engaged in figurative polychrome decoration in the the wooden synagogues of Mogilev, Kopys and Dolginov in Byelo-dorów, the walls and ceilings of the lofty wooden synagogue were painted by Israel, son of Mordecai Liśnicki of Jaryczów, about 1652;[37] this same artist, with Izak Baer and his son, painted the walls of the Gwoździec synagogue in the same year.[38] Although only a few of the names of the artists have been preserved, it does appear that there were families of synagogue decorators. Early in the eighteenth century Chaim, son of Izaak Segal of Sluck, a town on the estate of Prince Radziwill, decorated the wooden synagogues of Mogilev, Kopys and Dolginov in Byelorussia.[39] His repertory included an allegorical cycle based on a story in *Maasse Nissim* (Wondrous Tales) by Yuspa Shammas of Worms, published in Amsterdam in 1696. On the domed ceiling the city of Worms is depicted above a monstrous reptile – a play on its name – and between the Trees of Life and Knowledge. The synagogue artists drew their inspiration not only from biblical stories and medieval Jewish imagery but also from indigenous folklore; the signs of the zodiac and the Temple in Jerusalem were popular subjects as well as a profusion of animal and floral decoration. Some of the creatures conveyed a symbolic meaning – the stork (*hassidah*), for example, alluded to the pious people; the elephant symbolized endurance; the deer swiftness to obey God's will. Legendary beasts were also depicted, such as the behemoth, the leviathan and the unicorn, usually portrayed in a jungle of arabesques and scrolls. Izaak Leb, son of Yehuda Ha-Kohen of Jaryczów, painted the barrel-vaulted ceiling of the Gwoździec synagogue in 1729.[40] Another artist from Jaryczów, a town which produced a number of synagogue decorators, was an itinerant painter, Yehuda Leib, who signed his work in the synagogues of Przebórz (1760), Pinczów, Dzialoszyn and Szydlow.[41] This tradition of interior decoration continued well into the nineteenth century. The work of David Friedlander, who was a builder as well as a decorator, included the synagogues of Wyszogrod (1810),[42] and Grojec, where, in a scene representing the Babylonian captivity, musical instruments hang from trees in the garden of a four-storeyed tower of Babel.[43]

Since the time of Moses Isserles the authority of the Polish rabbis in spiritual and theological matters had been established in Bohemia and Germany. A number of them went to serve there and they, as well as migrant teachers and craftsmen, introduced the visual art and sometimes

OPPOSITE The exquisite early eighteenth-century interior of the synagogue at Vittorio Veneto, Italy, as is now installed in a room of the Israel Museum, Jerusalem.

Itinerant Jewish artists decorated many synagogue interiors such as this one at Orla, Poland.

David Friedlander was a builder as well as a synagogue decorator in the early years of the nineteenth century. His painting in the synagogue of Grojec, Poland, evokes a scene by the waters of Babylon.

Storks in medallions against a floral background. Part of Eliezer Sussman's decoration of the little upper-storey synagogue in the village of Unterlimpurg, near Schwäbisch Hall, Germany, executed in 1739. Other medallions framed smiling rabbits, an elephant and a stag.

also the form of the Polish synagogues to their new country of residence. For example, one of the inscriptions, apparently made in 1730, in the cage-work synagogue at Ellrich in the Harz mountains records the name of Aaron son of Rabbi Moshe of Vilna in Lithuania, and a number of the other inscriptions match those in the synagogue of Gwoździec in Galicia, the decoration of which in 1652 and again in 1729 has already been mentioned.

The best known of the artists from Poland who worked in Germany is Eliezer Sussman, who decorated at least four synagogues there between 1733 and 1740. He was a son of Solomon, the cantor of Brody in Galicia, and his artist's repertoire was that of his native country. In 1733 he painted the barrel vault, walls and furnishings of an earlier wooden synagogue at Bechhofen, a village in the Feuchtwangen district. The little building, which measured only 8.5 × 9 m and 7 m in height, was destroyed by the Nazis in 1937.[44] Two years after working at Bechhofen, Sussman decorated an even smaller synagogue, a half-frame building at Horb, in 1735.[45] After it ceased to function as a synagogue this edifice was used as a hay barn and so, to preserve it, it was dismantled and removed in 1914 to the Städtisches Museum at Bamberg, which has kindly loaned it to the Israel Museum, Jerusalem. The joyous decoration in warm colours includes a medallion with a liturgical inscription upheld by trumpet-blowing lions and a representation of the risen Jerusalem; on another wall lions hold up a baldachin between biblical texts below a medallion with liturgical inscriptions. On the ceiling, animals and birds, some of them exotic, some with human features, are depicted amid a riot of swirling leaves and flowers; at the apex of the vault are biblical inscriptions from Haggai 2:9 and Psalms 115:16. Sussman painted the synagogue at Kirchheim in a similar manner in 1739–40.[46] The painted panels and fittings of this synagogue were moved in 1912 to the Mainfränkisches Museum at Würzburg, where they perished in a fire in 1945.

The piers of the centrally placed masonry bimah in the synagogue at Nikolsburg were conceived by the architect as an organic part of the concentrically planned interior.

Sussman's other known work was in the synagogue of the village of Unterlimpurg, where Jews expelled from the town of Schwäbisch Hall had settled. The synagogue was on the upper storey of an inconspicuous house in the main street, reached by external stone steps and an external covered wooden stairway. Sussman's decoration of the interior of the synagogue room was executed in 1739[47] with polychrome panels depicting symbolic beasts in medallions against a floral background, as well as a representation of Jerusalem and Hebrew texts. The women's section was behind a wooden screen with peep-holes, which the artist contrived to incorporate in his decorative scheme. The dismantled synagogue is now preserved at Schwäbisch Hall in the Keckenburg Museum.

A simple wooden synagogue built in the latter half of the eighteenth century in the Transylvanian village of Naznánfalva by a Jewish craftsman, Isaac Moses Frankl,[48] also had a painted interior in the tradition of the Polish synagogues. Two plaques on the west wall were inscribed with prayers for the Christian lady who donated the land on which the synagogue was built and for the Emperor Josef II. In the seventeenth and eighteenth centuries Jews were forbidden to reside in the towns of Hungary, so communities formed in rural villages. Noble landowners often welcomed Jewish settlers on their country estates with a letter of protection (*Schutzbrief*): these permits invariably specified that the Jews should be allowed to build their own places of worship and celebrate their religion according to their customs.

Jews who fled from Poland at the height of the Chmielnicki massacres in 1648 were followed by waves of emigrants seeking better living conditions in the eighteenth century. Many settled in Bohemia and Nikolsburg, Moravia, where the Polish influence could be noted in the concentric plan of a number of synagogue buildings like those of Kuttenplan (1757) and Königswart (1764). The concentric plan with the bimah between the four supporting pillars of the nine cross-vaults was also employed in many masonry synagogues in Hungary, such as those of Bartfa, Bonyad, Csetje (1820), Gyöngos, Hunfalva (built 1821, architect Andreas Landherr), Stomfa and Trencsen. Immigrants from eastern Europe to Erez Israel who built the Ha'ari synagogue of the Ashkenazim in the town of Safed at the end of the sixteenth century (rebuilt after the earthquake of 1837) also employed the plan common in Poland: the four central supporting pillars form the built-in bimah.

6 *Western Taste and Fashion*

At the end of the sixteenth century the Jews in Bohemia found themselves in better conditions there than ever before and with apparently rosy prospects for the future: the Emperors Maximilian II and Rudolf II were well disposed to them and Ferdinand II distributed favours to Jews. In 1622 he granted armorial bearings and a patent of nobility to the leader of the Prague community, who became Jacob Bassevi von Treudenberg (1570–1634). This princely court Jew employed Italian artists and artisans to build his Prague mansion and instructed them to model it on the design of the palace of General von Wallenstein, with whom he leased the Imperial Mint during the Thirty Years War and debased the silver coinage to replenish the Emperor's depleted coffers.

David ben Solomon Gans (1541–1613), the distinguished geographer, mathematician and astronomer, published in 1592 a chronicle, *Zemah David*, in which he described the lifestyle and aspirations of the Jewish householders of Prague. Unlike that of the Jews of Poland, who tended to live in a secluded Jewish world of their own, the taste of the Prague Jews was assimilative: this attitude resulted in new departures not only in the decoration of the synagogue but also in its plan. The Maisl synagogue founded by Markus Mordecai Maisl, for which the Emperor Rudolf II granted a special licence in 1592, appears to have been built originally as a barrel-vaulted hall. Gans records that the architect was one Joseph Wal de Herz. According to a tombstone inscription at Prague a Jewish architect, Judah Coref de Herz (died 1625), was responsible for 'the whole building of the Pinkas synagogue and part of that of the Maisl synagogue'. In fact Judah Coref de Herz only enlarged and remodelled the medieval fabric of the Pinkas; it is not known to what extent he was involved with the Maisl, unless he is to be identified with 'Joseph Wal de Herz' as the original architect. The Maisl was enlarged and transformed into a basilical hall, the former synagogue becoming a broad nave to which were added side aisles with cross-vaulted galleries above them.

When the Pinkas synagogue was examined by experts in the course of restoration by the Czechoslovakian State after World War II, it became possible to identify Judah Coref de Herz's work on that building.[1] His architectural repertory was based on the Renaissance and baroque buildings of Prague but nothing is known of his origins or training. In his remodelling of the Pinkas synagogue in response to an urgent need for additional seating space, he displayed both imaginative talent and a ruthless disregard for the rhythm of the old Gothic structure. His transformation of a corridor into a south aisle by breaking four segmental arches in the south wall of the medieval synagogue was basically successful. A storey was added to the aisle to form a women's gallery and its parapet was finished inventively in the form of a little baroque balcony in each bay. Less successful was de Herz's initiative in cutting back the piers that remained of the south wall to make a little more floor space: this necessitated amputating the shafts of the Gothic vaulting and the effect is ugly. The remodelling appears to have taken twenty to thirty years, and by the time de Herz came to remake the east, south and west fronts he had absorbed more of the baroque style then flourishing in Prague. The outside doorway with pilasters and a broken pediment belongs to the later period.

PREVIOUS PAGE The synagogue at Lunéville in Lorraine, built 1785–8, reflects the elegance of eighteenth-century France. The Judaic symbols are skilfully incorporated into the neo-classical decoration.

The Klaus synagogue, built at the end of the sixteenth century, was modified at the end of the seventeenth. The building is surrounded on three sides by the grounds of the old Jewish cemetery of Prague, Czechoslovakia.

The Klaus synagogue has been attributed to the initiative of Markus Mordecai Maisl. The late sixteenth-century building was altered at the end of the seventeenth century: the barrel vault of the nave was stuccoed with the foliage, scroll and flower ornamentation which is found in contemporary buildings in Prague. The Vysoka or Hohe (High) synagogue, adjacent to the Jewish town hall, was also renovated in the seventeenth century. Its stark exterior belies the beautiful late Renaissance interior of the hall of worship on the first floor and the particularly fine stuccoed ceiling. The striking factor common to all the late sixteenth- and seventeenth-century synagogue-building and decoration in Prague is its conscious affinity with the local architectural idiom. This natural consequence of cultural acclimatization is even more evident in the seventeenth-century synagogues of the Netherlands.

Holland wrenched itself free from Spanish domination in 1572 and with the Treaty of Westphalia in 1648 Spain formally acknowledged the sovereignty of the United Provinces. The Dutch assumed an increasingly important role in European commerce until they attained the lead, handling grain and naval supplies from the Baltic, manufactured goods shipped down the Rhine from Germany, and spices and luxury goods from the Orient. The bulk of France's exports was carried in Dutch ships and Spain and Portugal depended on the Dutch for their grain imports and naval supplies; even the nautically powerful English relied substantially on Dutch shipping.

Once Holland was free from Spanish jurisdiction it was bound to appeal as a possible place of refuge to Jewish families living clandestinely in Spain and Portugal. In the early years of the seventeenth century Amsterdam, at the hub of international mercantile affairs with its Exchange Bank (instituted in 1609) and its bustling port, had already attracted a small colony of Sephardim who formed three congregations. By 1618, when the synagogue of Beth Israel was opened, each congregation had a permanent meeting-place: Beth Ya'acob (named after Jacob Tirado, in whose house in Vloonburg it first met), acquired a house in the Houtgracht in 1614 and added schoolrooms in 1620; opposite were the premises of the third congregation, Neveh Shalom. These immigrants aroused the attention of the staunchly anti-Catholic, anti-Spanish city fathers, who at first suspected the crypto-Jews of being crypto-Catholics gathering secretively to celebrate the Mass when they met to celebrate Jewish festivals and for prayer. As more Marranos arrived and began to take a useful part in the economic, social and intellectual life of the city and in diplomatic relations with foreign powers, the suspicion of the authorities changed to respect, tolerance and, eventually, approval, and the complaints voiced by the Calvinist elders also abated.

Thus the Golden Age of Amsterdam Jewry dawned as the Golden Age of Polish Jewry waned, but there was an essential difference between the attitude of the Amsterdam Jews and that of their co-religionists in eastern Europe, where they formed a compact, largely autonomous society, fairly insulated from the contemporary national culture, while enjoying various degrees of tolerance and privilege. The sponsors of Polish synagogue projects availed themselves of the technical abilities of Christian architects, builders and craftsmen, so inevitably some elements of the prevailing styles did find a place in Jewish monuments: however, it is clear that the architects were kept on a tight rein and their imagination was subordinated to the conservative requirements of the sponsors, which were dictated by, and rigidly rooted in, a narrow, fundamentalist interpretation of Halakah. Because of their different background, the Jews in Amsterdam, while orthodox in their religious practice, had an assimilative attitude to the prevailing national culture.

The majority of the immigrants to Amsterdam in the first half of the seventeenth century were Marranos, crypto-Jews whose families had contrived by accepting baptism to remain in Spain and Portugal after the orders of expulsion, and who escaped the vigilant Inquisition by simulating observance of the Catholic faith. Secretly they had clung to their Judaic tradition, and adhered as far as they could and dared to their ancestral beliefs. Succeeding generations, left without teachers, knew little or no Hebrew; they could only attempt to obey the Mosaic law surreptitiously and were usually unable to have their male children circumcised. Many families managed nevertheless to nurture among their descendants a keen desire to be able to return to a full and unrestricted observance of Judaism, even though they were outwardly part of the Catholic society in which they lived. It is remarkable that many immigrants to Amsterdam from Spain and Portugal belonged to families who had lived ostensibly as Christians for 100 or 150 years. In Holland the crypto-Jews were able to throw off their Christian-sounding names, resume their Jewish identity and return to the open practice of Judaism. They received religious instruction and the uncircumcised males were circumcised before admission to the community. However, after a long period of integration in Christian society, these Jews, a number of whom had been in Christian academic circles, were naturally disinclined to dissociate themselves culturally from non-Jews in a city which was then at the pinnacle of its importance, not only in commerce but also in science and the display of artistic genius. The Marranos knew that it was possible to participate in much of the national culture without endangering their attachment to Judaism – precisely because they had been obliged to do so in Spain and Portugal, and had managed it under the most contrary conditions. In Amsterdam, boys attending the Jewish school also took private lessons in secular subjects such as Latin.

Jewish–Christian dialogue was stimulated by some Calvinists who were excited by the eschatological aspect of the Jewish migrations; they connected the destiny of the Tribes of Israel with the ultimate salvation of mankind and inclined to search for signs to support their own belief in the imminence of the Parousia and the Millennium. Curiosity about Jews and Jewish worship was also animated by literary and artistic interest in Solomon's Temple. The painter Rembrandt (1606–69) was so interested in the Jews that he chose to reside among them in their quarter in Amsterdam: there he painted scenes of contemporary Jewish life and found inspiration for his biblical subjects.

The members of the Sephardic community, usually referred to generically as 'Portuguese', were active in the affairs of the Dutch East India and the Dutch West India Companies, in which several were substantial shareholders. Affluent Jews engaged in branches of high finance, banking, stockbroking, contracts to victual the army, and, on a humbler level, stockjobbing. The business activities of the Jewish inhabitants ranged from printing, in which they attained a high degree of proficiency and success, to diamond cutting and polishing, which became an almost exclusively Jewish industry. Many Jews were involved in the silk and tobacco industries. The most successful Jewish merchant was Isaac (formerly Antonio) Lopez Suasso, who was able to place two million guilders at the disposal of William III when he set out from the Netherlands to take the crown of England in 1688. Notwithstanding the fact that he was a Jew, Lopez Suasso was created a baron by King Carlos III of Spain in recognition of his diplomatic services. The Palache family of distinguished diplomats were influential members of the Amsterdam community; Samuel Palache, son of a rabbi at Fez, was the Sultan of Morocco's ambassador at The Hague and negotiated the first treaty between a Moslem state and a Christian state. One of Samuel's sons was the Moroccan ambassador to Denmark; another, the Dutch chargé d'affaires in Morocco. Samuel's brother Joseph succeeded him as ambassador at The Hague; of his sons, David succeeded his father as ambassador, Isaac was professor of Hebrew at Leyden University, Moses served as adviser to four sultans of Morocco, Joshua was an international merchant, and Abraham a financier and diplomat.

There were many clever physicians in the community. Isaac Orobio de Castro (1620–87), who was born in Portugal, had been a professor of metaphysics at the University of Salamanca until his arrest and imprisonment by the Inquisition for Judaizing; he was subsequently professor of pharmacy at the University of Toulouse in France before reaching Amsterdam, where he practised medicine and wrote works of philosophy. Zacutus Lusitanus, alias Abraham Zacuto (1575–1642), another illustrious Jewish physician, born in Portugal as Manuel Alvarez de Tavara, was circumcised on arrival in Amsterdam. A brilliant clinician, he was the first to describe blackwater fever and was the author of several medical works. Prince Maurice of Orange was attended on his deathbed by Dr Joseph Bueno, another Jewish immigrant, whose son, Dr Ephraim Hezekiah Bueno, was painted by Rembrandt as *The Jewish Doctor*. He was also an accomplished poet and translated the Psalms into Spanish.

The leading literary figure in Amsterdam Jewry was Daniel Levi de Barrios (1635–1701), born at Montilla in the province of Cordoba, who left Spain in 1655 and arrived in Amsterdam after sojourns in Algiers, Livorno (where he reverted to Judaism) and the West Indies. Although he joined the community in Amsterdam, Levi de Barrios lived outwardly as a Christian for another twelve years in Brussels as a captain in the army of the Spanish Netherlands, but on returning to Amsterdam in 1674 he professed Judaism openly. He has been called the poet laureate of Amsterdam Jewry, which he glorified in his works; he also exalted the Jewish faith, Sephardic culture, and the martyrs of the Inquisition, and began but never completed a poetic version of the Pentateuch in Spanish. He and his second wife, Abigail de Pina, may have been the subject of Rembrandt's painting *The Jewish Bride*.

The best-known Jewish exponents of the visual arts in Amsterdam were the engravers Jacob Gadella and Shalom Italia. Italia, who had arrived from Mantua in Italy by 1641, executed masterly copper engravings for *megillot* and portraits; he illustrated books, and worked as an illuminator. It appears that there were no Jews, however, among the city's versatile architects in the seventeenth century.

In the second quarter of the century the boisterous Dutch late Renaissance style with its ornate gables was superseded by a restrained classical style of which Jacob van Campen was the leading exponent. He designed the Coymans house about 1624–6 and the magnificent town hall (now the royal palace) between 1648 and 1655.

The three synagogues were described in 1636 by a French visitor, Charles Ogier,[2] as resembling 'the new Calvinist Temples'. He may have had in mind the Church of the Remonstrants in Amsterdam (1629) or the Protestant temple at Charenton near Paris, built by Salomon de Brosse in 1623 – halls with tiered galleries designed on a centralized ground-plan for acoustical efficacy. Ogier particularly noted the large bimah of the Beth Ya'acob synagogue. In the new Calvinist temples the pulpit supplanted the altar, reflecting the importance placed by Calvinists upon preaching.

The three Sephardic congregations amalgamated in 1639; their new Esnoga built in that year was an elegant building, its street façade distinguished by giant Corinthian pilasters rising to the cornice, sculpted fes-

OPPOSITE The façade of the Esnoga of 1639 built for the Sephardim of Amsterdam. It was later used as a banqueting hall after the new synagogue was built. Etching by Romeyn de Hooghe.

RIGHT The philosopher Baruch Spinoza (1632–77), on whom sentence of excommunication was pronounced from the bimah of the 1639 Esnoga in Amsterdam.

toons above the tall rectangular ground-floor windows, and a fanlight over the doors of the first-floor balustraded balcony in the middle bay. After its sale in 1675 the building functioned as a banqueting hall. It was finally demolished in the present century. An engraving of 1656 of the interior, which measured about 17 × 24 m, shows the long nave covered by twin timber barrel vaults supported by latitudinal beams on a framework standing on the barrel-vaulted galleries over the twin aisles, which were supported in turn by timber columns of the Tuscan order. Half-way along the wall of the north aisle stood the warden's tribune. The spacious bimah, a balustraded dais, was near to the west end of the nave on the axis of the tall tripartite Ark which stood against the east wall, enclosed by a balustrade. The great philosopher Baruch Spinoza (1632–77), born in Amsterdam of Marrano parents from Portugal, worshipped in this Esnoga and was educated in its school. However, his rationalist biblical exegesis which defied both Christian and Jewish tradition earned him the disapproval of the Parnassim and eventually, in 1656, exasperated by his insistence on voicing his opinions, they had a sentence of excommunication pronounced against him from the bimah, although he himself did not want to break with the community. In 1642 the Haham, Manasseh ben Israel, welcomed the English Queen, Henrietta Maria, and members of the ruling House of Orange to the Esnoga. A few years later, when Manasseh ben Israel went to England, Henrietta Maria was in exile and her husband had been beheaded by their arch-enemy, Cromwell, with whom the rabbi treated for permission for Jews to settle in that country.

In the thirty-five years since the formation of their congregation in 1635, the Ashkenazim, mostly from Germany, had become sufficiently numerous and prosperous to leave their makeshift meeting-place and commission the architect Daniel Stalpaert[3] to build them a synagogue. As Van Campen's assistant, Stalpaert had executed the splendid Amsterdam town hall. His synagogue, completed in 1671, is a handsome classical building in the manner of a substantial city mansion. The pleasing three-storey, three-bay pedimented façade was not improved by the later addition of a low vestibule which interrupts the harmony of the fenestration. The interior arrangement followed that of the 1639 Esnoga, except that Stalpaert's giant Tuscan columns rise to the barrel vault over the nave and the galleries of the aisles are abutted to their shafts. The men's seats were arranged in parallel rows in the aisles leaving a free passage down the nave from the Ark on the east wall to the bimah near the west end, resembling the Italian latitudinal plan.

In 1670 the United Portuguese Parnassim studied projects[4] for the enlargement in the 1639 Esnoga, which was already too small. After deliberation they decided on an ambitious new project – a spacious and grandiose place of worship with offices, a library and schoolrooms, on a site donated by 650 members of the congregation.[5] Of the plans or models submitted, the Parnassim selected the one by an Amsterdam master-builder, Elias Bouman. The style is that restrained interpretation of the classical idiom best described as 'Protestant baroque', reticent yet dignified, splendid yet sedate, serene rather than stern, an expression in classical architectural terms of the forthright character and sobriety of the Dutch Calvinists, with none of the tumultuous, overflowing grandeur of the baroque of the Catholic south. Bouman built a monumental place of worship devoid of any embellishment that could be considered idolatrous or ostentatious.

The four cornerstones were laid on 17 April 1671; owing to setbacks, the work took four years to complete. The pompous dedication ceremonies in 1675 were accompanied by an orchestra and choir. Ecstatically, the Dutch artist Romeyn de Hooghe extolled the new building in a poem as 'the glory of the Amstel and its senate',[6] and designed a commemorative broadside which was engraved by Emanuel de Wit; allegorical figures representing the Dutch Republic, Freedom of Conscience, and the High Priest with the Scroll of the Law pose benignly on clouds above the nave of the new Esnoga, which is filled with a smartly dressed crowd. A commemorative plaque on the east wall of the Esnoga names the Parnassim and the Gabay, the seven members of the building committee, and three 'zelosos favorecedores' (zealous benefactors), one of whom was the president of the congregation, Mosseh Curiel, in whose house William III, the Stadtholder of the Netherlands and King of England, stayed on a visit to Amsterdam twenty years later. On that occasion the King visited the Esnoga, a free-standing building in a courtyard with an ample forecourt approached through a *porte-cochère*. The interior, which measures 38 × 29 m, is a much grander and improved version of that of the 1639 building. The great wooden barrel vault over the lofty nave is supported by two rows of four giant Ionic columns on massive plinths; the columns at the east and west ends are engaged. Colonnades of six columns set further back on each side support the galleries over part of the aisles; the galleries are reached by stairs in the two pavilions which project from the east wall at the rear of the building. These galleries represent the first known occasion in the history of the synagogue when a section for women was an organic part of the initial design. The bimah and the warden's tribune are in the same positions as in the earlier synagogue; made of jacaranda wood imported from Brazil, both furnishings were donated by Mosseh Curiel. The magnificent tripartite Ark, which occupies the entire space between the engaged columns on the east wall, is surmounted by architectural pediments, crowns and obelisks; above the central bay, in an aedicule beneath a crowned pediment, are the Tables of the Law. According to the Spanish tradition, no paroketh hangs in front of the Ark.

During the day, light floods the synagogue through the many windows – six on the lower level, and seven on the upper, of both the north and south walls; four on each of two levels on the east wall, with an oculus above the upper row; and three levels of four on the west wall, with a matching oculus above the upper row. Electric lighting has not been installed. After sundown on a high holiday the Esnoga is a breathtaking sight when candles blaze from the four great candelabra which hang along the longitudinal axis of the nave, from the eight lesser candelabra hanging in the aisles and fourteen small ones under the galleries, as well as from the candlesticks on the bimah, on the balustrade of the Ark, and on the warden's tribune, and also from the sconces – four on each of the great free-standing columns and others on the tribune and the walls.

Jacob Judah Leon (1603–75), a member of the Sephardic community and an avid Hebrew antiquarian, published a treatise on Solomon's Temple which was translated into several languages. He also made a model of the Temple which attracted much attention: he showed it to many notable people including the Duke of York, later King James II of England. One must conclude that Bouman saw this model, because the concave buttresses on stepped bases of his synagogue building resemble those of Leon's model; in place of the round-headed niches between the buttresses of the model, Bouman placed round-headed windows on the north and south fronts, but at the rear of the synagogue, where the buttresses are much larger, there are niches. Leon, a versatile man, also designed a paroketh embroidered with the Ark of the ancient Israelites[7] for the synagogue at Middelburg.

The low buildings around the synagogue courtyard accommodate the offices, the schools, a marvellous library and a delightful small prayer-room. This little synagogue with panelled walls is like a room in a seventeenth-century private house except for the screened gallery behind the west wall; the Ark is a Dutch baroque armoire of the period, the work of a master cabinet-maker.

Later synagogues in the Netherlands were built in the classical style. The first at The Hague was built by the Sephardim in 1703; then Jacob Pereira gave the community the private synagogue he had built for his family. In 1726, Felis de Saart designed a handsome synagogue in the style of Daniel Marot, the royal architect. In 1725 the Jews of Rotterdam, Sephardim and Ashkenazim together, built a tall, narrow synagogue with a clock over the centre bay: the architect of this building, which was destroyed by bombs in an air-raid in 1940, was probably Titus Favre who built the Rotterdam Lutheran church and who went to Berlin in 1737 as court architect to King Frederick William I of Prussia. The Nieuwe (New), the second synagogue of the Ashkenazim of Amsterdam, was built in 1730 and enlarged in 1752 by Gerard Frederik Maybaum, who was director of the city works and buildings from 1746 until his death in 1768. It is a fine classical building with a breakfront centre bay, a balustraded parapet and a curvilinear dome above the roof.

The first Jews to settle in England since the Middle Ages were businessmen of Marrano extraction who arrived in London, mostly via Amsterdam, during the Commonwealth. The policy of the leaders of the congregation was to protect the growing community against molestation and help them to integrate into the civic life of London. This they eventually achieved, overcoming any adverse attitudes of religious bigotry and opposition based on commercial rivalry. In December 1656 the community acquired a twenty-one-year lease of a house in Creechurch Lane in the City of London and installed a synagogue on the upper floor. A visitor in 1662 described it:[8] the benches were in rows parallel to the north and south walls, the Ark at the east end, the warden's tribune at the west end, and the bimah between them. The women sat in an adjoining room from which they could hear the liturgy through a narrow lattice. In 1674 the synagogue was enlarged; the two rooms were united and the attic was converted into a gallery supported by an arcade with gilded Doric columns. Synagogues in Venice were fitted with galleries at about the same time (see p. 96). An unusual feature in the synagogue was a painting which, regardless of Judaic law, apparently hung above the Ark.[9] It depicts Moses indicating the Tables of the Law and Aaron on the other side holding a censer. This painting is now in the London offices of the Sephardic community. The painter, Aaron de Chavez, was a member of the community who, according to the *Encyclopaedia Neerlandica Sefardica*,[10] had belonged to the circle of the artist Jan Lievens in Amsterdam. The Parnassim paid for the canvas and frame and in 1675 paid de Chavez five pounds for painting the picture.[11] Engravings of Moses and Aaron with the Tables of the Law had appeared in a few Hebrew printed works in the seventeenth century, but de Chavez' inspiration appears to have been the painted or sculpted figures of Moses and Aaron flanking panels with the Ten Commandments, the Paternoster, or the Creed which hung at the end of some contemporary Protestant churches, such as those by Robert Streater in St Michael's Cornhill in the City of London.

The panelled room of the Creechurch Lane synagogue could accommodate 200 and the furnishings were quite sumptuous; an inventory of 1675 lists silver finials and silver candelabra for the bimah, which had a scarlet satin cover with a silver fringe, and silver candelabra for the walnut and gilt Ark, including one pair weighing five kilos for use at festivals. There were also silver dishes, a silver Torah crown and pointer, and silver *rimmonim* from the estate of one 'Deborah Israel the proselyte'; in 1684 a silver *ner tamid* was presented, and a 'great lamp with eight

Eighteenth-century engraving of the synagogue built by the Jews of Rotterdam in 1725. It was destroyed in World War II.

The New Synagogue, Amsterdam, built for the Ashkenazim of the city in 1730 and enlarged in 1752 by the city architect.

arms' of silver weighing nearly eleven kilos was acquired.[12]

Much of the congregation's precious silver was sold in 1703,[13] perhaps to help defray the cost of the stately new synagogue nearby in Bevis Marks which was opened in 1701 and still functions. It was built by a Quaker master-builder, Joseph Avis,[14] to a wooden model executed by an English joiner and adapted from the plan of the larger Amsterdam Esnoga; in Bevis Marks the galleries continue along the west end and are reached by a stair in the front vestibule. The Ark, undoubtedly the work of a London cabinet-maker, resembles the altar of London churches and in particular the reredos of the Wren City church of St Vedast, Foster Lane. Later furnishings acquired by the synagogue were also in the current English fashion[15] – purchased for the president of the congregation, a Chippendale chair of about 1750 has a pedimented back, carved arms terminating in lion masks, and chamfered legs, and is in the style of the Master's armchair of a London City guild. The circumcision chair of about 1790 is in the Sheraton style. The Ashkenazim of London built their first synagogue in 1722 in Duke's Place, near Bevis Marks, and another, the Hambro synagogue, in 1725 in Fenchurch Street, also in the City. Both were modelled on the Bevis Marks building.

The first Jews to reach the New World were enterprising members of the Spanish-Portuguese community of Amsterdam. Some who went first, in 1634, to Recife in Brazil, then a Dutch colony, went on in 1654 to New Amsterdam (now New York), settled there, and formed a congregation, Shearith Israel. Another colony of fifty arrived in 1651 in Curaçao, where they formed a congregation called Mikveh Israel. Descendants of some of the first settlers still belong to this congregation, as do descendants of the Parnassim responsible for building the present synagogue, which was dedicated in 1732. The four-storey building with curvilinear gables, standing in a tiled courtyard, has the appearance of

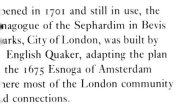

Opened in 1701 and still in use, the synagogue of the Sephardim in Bevis Marks, City of London, was built by an English Quaker, adapting the plan of the 1675 Esnoga of Amsterdam where most of the London community had connections.

a Dutch colonial mansion; the interior arrangement is influenced by the Amsterdam Esnoga of Bouman, long considered the 'mother synagogue' of the western Sephardim. It is the oldest synagogue building still in use on the American continent, closely followed by the Zedek ve Shalom synagogue at Paramaribo in Surinam (formerly Dutch Guiana), dedicated in 1737. An unusual custom of spreading sand over the wooden floor is still observed in the synagogues of Curaçao, Jamaica, and St Thomas: the origin of this practice, which is only followed in the Caribbean, is not known. One explanation, that it was because in Spain and Portugal the Marranos did this in order to muffle their footsteps when they assembled, seems as unlikely as an explanation proffered for the omission of the paroketh in front of the Ark doors in Spanish-Portuguese syna-gogues – that a curtain over a cupboard where the Torah was kept would have betrayed it as the sacred place. Surely the implacable spies of the Inquisition would not have been balked by such fragile subterfuges?

The Curaçao congregation, which included prosperous merchants and ship-owners, contributed to the building costs of the earliest synagogues in North America – at Savannah, Georgia, at Newport, Rhode Island, and in New York, where the Shearith Israel congregation purchased a site on Mill Street in 1728 and built a synagogue which was dedicated in 1730. It was a square building, about 10 × 10 m, with a gallery on three sides. The bimah and some of the other fittings are still preserved in the present Shearith Israel building on Central Park West.

At Newport the Touro synagogue, named after its first rabbi, Isaac Touro, and his sons, who were its benefactors, was designed by the first skilled architect in New England – and the most academic, before Jeffer-son – an English immigrant, Peter Harrison (1716–75). He has been referred to by one critic as 'the prince of the Colonial amateur archi-tects'.[16] Harrison's civic buildings in Newport – the Palladianesque Red-wood Library with a full temple portico, and the Brick Market – and his churches (King's Chapel, Boston, and Christ Church, Cambridge, Mass.) are careful, well-proportioned edifices based on designs in English archi-tectural books: Kent's *Designs of Inigo Jones* (1727), Gibbs's *Book of Architecture* (1728), Batty Langley's *Treasury of Designs* (1745) and Ware's *Designs of Inigo Jones and Others*. For the Touro synagogue, started in 1759 and dedicated in 1763, Harrison resorted to the same sources, but he must have consulted members of the congregation about the internal scheme because it is based on the Bevis Marks building and consequently ultimately derives from the 1675 Amsterdam Esnoga. It is a rectangular hall, about 13.35 × 10.75 m, with two tiers of columns, the lower Ionic, the upper Corinthian, supporting the galleries on three sides and the ceiling, which has a handsome cornice. The interior is now painted in grey and white; originally it was apple green, a favourite colour in decoration of the Georgian period. The building was designated a National Historic Site in 1946. In a book published by the Society of Friends of Touro Synagogue in 1948 and since several times reprinted, a former rabbi of the congregation, Dr Morris A. Gutstein, made the following delectable assertion: 'The plan of the interior is a miniature parallel to the ancient Holy Temple in Jerusalem and resembles closely the plan of a Masonic Lodge Hall.'[17] He omits to mention whether he

OPPOSIT
ABOVE This gilded wrought-iron doo
dated 1763 in Hebrew, is on a wa
cupboard on the bimah-balcony of th
synagogue at Cavaillon, France, whic
is entirely decorated in the style o
Louis xv

BELOW Detail of the interior of th
synagogue at Casale Monferrato, Italy
sumptuously gilded and painted in th
eighteenth century. The delicate gril
encloses the women's gallery

FOLLOWING PAGE
LEFT Detail of a wall from th
synagogue at Isfahan, Iran, now in th
Jewish Museum, New Yor

RIGHT Ruined monuments of ancie
Rome surround the imposin
synagogue of modern Rome, th
Tempio Israelitico, completed in 190

had Solomon's or Herod's building in mind but his endearing howler is surely prizeable.

In the first half of the eighteenth century there were a number of highly skilled Jewish professional embroiderers in Germany executing secular and religious tapestries, as well as proficient amateurs like Bluma Kassel, who in 1744 presented to the Kassel synagogue her beautiful paroketh depicting a pelican in her piety[18] – a known Christian symbol of the sacrifice of Jesus on the cross, but obviously intended here as a symbol of charity. Of the professionals, Elkanah Naumburg from Silesia, who was also a cantor, embroidered parokethim for the synagogues of Augsburg and Hildesheim (1714) and for the Hambro synagogue in London and worked for the Episcopal Court at Fulda;[19] Gershon Meyer made a new cover for the Emperor Henry II's tomb at Bamberg in 1738. At Königsberg in East Prussia, Moses Samuel started a silk embroidery industry in 1720. There were also embroiderers among the many skilled Jewish craftsmen – jewellers, goldsmiths and silversmiths, and businessmen – purveyors to the army and contractors to the mint – who formed a congregation at Berlin at the end of the seventeenth century. They enjoyed the protection of the Elector, who recognized the usefulness of these clever inhabitants. King Frederick William I of Prussia appointed Solomon Isaac his court embroiderer. When the first Berlin community synagogue was completed in the Heidereutergasse in 1714, the King attended the dedication, during which the wedding of Solomon Isaac's daughter was celebrated. The building, in the sedate Protestant baroque fashion, was the work of a master-carpenter, Michael Kemmeter, who had constructed the Neue Kirche (New Church) in the Gendarmenmarkt (1701–8). For the Ark, however, Kemmeter abandoned the formal rigorism of the rest and created a grandiose wooden shrine which reached the cornice in a series of columns and exuberant curves.

In 1746 another German ruler, the Margrave of Ansbach, who patronized the Jewish artist Judah Pinhas (1727–93) and kept him at the court as miniaturist and calligrapher, ordered the construction of a synagogue, to be paid for by the community. He entrusted the work to his court architect Leopold Retti (1705–51), a member of a family of north Italian stuccodores and painters working in Germany. The Ansbach Ark with twisted columns and the fanciful bimah, an urn-capped octagonal kiosk with twisted columns, are in surprising contrast to Retti's sober façade and interior but are explained by the range of his repertory, which over a twenty-year period in Ludwigsburg, Stuttgart and Ansbach reflected a development from the Italian baroque tradition through the French rococo style to classicism. That there was a vogue for fancy synagogue furnishings in Germany can be seen from an Ark (now in the Jewish Museum, New York) made about 1720 for the small synagogue of Weilheim in upper Bavaria. It was made by a carpenter used to working on church altars and the gaily painted cupboards in domestic use in south Germany. Two naïvely carved lions, with that human appearance which is common to beasts in folk art, uphold the crown and inscribed cartouche above the pediment like the heraldic supporters of armorial bearings. The beautifully carved bimah of the now disused synagogue of Carmagnola in Piedmont, Italy, is a more ornate version, with an intricately carved

OPPOSITE Detail of the painted and gilded bimah of the synagogue at Stockholm, Sweden (1878). The decorative style anticipates that of the English arts and crafts movement.

rococo open canopy, of Retti's bimah at Ansbach, a free-standing octagonal kiosk with twisted columns. This type became popular and with variations was used in synagogues in Germany and Austria and later in central and eastern Europe.

If the engraving of the Great Synagogue of Breslau in Silesia (now Wroclaw, Poland) by Johann Christian Sander is a correct representation, it had in 1746 a most extraordinary furnishing – a sort of tiered double baldachin in which, of all things, were statues of Moses with a Table of the Law and Aaron with a censer: on the back wall was a portrait of the sovereign, Frederick the Great, who had then permitted Jews to return and settle in the city.

Eighteenth-century redecoration of synagogue interiors in Italy was often lavish. The Livorno synagogue was the most distinguished and the gilded Ceneda (Vittorio Veneto) synagogue the most intimately elegant, but none was more lushly opulent than that of Casale Monferrato in Piedmont. The synagogue built there in 1595 was replanned and redecorated in the eighteenth century in the manner of Piedmontese baroque-rococo churches. The great gilded Ark of 1787[20] above three steps is in an enclosure like the sanctuary area of a church with an ornate wrought-iron grille and gates; it occupies about one-quarter of the space of the hall, which was lengthened in 1866 and measures 9.5×19 m. The longitudinal seating arrangement, with benches facing the Ark in rows on either side of a narrow central aisle, and the balcony-pulpit of 1765[21] projecting from the side wall above the heads of the worshippers both add to the church-like appearance. However, the women's gallery of 1720[22] with its delicate rococo gilded lattice-work screens, the Hebrew inscriptions on the walls in rococo-style cartouches, and the Hebrew letters in the painted sky of the magnificent painted and stuccoed ceiling all remind the visitor that this is a Jewish place of worship, worthy of one of the inscriptions which is based on Haggai 2:9: 'The latter splendour of this house shall be greater than the former.' The marble floor, the gift of Baron Guiseppe Raffael Vitta, was laid in 1823.[23]

The ceiling of the synagogue of Rohonc (Rechnitz) in Hungary, built by the community there in 1718[24] under the protection of Count Batthyany, was painted and stuccoed in the same florid manner as that of Casale Monferrato and also had Hebrew inscriptions in rococo cartouches, but here there were in addition paintings of biblical scenes in elaborate stucco frames on the ceilings, in a style which recalls that of the Austrian village church of the period. The synagogues of Csabrendek and Tapolcza in Hungary had similar biblical paintings and frescoes. A less exuberant painted interior, with non-figurative decoration, was that of Mährisch Aussee in Austria.

Reconstruction of the early seventeenth-century synagogue of Livorno (Leghorn) began at the beginning of the eighteenth century and continued sporadically until the new façade was added in 1789. As Rachel Wischnitzer has remarked, although its scheme derives from the 1675 Amsterdam Esnoga and northern Protestant church designs, it had no northern austerity.[25] One reason for this was the beautiful arcading of the two tiers of galleries on three sides of the hall (28.2×25.8 m), which gave the impression of a small theatre. The marble Ark of 1742 was the work of a

Detail of the gaudily painted Ark from a synagogue at Weilheim in Upper Bavaria, now in the Jewish Museum, New York. The human appearance of the exuberant, naïve lions follows closely the regional folk-art.

The eighteenth-century bimah of the synagogue at Carmagnola, Italy, is in the same gaily ornate style as the contemporary rococo furnishings of Piedmontese churches.

Carrara sculptor, Giovanni di Isidoro Baratta, who sculpted the high altar in Livorno Cathedral and much church statuary;[26] the marble balustraded bimah was made in 1745. This synagogue, of which drawings, paintings and engravings survive, was destroyed by bombs in an air-raid in World War II.

The medieval synagogues of Cavaillon and Carpentras in France which were rebuilt in the eighteenth century were decorated in the delicate style of *salons* of the reign of Louis XV. Both synagogues retained the curious arrangement, apparently of long standing (see p. 68), of having the bimah on a lateral balcony on the west wall above the congregation, and the Ark on the floor below. The little synagogue at Cavaillon, 8.4×7.2 m and 8.3 m in height, on the first and second storeys of a medieval building, was reconstructed by the local master-masons Antoine Armelin and his son Pierre; the very detailed legal contract for the work, drawn up between them and representatives of the community in 1772, has been preserved.[27] A sculptor was also engaged, an artisan named Jean-Joseph Charmot from the neighbouring town of l'Isle-sur-Sorgue, who had worked on the Cavaillon town hall. The fine *boiseries* of the interior are his work, as are the entrance sculpted with medallions, shells and palmettes, and in a cartouche a verse in Hebrew from Psalms 118:20: 'This is the gate of the Lord; the righteous shall enter through it.' The delicate wrought-iron work of the grilles and banisters was executed by a local locksmith, François Isoard, who, too, had worked on the town hall. The synagogue is now cared for by the municipality and is open to the public: many visitors come to admire the place, which has been described as 'a precious casket carved like a jewel'[28] and as 'a jewel of French Judaic art'.[29] A Chair of Elijah, in the contemporary *salon* style, presented in 1774, is set high up in one corner on a stucco cloud. The alms-boxes are labelled for the communities of Hebron, Safed, Tiberias and Jerusalem.

The synagogue built between 1785 and 1788 at Lunéville in eastern France also exemplifies the French taste of the period. Its façade, like that of a small but very superior urban residence, is ornamented with a discreetly Judaic symbol entirely in keeping with neo-classical taste – festoons of vine leaves and grapes.

In Germany, as the eighteenth century drew on, the position of the Jews improved in those states where they were favoured by the more progressive rulers. Most of the monarchs admitted court Jews to their entourage. These emancipated Jews and the sons of the Jewish artisans, who were protected for their commercial usefulness, began to gain admission to the universities and academies and to penetrate the fringe of non-Jewish society, especially the intellectual circles. In 1761 a Jew from Dessau, Moses Mendelssohn (1729–86), defeated Immanuel Kant and another competitor for the Prussian Academy of Science's prize. Subsequently, Mendelssohn translated the Hebrew Pentateuch into German. He was tireless in his efforts to reconcile Judaic philosophy with the current ideas and ideology of Germany in the Age of Enlightenment and to defend Judaism as being at once an inherited faith revealed by divine legislation and a manifestation of the universal religion of reason. In the climate created by Mendelssohn and his followers, who urged Jews to become westerners, it is not surprising that their new synagogues expressed the new classicist idiom which, with its conservative tendencies, was favoured by the enlightened but absolutist German monarchs – whose ideology, like that of the Jews, was authoritarian. The new architectural classicism with its clear lines and uncomplicated forms shied away from the voluptuousness of the preceding century and strove for that discipline which Winckelmann described as 'noble simplicity and great calmness'. The synagogue built in 1789–90 for the community of Wörlitz by the Duke of Anhalt-Dessau in his park there reflects this trend. The architect, the Duke's friend and confidant Friedrich Wilhelm von Erdmannsdorf (1736–1800), had spent time in Italy where he studied Roman architecture and met Winckelmann, father of systematic archaeological research. He chose the Temple of Vesta as his model for the Wörlitz synagogue, a circular building with a conical roof; a semi-circular gallery supported by six Doric columns ran around one-half of the twelve-bay domed interior, lit by an oculus high up in each bay.

This synagogue, built in the park at Wörlitz in 1789–90, was commissione[d] for his Jewish subjects by the Duke o[f] Anhalt-Dessau and designed by his court architect Friedrich Wilhelm vo[n] Erdmannsdorf, an enthusiastic classicist who chose the Temple of Vesta in Rome as his model.

The synagogues of Karlsruhe (1798–1800) and Düsseldorf (1803) reflected the current classical trend but in a less extreme manner than the synagogue of von Erdmannsdorf, who attempted to realize the teachings of Winckelmann in his work and was influenced by the English neo-classicists Adam and Chambers. The Karlsruhe synagogue was designed as part of a whole city building project by Friedrich Weinbrenner (1766–1826). The street entrance, with a lofty Gothic archway between two towers, led to the colonnaded forecourt of the synagogue, a neat, pedimented, neo-classical edifice hidden from the street. Peter Joseph Krahe (1758–1840), architect, engineer and professor of painting and perspective art at Düsseldorf, designed the synagogue there, which he masked from the street by a perfect, small, neo-classical five-bay mansion through whose vestibule and a semicircular courtyard behind it the prayer-hall was reached. This rectangular building in the neo-classical style had galleries on three sides and a large rectangular central bimah.

A book much larger than this one could be devoted to the study of the development of synagogue architecture in the nineteenth century and the social-cultural-economic reasons behind the choice of each of the western fashions that succeeded one another – Romantic Neo-Classicism with its Greek Revival and Egyptian Revival trends, Gothic Revival, Romanesque Revival, Byzantine Revival, Neo-Baroque, Neo-Gothic, and one which the synagogue could claim almost as its own and which is treated in Chapter 7, Moorish Revival.

Jewish emancipation in France in 1790 after the revolution was followed by equality of citizenship for Jews in Holland in 1796. In 1801 the first Jewish lawyer in France petitioned the Congress of Continental Powers at Lunéville to extend these rights to all Jews in Europe. They responded slowly: in the German states civil rights were granted first in Kassel in 1833 and then in Brunswick in 1834, but full emancipation was not given in Baden until 1862 and in Saxony until 1868 and was only extended to all the states by the German Imperial Constitution of 1871. Jews were fully emancipated in the Kingdom of Sardinia in 1848, in Denmark in 1849, in Austria-Hungary (where there had been an Edict of Toleration in 1781) in 1867, and in 1870 in Sweden and in newly united Italy. In eastern Europe obscurantist attitudes persisted. The ghetto remained a reality in the vast Russian empire and from 1881 until the 1917 revolution the Jewish communities were subjected to intermittent pogroms – mob attacks on persons and property approved, or at least condoned, by the authorities.

In the early years of the course towards civil equality most western Jewish communities sought to erect synagogues that would differ as little as possible in style from the national religious buildings; desire for expression of their Jewish identity was to come later. Moses Mendelssohn's disciples, the Berlin Haskalah, publicized the advantages of secular education, urging that subjects such as German, mathematics, literature and history should take precedence over the traditional Jewish curriculum. Consequently modern Jewish schools were established on this model in several German cities. The westernized Jewish bourgeoisie which arose sought a new definition and expression of Judaism – one divested of alien customs and adapted to the surrounding cultural, social and intellectual norms. Almost simultaneously in Germany and in the United States (at Charleston, South Carolina), rabbis responded to this trend by proposing or introducing reforms in the synagogue ritual. In Germany, where the Reform became institutionalized in the 1840s, the theological rationalization went as far as to abolish not only the dietary laws but even circumcision, and Messianism was abandoned. German Reform Jews who emigrated at this time to North America gave impetus to the nascent Reform movement there and their ideology struck root with such rapidity that by 1880, before the waves of immigration of Orthodox Jews from eastern Europe, the majority of the 200 synagogues in the United States had embraced Reform. The most vigorous spokesman in its favour was Rabbi Isaac Mayer Wise (1819–1900) of Cincinnati, Ohio, who had emigrated to America from his native Bohemia in 1846.

The effect of Reform on the appearance of the synagogue was to make it more like a Protestant church. With the abolition of segregation of the sexes, family pews were introduced, aligned in rows to face the Ark; the bimah was moved up to the east end, becoming eventually the actual platform on which the Ark also stood. One lectern and sometimes two, for preacher and reader, were placed directly in front of or to the side of the Ark, on this platform. This tendency began as early as 1810 in a 'Reform Temple' built at Seesen by Israel Jacobson, who had been appointed President of the Israelite Consistory under Bonaparte rule in Westphalia. There the pulpit was so close to the Ark that the *ner tamid* in front of the Ark illuminated it too.[30] The practice of moving the bimah to the front did not spread without much opposition: in 1886 the rabbis of Hungary (where the first synagogue with a decentralized bimah had been built at Papa in 1846)[31] and Galicia issued a *herem* fulminating against the practice, but it spread nevertheless, even among Orthodox congregations. With the bimah at the east end the architectural problem of the two focal points of the synagogue ceased to exist and the plan of a Christian church with its longitudinal thrust was no longer unacceptable. Indeed, a number of American Jewish congregations purchased church buildings and used them as synagogues with little adaptation.

An early example of the many to follow was the first synagogue owned by the Ashkenazim in New York in 1826, the Elm Street synagogue of congregation B'nai Jeshurun, which had previously been a Protestant mission church. Orthodox congregations acquired former churches so long as they had not contained 'idols', so Roman Catholic buildings were avoided – anyway, they were rarely on the market in the nineteenth century. Today, with the rapid shifts of population in urban America, the pendulum has swung in the other direction and purpose-built synagogues which have lost their congregations have been sold, usually to Christian ethnic minorities who have moved into the area, for use as churches. One synagogue on New York's Lower East Side, now a Spanish-American Pentecostal church, sports a sign '*Jesus Sana y Salva*' ('Jesus heals and saves') beside the original Hebrew inscription surrounded by *magen Davidim*.

The 'enlightened' Jews of Vienna in the nineteenth century vied with those of Berlin in prestige and elegance. Franziska (Fanny) Itzig, from a prominent Berlin banking family, and her husband Freiherr (Baron) Nathan Adam von Arnstein of Vienna were the most prominent Jewish couple of their time in the Austrian capital. Fanny von Arnstein entertained the participants in the Congress of Vienna and the chancellor, Prince Metternich, frequented her brilliant *salon*, a gathering place for politicians, magnates, intellectuals and aristocrats. A new Vienna synagogue in the Seitenstettengasse, erected in Baron von Arnstein's lifetime, was dedicated in 1826 – its construction had been delayed by controversies between the Reform and Conservative parties in the congregation.[32] One of the debates was whether or not to have an organ. In this the composer Meyerbeer supported the cantor and the anti-organ faction on the grounds that it would be detrimental to Jewish liturgical music, which has a quicker tempo than that of the Church. Nevertheless, the organ was to find a place in the synagogues in the nineteenth century and became generally accepted. The architect of the Seitenstettengasse building was the highly considered Josef Kornhäusel (1782–1860) whose work was dominated by his attachment to classicism. He also designed the accessories of the gracious synagogue, which lies behind a domestic façade wedged between two houses. It has an elliptical dome and a narrow two-tier gallery carried by a twelve-bay giant Ionic colonnade.

The neo-classical synagogue in the Rue Notre Dame de Nazareth in Paris, dedicated in 1822, also stood in a courtyard behind a neat, domestic-type street façade. The architects were Philippe-Jérome Sandrié, who had designed the synagogue in the Rue Notre Dame de Lorette (1819–20), and Jacob Silveyra. A French architect, Jean-Baptiste Métivier (born 1781), designed the Neue (New) synagogue of Munich, which was dedicated in 1826 in the presence of King Ludwig I (who contributed to the building costs) and Queen Thérèse of Bavaria; it, too, was a neo-classical building, with a fine coffered barrel vault over the prayer-hall. The capitals of the red marble columns were decorated with white and gold palm leaves, a feature of the Egyptian Revival style which had become fashionable since Napoleon's campaign in Egypt. In another capital, Copenhagen, the synagogue was built by a German-born architect, Gustav Friedrich Hetsch (1788–1864) who had settled in Denmark in 1815 after meeting the Danish sculptor Thorvaldson and his circle in Rome, and who married in turn the two daughters of Denmark's leading architect,

etail of the neo-classical portico and
-diment of the Obuda synagogue,
dapest, Hungary, built in 1820–1
András Landherr. It was the first
nagogue in the Greek Revival style,
th a temple front.

e municipal architect of Avignon,
ance, designed and built this
ccessful neo-classical synagogue, a
cular domed temple, for the Jewish
mmunity of the town in 1846–8.

C. F. Hansen, with whom he became associated. Hetsch was a prolific designer of furniture, silver and *objets d'art* as well as buildings, of which his most important are considered to be the Catholic church in the Bredgade (1842) and the synagogue in the Krystalgade (1833), in which he successfully blended Egyptian Revival elements and Greek Revival forms – the classically framed Ark, for example, has an Egyptian coved cornice and the main doorway has trabeated jambs and a coved lintel. The splendid gold and white interior has been visited by each successive king of Denmark. A distinguished American architect, William Strickland of Philadelphia (1788–1854), who had a wide neo-classical repertory, chose an Egyptian Revival design for the synagogue he built there on Cherry Street for the Mikveh Israel congregation in 1822–5. A full study of this building has been made by Alfred Bendiner under a Penrose Grant.[33]

The first synagogue building in the Greek Revival style with a prostyle temple front, which was to become popular in many countries for a long period, appears to be the Obuda synagogue beside the Danube in Budapest, built by the architect András Landherr between 1820 and 1821, possibly in collaboration with Mihály János Pollack (1773–1855) and inspired by Pollack's Evangelical church in Deák Square in the city. In turn it became the model for other Hungarian synagogues: Hunfalu (1821) probably also by Landherr, Várpalota (1835–40), Liptószentmiklós (1842), Baja, Abony and others. By the 1830s the style had spread to Poland. It was adopted for an American synagogue, at Charleston, South Carolina, which was built in 1840–1 by David Lopez (1809–84), a member of the Beth Elohim congregation, to a design by a little-known New York architect, Cyrus L. Warner. In 1845 a Greek Revival synagogue was dedicated at Baltimore, Maryland, with a prostyle Doric temple front. Here was an early instance of positioning the bimah directly in front of the Ark in the synagogue of an Orthodox congregation. The first purpose-built synagogue in South Africa, the Old Synagogue, Cape Town, dedicated in 1863, is a Greek Revival building with a handsome hexastyle Corinthian portico; it now houses a Jewish Museum, opened in 1958. In the United States, where the lasting appeal of this classical idiom appears to be that it is considered respectable and dignified, owing to its association with the colonian period, it was revived for churches and public buildings in this century. In 1949 a synagogue with a white octastyle portico was built in Worcester, Massachusetts, on the corner of May and Chandler Streets.

One of the most agreeable essays in neo-classical synagogue architecture is the synagogue of Avignon, in the south of France, built in 1846–8 by the municipal architect, Joffroy. It is a circular, domed temple: the bimah is in the centre and a pulpit is attached to one pier of the elegant two-tier colonnade, Ionic and Corinthian.

David Mocatta, a Jewish architect who specialized in railway stations, was associated with Nathan M. Rothschild's architect, John Davies, in building the New Synagogue in Great St Helens, City of London, in 1838. The building was greatly admired: the *Architectural Journal* commented favourably on the use of stained glass to highlight the built-in Ark in the lofty apse, and *London Interiors* of 1841, in which an illustration of the synagogue appeared, claimed effusively that it 'eclipses every one of our modern churches'. In fact this synagogue, which had a commodious lobby with a committee room above it, a dignified and impressive hall of worship rising two storeys in height, and apartments for the officials, was taken as a model for many others. The style of the interior was neo-classical; the round-headed windows and arcade of the front were an early sign of a simplified Romanesque Revival style which was to be widely adopted in synagogue architecture.

A Jewish architect, Leopold Eidlitz (see p. 168), with Otto Blesch, made an academic attempt at Romanesque for a neat synagogue which they designed on Wooster Street, New York (1847). In Germany, where the *Rundbogenstil* made its appearance about 1830, it was favoured by many synagogue architects, but the buildings were often awkwardly proportioned and incoherently ornamented. In 1855 the synagogue of Gothenburg, Sweden, was built in a pleasant adaptation of this style with a Moorish interior (see p. 164). While designs rooted in serious historicism resulted in impressive Romanesque synagogues like those at Düsseldorf and Munich, the increasing eclecticism of taste in the middle of the nineteenth century resulted in the combination of the Romanesque idiom with the most disparate details of other styles – Gothic, Saracenic, Byzantine, and eventually Islamic. By the late 1860s a basically Romanesque Revival style in a range of versions had been applied to synagogue designs all over the world, from, for example, the Mikveh Israel synagogue of 1860 in Philadelphia by the architect John McArthur Jr (1823–90), to the Postepowa synagogue (known as 'the Temple') in the Kazimierz suburb of Cracow, Poland, built in 1862, the Temple Algérois at Constantine in Algeria, the synagogue of Steenwijk in Holland (1869) and synagogues in South America. One version of Neo-Romanesque which occurred in synagogues was a façade dominated by a huge semicircular gable framing a rose-window, and surmounted by the Tables of the Law. This feature, which might be called 'Judaeo-Romanesque', seems to have appeared first in 1861 on the synagogue of Nancy in France. The Parisian architect Alfred Philibert Aldrophe (1834–95) employed it functionally on the façade of the Rue de la Victoire synagogue in the French capital in 1874 to terminate a barrel vault of the majestic interior, one of the first to give a truly cathedral-like effect. Similar façades with the same elements are found on the Serfati Siami synagogue in Algiers, completed in 1892, and on the synagogue at Deventer in Holland of the same year where the use also of Islamic horseshoe arches and little minarets gives a more oriental effect. On the 1886 synagogue of the Khal Adath Jeshurun congregation on Eldridge Street, New York, which is now falling into decay, the architect skilfully combined Moorish horseshoe arches with a traditional Romanesque façade.

The Gothic Revival in religious buildings remained largely the preserve of the Christian Church (and more particularly the Roman Catholic Church) but, nevertheless, late in the century some synagogues appeared in the Neo-Gothic style. One example may be seen at Budapest, in Leo Frankel utca, built in 1888 by Sandor Fellner, a Gothic enthusiast who later designed the Ministry of Finance and Ministry of Justice buildings. The little synagogue with a high pointed arch over the Ark and pointed stained glass lights stands in the inner courtyard of a tenement building

which was once occupied by members of the congregation. In Holland, the Haarlem synagogue, built in 1841, was originally a little Romanesque-style hall but it was gothicized and two wings were added in 1896, after which it was indistinguishable from a Neo-Gothic church except for the Hebrew inscription over the doors. The remodelling of the Old Maisl synagogue in Prague between 1893 and 1905 by the architect Alfred Grotte transformed it into a Neo-Gothic building of considerable charm.

Robert Mook's synagogue built on West Nineteenth Street, New York, in 1860 for the Shearith Israel congregation is said to have introduced the Neo-baroque style to the United States.[34] These were the years when many Jewish congregations were adventurous in their plans. In 1859 the small community at Geneva, Switzerland, built their synagogue on a plan based on ninth-century Byzantine churches. At Kremsier, Czechoslovakia, the community opted for a curvaceous vernacular Neo-baroque style. The community of Potsdam in Germany, having rejected a Romanesque project in 1899,[35] built between 1901 and 1903 in a full-blown Revival style which was based on the early eighteenth-century Bavarian baroque and known as *Wilhelminisches Barock* because Kaiser Wilhelm II favoured it: in fact he took a personal interest in the building of the Potsdam synagogue.[36] The Great Synagogue built in 1878 at Sydney, Australia, where most of the congregation had come from England, is a splendid example of the English High Victorian Gothic style. It is interesting to note the semi-centrally planned seating arrangement in this building, which differentiates it radically from a church.

With all the changes in architectural style there often remained, even in westernized congregations, a conservative resistance to minor innovations. In 1879, for example, a dissident faction of the Bevis Marks congregation broke away and erected their own synagogue in Mildmay Park, north London, only because they stubbornly disapproved of the cantor's

ABOVE The architects Kohn, Butler and Stein drew on the repertories of Romanesque, Byzantine, Gothic and Islamic architecture to achieve the imposing Temple Emanu-El on Fifth Avenue in New York City.

RIGHT For their synagogue built in 1878 the Jewish community of Sydney chose the High Victorian style.

OPPOSITE This detail of the façade of the Maisl synagogue in Prague shows the Neo-Gothic rebuilding executed by Alfred Grotte.

wearing a silk top-hat instead of the customary tricorn hat – a seven-teenth-century fashion which had come from Amsterdam but to which they seem to have attached some religious significance. Today, top-hats in synagogues can seem as incongruous as the broad-brimmed, fur-trimmed hats of the eighteenth-century Russo-Polish bourgeoisie do when worn by the Hassidim in hot, sunny Israel.

The Rue de la Victoire synagogue in Paris was not the only one to achieve a cathedral-like effect. One close rival was the Great Synagogue of Pilsen in Czechoslovakia, but none can compete in this with a much later building, New York's Temple Emanu-El built by Robert B. Kohn, Charles Butler and Clarence B. Stein, and dedicated in October 1930, three months after the Wall Street stock-market crash which affected many members of the congregation. The basilical synagogue, about 61.5 m in length and 30.75 m wide, has its imposing single-bay façade on Fifth Avenue, with a rose-window in the high arched portal surmounted by a stepped arcade. On the Sixty-fifth Street side the syna-gogue adjoins the community building which has a prominent campanile-like elevator-tower. The long, lofty nave is dimly lit from the high cleres-tory and the tall stained-glass windows to produce an effect of sanctity and solemnity. Shallow galleries are fitted over the narrow side aisles: the visual thrust is entirely to the huge eastern arch with a Moorish-style horseshoe arcade and screen perforated with stellar interlace over the Ark. The 'feeling' of Temple Emamu-El is Gothic, perhaps because of its lofti-ness; the architects have in fact drawn on the repertories of Romanesque, Byzantine, Gothic and Islamic architecture in the creation of this syna-gogue. They synthesized, in a way, in a twentieth-century building which made use of modern technical advancements, several of the architectural currents of the nineteenth century which were dear to this congregation. It had started its life in a little Neo-Romanesque former Methodist church on Chrystie Street in 1848, moving to a Gothic Revival former Baptist Church with a steeple on East Twelfth Street in 1854, and then settling in a Moorish-style synagogue which they erected in 1868 on Fifth Avenue at Forty-third Street. This is discussed in Chapter 7 (see p. 168).

7 The Oriental Influence

Early in the nineteenth century David d'Beth Hillel left his birthplace, Vilna in Lithuania, and after spending some years in Safed, set out on an overland journey to India. His *Travels from Jerusalem through Arabia, Kurdistan, Part of Persia and India to Madras 1824–1832* was published in Madras in 1832. This detailed account of the Jewish communities he encountered is an important source of information on the oriental Diaspora; he spent a year in Baghdad and four months in Cochin, where he visited the Paradesi synagogue of the 'White' Jews, and also the synagogue of the 'Black' Jews.

Only 300 copies of d'Beth Hillel's travelogue were printed but his enterprise may have helped to fire the imagination of a romantic Romanian Jew who set off in 1845 to search for the lost ten tribes. The young man, Israel Joseph Benjamin (1818–64), then in his late twenties, had devoured the travel diary of the twelfth-century traveller Benjamin of Tudela whom he wished to emulate, and called himself Benjamin II. Benjamin of Tudela's *Itinerary* had been reprinted in Hebrew at Zolkiev in 1805 and nineteenth-century historical interest in the medieval travelogue had resulted in the publication of a French translation at Paris in 1830 and an English translation in London in 1840, and had stimulated the *Notice historique sur Benjamin de Tudèle*, published at Brussels in 1852.[1] The five-year journey of exploration of the nineteenth-century Benjamin II took him to Egypt and Palestine and through Syria, Armenia, Iraq, Kurdistan and Persia to India and China. He returned to Europe via Afghanistan. Everywhere he went he collected information on the Jewish communities and his account *Cinq années de voyage en Orient 1846–1851* excited much interest: a Hebrew version was published at Luck in 1856 and an English translation in 1859. Benjamin II made a second journey from Vienna through Italy to Libya, Tunisia, Algeria and Morocco. He spent three years in North America during 1859–62, and died in London in 1864.

Information on the communities of the Sephardic Diaspora in North Africa and Asia came too from other writers. Mordecai Manuel Noah, born at Philadelphia in 1785, an early Zionist, served as United States consul at Tunis in 1813. An account of Jewish life there appeared in his *Travels in England, France, Spain and the Barbary Coast*, published at New York in 1819. Non-Jews were fascinated by the long-standing Jewish settlement at Kai-Feng in central China; James Finn, the British consul at Jerusalem, corresponded with them in 1842 and published his *The Jews in China* in 1843. Finn was also author of *Sephardim: or the History of the Jews in Spain and Portugal*, published in London in 1841. In 1850 the London Missionary Society sent envoys to investigate the remainder of the Jewish community at Kai-Feng: the missionaries brought back their genealogical register, illuminated manuscripts, and prayer books, some of which are now in the Hebrew Union College in Cincinnati. Bishop Smith of Victoria, who was one of the group, published his *The Jews at Kai-Feng Fu* in London in 1851.

Persecutions in Baghdad in the 1820s caused many Jews to emigrate from there to British India. The Sassoon family, who had founded textile mills and factories in Bombay, settled there in 1832. They wielded tremendous power through their commercial empire which eventually

PREVIOUS PAGE Of all the synagogues built in the Moorish style the interior of the Florence synagogue in Italy is certainly the most opulent and the most distinguished. This view of the vestibule gives an idea of the extravagant decoration of the whole prayer-hall.

Interest in the exotic diaspora of Africa and the East attracted Jewish travellers to the synagogues of far-flung communities such as the Paradesi synagogue of the 'White Jews' at Cochin in Kerala, southern India. The blue-and-white floor-tiles were imported from China in the eighteenth century.

extended to China, and their wealth enabled them to help the ancient Jewish communities which had been in India for centuries on the Malabar coast. Abdulla (later Albert) Sassoon (1818–96) who built the Magen David synagogue at Byculla, a Bombay suburb, in 1861, moved to London; he was awarded a baronetcy for his role in the industrialization of India. Sir Albert's sister-in-law, Flora Sassoon, was a Hebrew scholar and learned Talmudist; her wealth enabled her to travel across the world with her personal *shohet* and a *minyan*. Two half-brothers of Sir Albert were intimates in the circle of the Prince of Wales, later Edward VII, and a nephew, Sir Jacob Elias Sassoon, built the Keneseth Eliyahu synagogue in Bombay as well as a general hospital and the Central College of Science. The immense wealth of this family, called the 'Rothschilds of the East', as well as their magnanimous philanthropy and dazzling lifestyle, aroused curiosity in their eastern Jewish background.

Moroccan Jews had emigrated to North America in the eighteenth century. One of them, Isaac Pinto, helped to arrange the treaty between the United States and Morocco in 1787; David Yulee, the first United States senator (1818) of Jewish origin, was the son of an immigrant from Morocco. In 1827 the Sultan appointed a Jew, Meyer Macnin, as his ambassador to England. Macnin's secretary in the London Embassy was his nephew, Solomon Sebag, who had been sent to England from Morocco to manage the family's mercantile interests there and became connected with the leaders of British Jewry through his marriage to Sarah Montefiore, elder sister of Sir Moses. In London, Sebag published

English translations of Moroccan Jewish authors including, in 1836, Moses Edrehi's *An Historical Account of the Ten Tribes*, which was read by both Christians and Jews.

Interest in the Jewish communities in the other countries of North Africa was stimulated by events in the political sphere. Debts accumulated over many years by the French government to Jewish grain suppliers in Algeria caused diplomatic incidents which resulted in the French conquest of Algiers in 1830 and brought thousands of Algerian Jews into the French orbit: in 1870 French citizenship was granted *en bloc* to 35,000 Jews in Algeria. Opulent Tunisian Jews who held government posts had attracted attention in Paris when they came in the retinue of the Bey of Tunis on a state visit to King Louis-Philippe. A few years later in 1857, after the next Bey had had a Jew executed for blasphemy, the squadrons of Napoleon III lined up in front of La Goulette in a show of force in order to coerce the Bey to grant equal civil rights to all inhabitants. As a result the *Pacte Fondamental* was signed in September 1857, removing all discrimination against the Jews of Tunisia, who numbered about 50,000. The French painter Eugène Delacroix (1798–1863), who was fascinated by the Orient, painted his *Two Hindus* as early as 1822–3. His visit to Morocco, however, was to inspire him for the rest of his life. On his return he painted *Algerian Women in their Apartment* and later *The Fanatics of Tangier*; his *Jewish Nuptials in Morocco*, exhibited at the Paris Salon in 1841 and now in the Louvre, brought to the notice of the public the existence of the exotic Jewish communities in that country.

The most famous Jewish philanthropist of the nineteenth century, Sir Moses Montefiore (1784–1885), was the scion of a family of straw hat importers in London, where they had come to settle from Livorno in the eighteenth century. From the time of his first visit to Erez Israel with his wife in 1827, he used his wealth, social position and political influence to help unfortunate Jewish communities, especially those who were victims of poverty or injustice in the countries of the Turkish empire. He lived to enjoy his hundredth birthday, which was celebrated as a holiday by Jewish communities throughout the world. The successful intervention in 1840 of Sir Moses, together with Isaac Adolphe Cremieux, in the appalling events remembered as 'the Damascus Affair' drew not only the concerned attention of western Jewry but of world public opinion to the life of the long-standing Jewish communities in Syria. The bungling and animosity of the anti-Jewish French consul, who was officially charged with the protection of the Catholics in Syria, had resulted in the death under torture of Jews apprehended by the authorities on a blood-libel charge and the arrest of sixty-three Jewish children, held as hostages in order to extract 'confessions' from their mothers. Eventually the Austrian, British and United States governments also intervened on behalf of the Jews. The interest of the western powers in the Middle East was largely dictated by their watchful concern for the *status quo* of Imperial Turkey; the question of Jewish settlement in Palestine was considered mainly in this light.

Cremieux' and Montefiore's action in going to Damascus was a stimulus to international Jewish solidarity and to a renewal of Jewish cohesiveness which resulted eventually in the foundation in 1860 in Paris of the first

Jewish international organization, the *Alliance Israélite Universelle*. Cremieux, who came from a Jewish family of the Comtat Venaissin, served as Minister of Justice in France under two regimes, and became President of the *Alliance* in 1864 despite opposition in some circles because he had permitted his wife to have their children baptized; in 1872 he was parliamentary deputy for Algiers. The aim of the organization was to form an association of responsible 'fortunate' western Jews to help 'unfortunate Jews' by working for emancipation and moral progress. In the process it inevitably invited the attention of its members to the culture of the Jewish communities that they assisted, and by the 1860s the *Alliance* had opened and financed schools at Tetuan and Tangier in Morocco and at Baghdad. On the cultural level the *Monatsschrift für Geschichte und Wissenschaft des Judenthums* (organ of the positive-historical school of Jewish thought, founded in 1851 by Rabbi Zacharias Frankel and soon the leading Jewish periodical in the world) revived the interest of Jews in their cultural background and sought to increase their self-respect by disseminating scientific knowledge of Jewish cultural history.

In 1856 the *Monatsschrift für Geschichte und Wissenschaft des Judenthums* published an article on the 'Transito' synagogue in Toledo (see p. 75) by Heinrich Graetz entitled 'Die Hebräische Inschrift in der Kirche San Benito oder del Transito in Toledo und ihre Geschichte'. A description and illustration of the 'La Blanca' synagogue of Toledo (see p. 75) had already appeared in print in *Toledo Pintoresca* by José Amador de los Rios, published in Madrid in 1845, and in 1848 the same author published his historical, political and literary studies of the Jews in Spain.[2] In 1857 Gustavo Adolfo Bécquer included in his *Historia de los Templos de España* descriptions and illustrations of both the 'La Blanca' and the 'Transito' synagogues.

In his *Kasseler Synagogengeschichte* (1932), Rudolf Hallo discusses the synagogue built by Gottfried Semper (1803–79) at Dresden in 1839–40 as the first synagogue building of the Oriental Revival movement and in her study of European synagogue architecture Dr Rachel Wischnitzer follows this hypothesis. The synagogue at Dresden, built while Semper was professor of architecture there and chairman of the Architectural School of the Academy of Arts, has been demolished: the one – unsatisfactory – illustration of it shows a handsome building mainly Romanesque in style with a pyramidal roof, a feature found in German Christian medieval building, intended here to evoke the biblical Tent of Meeting in the wilderness. The interior was decorated with Saracenic ornamentation executed in polychrome stucco, wood and ceramic. All this, however, resulted from Semper's keen personal interest in antique polychromy, on which he published a learned work, and from his own enthusiasm for the medieval architecture of Sicily which he had observed on an architectural tour there in the late 1820s. The style of the Dresden synagogue – a free amalgamation of Lombard-Romanesque and Byzantine elements in a square ground-plan with four main pillars supporting an arcaded gallery and two domed towers flanking the entrance porch – resulted from Semper's Protestant rejection of Gothic and his individualistic architectural repertory.

It can be more easily argued, therefore, that the Moorish Revival in synagogue architecture began as a movement some years after the Dresden synagogue – in the 1850s, with the Leopoldstadt synagogue in Vienna (begun 1853, finished 1858) and the Dohany utca synagogue in Budapest (begun 1854, finished 1859), both designed by Ludwig von Förster, and the Leipzig synagogue (1855) by Otto Simonson. On 12 October 1855 the synagogue of the community of Gothenburg, Sweden, designed by August Krüger, was opened. The pleasing interior decoration is Moorish – one of the earliest examples. The exterior of the building, however, is in *Rundbogenstil*. This small but progressive community, which had completed an adjoining school building in the same year, introduced Swedish into the synagogue service.

The Pest community acquired the Dohany utca site in 1844 and in the following year the committee formed by Rabbi Löw Schwab decided that the projected synagogue should have an organ and choir. Architects were invited to submit plans. A classical basilica design submitted by József Hild in 1848 was rejected, as was a design for a handsome Byzantine building with cupola submitted in 1850 by Frigyes Feszl, the architect of the Vigadó Theatre in Pest, and his associates.[3] Eventually the committee opted for a Moorish-style synagogue designed by the German-born architect Ludwig von Förster, for which the Budapest municipal authorities granted a building permit on 10 October 1853.[4] Förster, whose Moorish Revival synagogue in the Leopoldstadt sector of Vienna had just been begun, had spent his adult life in Vienna as professor of architecture at the Academy and he drew up and partly executed the new city plan. The Dohany utca congregation archives record the names of all the suppliers and artisans involved in the construction and decorating. In Förster's absence the work was directed by the architect Ignac Wechselmann; the architect Frigyes Feszl, whose design had been rejected, was called in to assist, especially with the decoration of the majestic interior. It appears that he may have been the designer of the imposing Ark. No precious materials were used because the exterior had been so costly. The cornerstone of the building was laid in September 1854; 26 m high internally, 56.1 m in length and 26.55 m in width, with twin onion-domed minarets 43.61 m in height on the front, it took five years to complete. It is still the synagogue with the largest seating capacity in Europe, having 1492 seats for men in rows across the nave and the two aisles, and 1472 seats for women in the two tiers of galleries which run along the north, south and west sides. Iron piers support the three great semicircular lobate arches over the north and south galleries; twin pulpits rest against the piers on either side of the first and second bays. Liszt and Saint-Saëns both played on the organ of this synagogue. The construction of the ambitious building was not executed perfectly: only five years after its completion cracks appeared in the ceiling and important repairs had to be carried out under the direction of Adam Clark.

Otto Simonson's Moorish synagogue at Leipzig was being built at the same time as Förster's in Vienna and Budapest. In a book published by Simonson at Berlin in 1858 about the Leipzig synagogue, *Der neue Tempel in Leipzig*, the architect states categorically: 'The Temple is built in the Moorish style which I believe is the most characteristic. Judaism is faithful to its history, its laws, its customs and practices, the organization of

Detail of the façade of the synagogue on the Dohany utca in Budapest, Hungary. It was begun in 1854, and built in the Moorish style with onion-domed minarets after the community leaders had rejected Classical and Byzantine designs.

OPPOSITE A gilded capital in the splendid synagogue of Szeged, Hungary, designed by Lipot Baumhorn and completed in 1903.

FOLLOWING PAGE LEFT One of a series of windows depicting the Creation in the Jacob Obrechtplein synagogue, Amsterdam, Netherlands (1928).

RIGHT The Jewish chapel on the campus of Brandeis University, Waltham, Massachusetts.

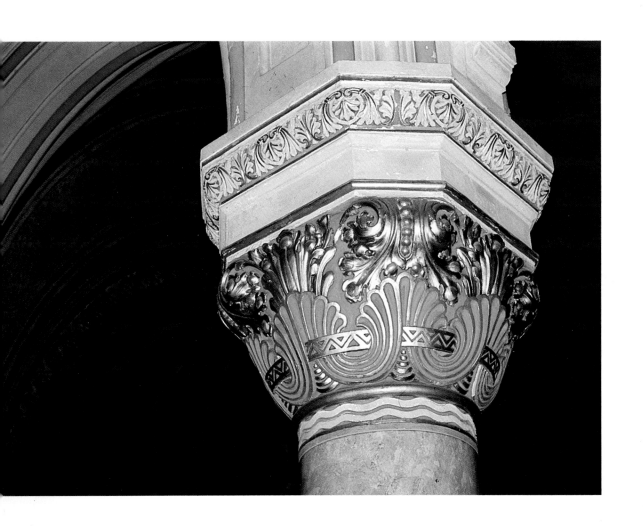

its ritual; its whole substance is embedded in the East, its motherland.' These were the ideas circulating in the 1850s in Dresden (where Simonson had studied architecture under Semper), promulgated by the advocates of the positive-historical school who gravitated around the publication of the *Monatsschrift für Geschichte und Wissenschaft des Judenthums*. This group eagerly equated Moorish architecture with Jewish aesthetic and spiritual values and especially with the wonderful flowering of Judaic culture under the Moslem caliphate in Spain in the Middle Ages.

Simonson explained in his book that his Moorish Revival style for the synagogue was not 'a blind imitation but rather an adaptation of available motifs to the requirements of the age'. Knowledge of Islamic architecture was, however, limited. Information about the Toledo synagogue was in circulation and there were verbal reports, letters, and possibly photographs of the old synagogues of Syria, Egypt and the other North African countries visited by Jewish luminaries, but paucity of material on the synagogue obliged the architect to turn to the mosque and to Islamic secular buildings for inspiration. Some details of these buildings could be gleaned from the two volumes of Texier's *Description de l'Arménie, la Perse et la Mésopotamie*, published in Paris 1848–52, and from Xavier Hommaire de Hell's *Voyage en Turquie et en Perse*, the first volume of which appeared in Paris in 1853. Coste, who collaborated with Flandin in a *Voyage en Perse* published in Paris in the 1850s, did not publish his informative illustrated architectural survey, *Monuments de la Perse, mesurés, dessinés et décrits*, until 1867. Descriptions of the Alhambra at Granada, popularized in literature by Washington Irving, were available;[5] restoration work on the buildings, which had been damaged by an earthquake, had been under way since 1828. Generically 'oriental' and also available to architects were the designs published in 1838 of Nash's Royal Pavilion at Brighton, England (1815–23), built in the romantic Hindu-Gothic or so called 'Indian Revival' style which was short-lived and had no sequel. Because of the dearth of Islamic architectural source material the synagogues of the Moorish Revival were generally Byzantine in plan – often a Greek cross inscribed in a square and capped by a central dome. The interior decoration, however, made generous use of Moorish motifs and the structure was usually endowed with bulbous domes and domelets and an array of Islamic elements such as the minaret-like tower, the horseshoe arch and the *iwan*, a vaulted niche or open porch framing a portal for emphasis. These elements were eventually used with little discrimination and with increasingly mechanical and banal results.

Simonson's Leipzig synagogue was unmistakably mosque-like; the Ark and bimah were treated as the *mihrab* and *minbar*. It was a sensational success and because large numbers of Jews from many European countries came to Leipzig annually to attend the international fair, the fame of the Moorish synagogue spread rapidly. Only two years after it was built and while Förster's synagogues at Vienna and Budapest were still not completed, the Moorish Revival style for the synagogue was widely enough discussed for the Jewish architect Albrecht Rosengarten (1809–93), who had himself designed synagogues at Hamburg and at Kassel, to pontificate in his *Die architektonischen Stilarten* (1857) that the Moorish style was entirely unsuitable for the synagogue and that Moslem

PPOSITE The boldly designed
nagogue by the eminent Frank
loyd Wright built in 1959 for the
eth Shalom congregation at Elkins
ark near Philadelphia, Pennsylvania.

architecture lacked the uplifting effect that the Romanesque type, which he preferred, could create. The Jewish outlook in Germany had, however, undergone a metamorphosis in the twenty-five years since the community in Kassel had rejected an Egyptian-style design for a new synagogue on the grounds that Jewish history was linked with the west rather than the east, and had remarked that the Christian Church, which also originated in the east, had not adopted oriental building forms.[6] The Moorish style received an enthusiastic response. In 1856, the year after the Leipzig synagogue of Simonson, the architect Ernst Friedrich Zwirner (1802–61) embarked on a splendid Moorish Revival synagogue for the community of Cologne.

Zwirner, who had been in charge of the restoration and reconstruction of Cologne Cathedral, was a devotee of Gothic and had built a number of Gothic Revival churches, but he abandoned his predilection in the case of the synagogue and declared that he considered an Islamic style more expressive of Judaism. However, he was unable to purge his design of Gothic features: behind the Ark, which was framed by a horseshoe arch between two slender minarets, Zwirner placed a Gothic rose-window in the east wall under the lofty horseshoe arch which supported the central dome. The arcade of the two tiers of galleries recalls the north arcade of the Patio de los Arrayánes (the Court of Myrtles) of the Alhambra at Granada.

A rash of Moorish Revival synagogues followed in the 1860s. In Hungary during that decade they were built at Székesfehèrvar in 1862 by the architect Bernardin Cometter, at Temesvar by the Viennese architect Ignatz Schumann, in the Öntöház utca in Budapest in 1866 by the architect Ignac Knabe, and at Pecs in 1869 by the architects Karoly Gerster and Lajos Frey. The great Moorish Revival synagogue crowned by a prominent bulbous dome begun in 1859 in the Oranienburgerstrasse in Berlin was completed in 1866 after the death of the architect, Eduard Knoblauch of Berlin (1801–65), a co-founder of the Architects' Circle, and of his colleague, the King of Prussia's architect, August Stüler (1800–65). In this synagogue Knoblauch combined the use of polychrome brick and cast iron; it was considered by contemporary critics to have exceeded all Knoblauch's other work, both in the maturity of the planning and the beauty of the interior decoration. Knoblauch had specialized in urban dwellings in Berlin and was a master of detail. In plan the synagogue had many similarities with Förster's in the Dohany utca, Budapest – a longitudinal arrangement with the domed Ark raised on a podium above steps at the east end. The decoration of the Berlin synagogue was richer and more lavish, but it had only one tier of galleries under the great semicircular lobate arches. An American Jewish periodical published a newsletter from Berlin in 1864 reporting the construction of the Oranienburgerstrasse synagogue as 'a large and magnificent synagogue which will be ranked among the most splendid public edifices'.[7]

Inspired by the Moorish synagogues in Germany, two German Jewish congregations in the United States undertook to build in that style at this time. Both the Temple Emanu-El on Sutter Street, San Francisco, California, begun in 1864 and completed in 1866, and the Isaac M. Wise Temple of the B'nai Jeshurun congregation on Plum Street, Cincinnati,

Woodcut showing the interior of the splendid Moorish style synagogue built in the Oranienburgerstrasse, Berlin, between 1859 and 1865. Designed by the architect Eduard Knoblauch and completed by August Stüler, it won world-wide acclaim.

OPPOSITE The exotic silhouette of a minaret of the Central Synagogue, Lexington Avenue, New York City (1872), contrasts splendidly with the modern skyscrapers of mid-town Manhattan.

Ohio, were basically Gothic basilicas in plan, on to which Moorish elements were grafted. The San Francisco synagogue, by the architect William Patton, was in fact a Neo-Gothic cathedral-like building, orientalized by gilded bulbous domes on its twin towers. It perished in the earthquake and fire of 1906 which destroyed the central business district of the city. The basic concept of the Cincinnati synagogue, which is still in use, is also Gothic – nave with clerestory, side-aisles, transept, and rose-window; but the Gothic elements in the strikingly Islamic façade are not immediately evident and in the interior the mural decoration, the domes and the rectangular frame with towers which surrounds the Ark produce a pronounced Moorish effect. The congregation was certainly convinced that they had a Moorish-style synagogue: Rabbi Isaac M. Wise described it in euphoric terms as an 'Alhambra temple with slender pillars and thirteen domes'.[8] The architect was an American, James Keys Wilson.

The most prominent Reform congregation in New York commissioned two European-born architects, Leopold Eidlitz (1823–1908), a native of Prague who had studied in Vienna, and Henry Fernbach (1828–83), a native of Breslau who had studied in Berlin, to design their new synagogue, the Temple Emanu-El on Fifth Avenue at Forty-third Street. Eidlitz, who was a Jew, had already built a synagogue in the city on Wooster Street (in 1846–7) for the congregation Shaaray Tefila. It was a neat essay in the Romanesque Revival style which, it may be noted, was at the time considered to reflect the oriental origins of Judaism and was thought by the congregation's cantor, Samuel M. Isaacs, to have been the style of the buildings of Jews in the Middle Ages, particularly in Portugal.[9] In a published description of the new building in 1846 Cantor Isaacs wrote of 'the imposing grandeur of the style, together with its Oriental origin ...'[10] In 1848 Eidlitz was commissioned to design new furnishings for Temple Emanu-El, which then occupied a former Methodist church on Chrystie Street. In the same year he designed a villa for P. T. Barnum at Bridgeport, Connecticut, named 'Iranistan' and modelled on the oriental-looking Hindu-Gothic Brighton Pavilion. The new Temple Emanu-El on Fifth Avenue, built 1866–8, was basically another Neo-Gothic building, more Moorish-looking inside than out, orientalized by the imposition of domes and spirelets on Romanesque colonettes flanking the façade and by the lavish use inside of horseshoe arches and Mudejaresque polychrome decoration. The transept of the Gothic plan of the building was a spatial asset as the reader's desk and the pulpit were all moved up to the east of the building.

Fernbach, Eidlitz's collaborator on the Temple Emanu-El, which was dedicated in 1868, designed on his own the Central Synagogue on the corner of Lexington Avenue and Fifty-fifth Street, New York City, for the congregation Ahavath Chesed, which was composed of immigrants from his native Bohemia. The synagogue, dedicated in 1872 and now a classified monument, is still in use; its twin towers with gilded domes make a delightfully exotic and alien silhouette against the background of the surrounding Manhattan skyscrapers. Fernbach himself admitted, 'The style is mainly Moorish, although the arrangement is Gothic,'[11] but he was a skilful architect and the amalgamation is aesthetically successful.

Rabbi Isaac M. Wise, the champion of Reform Judaism in the United States, wanted for his congregation at Cincinnati a synagogue that was truly grand both in design and size. He described the building on Plum Street which was dedicated in 1866, as an 'Alhambra Temple with slender pillars and thirteen domes'.

The façade of the Moorish Revival synagogue in Turin, built between 1880 and 1885.

It is obvious that the architect had a grasp of Islamic architecture and was able to introduce and handle its elements boldly and with precision, so that the Moorish effect is convincing.

Although synagogues were built in other styles in the 1870s and 1880s, Moorish Revival held its own both in Europe and North America. The synagogue of the Reform congregation of Nuremberg in the Hans Sachs Platz with many Moorish details, dedicated in 1874, was destroyed in 1938. That of the Reform congregation of Kaiserslautern, dedicated in 1886, was a convincing Moorish essay with a great horseshoe arch over the portal: it has been demolished. The Moorish-style synagogue at Karlsbad, Czechoslovakia, dedicated in 1877, which had a brilliant interior décor, was another of the many synagogues destroyed by the Nazis in 1938.

The synagogue in the S. Rumbach utca, Budapest, begun in 1872 and finished in 1875, was the first important project of the eminent Viennese architect Otto Wagner (1841–1918), who was to become a leader in the modern architectural movement. The synagogue, with slender minarets rising on each side of the entrance, is still standing but it has been put to secular use. The panels over the semicircular lobate arches of the eight bays of the octagonal prayer-hall are painted with a design which was executed in the Mudejar stucco-work of the 'Transito' synagogue at Toledo (see p. 75). In the Spanish synagogue at Prague, built in the Dušni ulice in 1882 for the Sephardic community by the architect J. Niklas, the interior is superbly ornamented with actual stucco decoration in the Mudejar manner also copied from the work in the 'Transito' at Toledo and from the Alhambra of Granada. This synagogue, whose style is described as 'Moorish-Renaissance' in a modern guide to the city,[12] is now a section of the State Jewish Museum, housing a collection of Jewish textiles.

The most outstanding Moorish Revival synagogue must be the one begun in 1874 at Florence in Italy, and completed in 1882 with the collaboration of Mariano Falcini (1804–85), Vincenzo Micheli (1830–95), and Mauro Treves (1814–97), who was a Jew. Davide Levi, the president of the Council of the Florence Jewish Community, by his will dated 15 March 1868 left his entire estate for the building of 'a monumental Temple worthy of Florence'; he died in February 1870 and assets totalling 1,492,000 lire became available for construction.[13] The plan, which was Falcini's, is of Byzantine derivation, inspired by Santa Sophia in Istanbul. The building is centrally planned with a dome-crowned drum over the crossing and barrel vaults over the four equal arms; these terminate externally in huge, round gables. The gable over the entrance at the front is flanked by octagonal turrets with bulbous domes rising from the twin staircase towers. All the windows and the three-bay arcade of the porch have horseshoe arches, most of them in rectangular frames; these, together with the domes and the horizontal banding, produce the desired Moorish effect externally. It is the excessively ornate exotic interior which is exceptional (see p. 155).

The walls and ceiling of the vestibule, the prayer-hall and the galleries are relentlessly covered in a *tour de force* of *horror vacui* decoration with Mudejar-style patterns, some of which are found in the 'Transito' of Toledo. Ornately carved and decorated wood, ornately worked bronze, polychrome tile, mosaic and glass combine to overwhelm. The Ark, whose horseshoe arches, one recessed behind the other, have intricately interlaced lobes, stands at the back of the apse with the bimah before it in an enclosed sanctuary area like that of a church; the pulpit, reached by a stair and supported by one column, is at the east and also against the north wall of the nave.

In his Moorish Revival synagogue built at Turin between 1880 and 1885, the architect Enrico Petiti (1832–98) employed many of the Islamic motifs used at Florence and added others like the Mameluke parapets of the four rectangular corner towers with domes, but neither the exterior nor the interior can compare with the Florence synagogue in grace, unity, or richness of decorative detail.

Rich, elaborate decorative detail was also a mark of the later Moorish synagogues in the United States, and it must be remembered that by the 1880s a number of books with illustrations of Islamic architectural decoration were available. The Park East synagogue of 1889 built on East Sixty-seventh Street, New York City, between Lexington and Third Avenues for the Zichron Ephraim congregation formed of immigrants from Germany, is still functioning as the place of worship of the same

The interior of the Park East synagogue of congregation Zichron Ephraim, built in 1889, is designed and decorated in a conservative and individualistic interpretation of the Moorish idiom.

congregation. This is unusual for an Orthodox congregation in a city where the population patterns change frequently, and in 1977 a son of Dr Bernard Drachman, the first rabbi, was still a member. In 1890 this was the first Orthodox congregation in the United States to introduce preaching in English; another innovation was the early installation of a steam-heating system around the cast-iron columns of the nave. The building, with a picturesque Byzantine-Moorish façade, is basilical: a lofty nave with a clerestory is flanked by lower aisles, but the fittings are Moorish – the arches supporting the roof of the nave and the arches of the arcade of the galleries are lobate horseshoes. The decoration is rich but the impression is sumptuous rather than dazzling and it does not overwhelm: the walls are plain and the colour scheme is subdued; the triple lights in each bay of the clerestory are fitted with brown, pink and blue coloured glass. The rose-window above the choir loft, over the many-domed and domeletted Ark at the east end, and the one in the gallery over the vestibule at the west end represent the moon and sun respectively. The women now sit in the roped-off aisles.

The architects Schneider and Herts, who built the synagogue for congregation B'nai Jeshurun in New York City in 1918, decorated the ceiling with *muqarnas* stucco work inspired by the great buildings of the Moorish Caliphate in Spain.

The Moorish Revival synagogue built by the architect Shaposhnikov at St Petersburg (Leningrad) in 1893 had been planned ten years before but as late as 1906–8 the Jubilee synagogue was built in the Jeruzalémská ulice in Prague. It is in a drab pseudo-Moorish style; the tawdry banality of its façade is not alleviated by the prosaic buildings which hem it in on either side. The metal minarets, now painted maroon colour, rise high above the façade. The mish-mash of horseshoe arches, imitation *mushrabiyya* in pointed windows, frieze, Tables of the Law, and frilly parapet, is made even worse by the medley of colour – green and brown marble columns with black plinths, blue paint around the main arch, and maroon and beige banding across the whole façade. However, in 1906 the Great Synagogue at Groningen in Holland was built in a robust and visually successful version of Moorish Revival; it is now an Apostolic church.

Traditional Moorish motifs were still used in 1918 by the architects Walter S. Schneider and Henry B. Herts for the synagogue of the B'nai Jeshurun congregation at 270 West on Eighty-eighth Street, New York City, both on the original façade, where all the elements are reduced to a minimum except for the massive portal, and in the interior with Moorish decoration and a delightful *muqarnas* ceiling.

Schneider, who built the Park Avenue synagogue in 1926 in collaboration with another architect, again used Moorish decoration in the interior, while Herts, collaborating with Charles B. Meyers in 1928 on the auditorium-synagogue of the Yeshiva University on Amsterdam Avenue, introduced arabesque grilles. And with arabesque stencilled frescoes the oriental style went out with a whimper in the west.

North African synagogues built in an indigenous Islamic style with beautiful tile, mosaic and wood carving, exist in Tunisia at Djerba, Tunis and Kairouan, and in Morocco at Meknès and Fez.[14]

In Israel, Sephardi settlers from the Arab world brought with them synagogue customs and styles acquired during their centuries of residence there – the double Ark from Iran and Persia (purported by oral tradition to have been for housing the Koran as well as the Torah), the practice of seating the congregation on the floor, fine filigree-work objects from Yemen, and splendid rugs from Bokhara. In their new setting these oriental fashions and artefacts are often introduced indiscriminately with some western discoveries such as multicoloured fluorescent strip-lights, to produce an effect which ranges from the garish to an endearing expression of popular art. The most elegant oriental work in any Israeli synagogue is probably the handsome panelling, intricately carved and inlaid with ivory in the Syrian fashion, of the east wall with the Ark (a gift sent from Damascus) in the synagogue of a Syrian congregation which started with 180 families brought from Aleppo in the last century by Rabbi Isaac Adis. This synagogue, which is visited by many pilgrims, is known colloquially as the 'Synagogue of the Twelve Tribes'.

8 *The Search for a Style*

In the course of the nineteenth century the bourgeoisie, sovereigns of the industrial revolution, had emerged as the new ruling class, first in France, where the 'July' or 'Bourgeois' monarchy of 1830 had ushered in an era of radically changed political and social conditions, and then in other western European nations. At the same time the aristocracy gradually faded into the background, where it was to appear more and more a *tableau vivant* of traditions and titles. The proletariat grew in awareness of its separateness from either group. For more than seventy years, these were the elements that would characterize what is commonly understood as the nineteenth century.

In architecture, a surge of imaginative experiment had really begun at the end of the eighteenth century. The British architect Sir John Soane (1753–1837) designed such impressive buildings as the Bank of England and his own house in Lincoln's Inn Fields. In France, Etienne-Louis Boullée (1728–99), though not of much interest as a practical architect, prepared a set of drawings in the 1780s and 1790s that are nervously mega-lomaniac and uncompromisingly heroic. Claude-Nicholas Ledoux (1736–1806), his contemporary, had not the same chimerical imagination but was more successful. His Parisian town houses and public buildings were in a thoroughly re-thought classical style which did not simply rely on slavish imitation of the past. In 1806 he published a plan for an ideal city which included such 'socially aware' buildings as a 'Palace dedicated to the Cult of Moral Values'. In Germany, Friedrich Gilly (1772–1800) designed two masterpieces which were never carried out: a monument to Frederick the Great and a National Theatre for Berlin. Both these buildings used classical elements in bold new ways.

It would have seemed only too natural for the nineteenth century, which was so enterprising in industry and commerce, to champion such independent ideas. But, as Pevsner points out, 'It is the things of the spirit in which the Victorian age lacked vigour and courage. Standards in architecture were the first to go; for while a poet and painter can forget about their age and be great in the solitude of their study and studio, an architect cannot exist in opposition to society....' By 1830 an alarming social and aesthetic situation in architecture had arisen.

Architects believed that anything created by the pre-industrial centuries must of necessity be better than anything made to express the character of their own era. Architects' clients had lost all aesthetic susceptibilities, and wanted other than aesthetic qualities to approve of a building. Associations they could understand. And one quality they could also understand and even check: correctness of imitation.[1]

Pattern-books had been available since the middle of the century for a vast assortment of styles: Gothic, Classical, French Renaissance, Tudor, Italianate, Oriental and others. The choice varied according to local fashion. Certain styles, however, were found to be particularly suitable for particular buildings, often on associative grounds – hence the Jewish predilection for Moorish and the choice of Gothic for nineteenth-century churches.

Towards the end of the nineteenth century the assimilation of many western middle-class Jews into the flourishing European and North

PREVIOUS PAGE Of the twenty-four synagogues built by the architect Lipot Baumhorn, the most impressive and the most successful is this one at Szeged in southern Hungary, completed in 1903.

American bourgeoisie was almost complete. The advent of Zionism, however, and the anti-Semitic shock waves of the Dreyfus case were to disturb the equanimity of the assimilated Jews and cause them to question the security of their prosperity, freedom and apparent integration. In consequence they began to reassess their ethnic, cultural and religious identity. This process was further stimulated in the next century by the impact of World War 1.

When the Jews had not clothed their synagogues to recall the heyday of Jewry under the western caliphate, they had drawn on the 'safe' adaptations of Romanesque, Byzantine, Classical and Gothic. None of these styles, however, aroused the spiritual meditations that Moorish could evoke; on the other hand they did coalesce with the cityscape, which pleased communities that had only recently experienced emancipation and had no desire to appear extravagantly alien.

Of the revival styles, Gothic had met with the least popularity in European Jewish circles. This is not difficult to understand, given the overwhelmingly Christian associations it held. In fact, that great exponent of this style, Augustus Welby Pugin (1812–52), felt that a revival of the Gothic ideal in the arts and crafts required a 'return' to the Catholic way of life.[2] The Gothic magnificence of the French cathedrals had played a part in his own conversion to Roman Catholicism (he was born a Protestant). Some Jews, too, were emotionally drawn to Catholicism in the nineteenth century through their aesthetic affinities with the Romantic movement. Dorothea, the daughter of the Jewish scholar Moses Mendelssohn and aunt of the composer Felix Mendelssohn, became a Catholic along with her husband, Friedrich Schlegel, at a time when the Gothic style was thought to epitomize the truest expression of the German spirit and more specifically, a German Catholic spirit.

Like Gothic, Romanesque had been associated with Christian ecclesiastical buildings, but nineteenth-century Jews had few misgivings about its use in synagogue-building. This was especially true in Germany where the term *Rundbogenstil* had been coined to describe the composite of Renaissance and Romanesque that was in use. The successful synagogue architect Albrecht Rosengarten (1809–93) was a keen exponent of this style. He had been the first Jew in Germany to write on synagogue architecture and in 1840 the *Allgemeine Bauzeitung* of Vienna had published an article which gave his reasons, theological and historical, for rejecting Solomon's Temple as a model for the modern synagogue. His preference for Romanesque had been based on its 'solemn and uplifting effect on the mind'.[3] In northern Europe this style had been in general use; indeed its revival had been as great in Germany as that of Gothic in England. Thus Romanesque synagogues had looked comfortably at home in northern Europe, where the process of assimilation had advanced considerably by the end of the century.

The neo-classical style, though it had continued in general use in the United States, had lost ground to Gothic and Romanesque in Europe. For the synagogue, however, it had the advantage of treading neutral ground with few religious associations of its own.

By the last two decades of the nineteenth century the over-use of all these styles, and the demand for more and more decoration as a remedy for the dearth of structural invention, had led to an indiscriminate combining of elements in the search for novelty. Most architects were still trained to apply decoration to a more or less stock catalogue of shapes and sizes. The best architects had received sound instruction in Greco-Roman forms and had an urbane familiarity with Gothic, Romanesque and Italianate styles.

A number of synagogues had combined diverse styles in the same building, but this may have been due to a time-lapse in construction or the choice of a different style for the interior, as at Gothenburg, Sweden. A truly eclectic building in Sweden, however, is F. W. Scholander's synagogue, built in 1878 for the Stockholm community, which was greeted as a pleasing novelty when it was erected: there is certainly no other building like it. Built on a simple rectangular plan with side galleries, the style is a cerebral and interesting mixture, not without wit and a subdued gaiety. The tall, pointed windows have remote Gothic ancestry while the arch surrounding the Ark is Moorish; some of the decorative motifs derive from the Egyptian Revival. The elaborate painted and gilded woodwork anticipates the kind of work produced by the exponents of the arts and crafts movement in England.

A new synagogue at Turin was begun in 1863; its builder, the architect and engineer Alessandro Antonelli (1798–1888), has been aptly described as 'a man of genius, original, dogged, opinionated, and one who walked with grandiose visions'.[4] The choice of such an architect and the approval of his 'grandiose' scheme is an indication of just how far emancipation had progressed among the Italian Jewish communities, especially in Turin, the capital of the Savoy rulers who were soon to become kings of the new secular Italian state. As a contemporary writer put it: 'With the dawn of new times and broader liberties, the persecutions and restrictions that had afflicted the Jews ceased and they were called to share the same call to private and public life of all citizens, brothers and freemen like all the others, and in many cities temples arose that were not without a certain grandiosity and elegance.'[5] The community decided to erect a building that would house 1500 worshippers as well as provide facilities for a school auditorium, ritual baths, wedding and funeral rooms, and residential quarters for the rabbi and the caretaker, in addition to rooms for other administrative, didactic and liturgical purposes.[6] Antonelli's original scheme was considerably more modest than the final building: as work progressed he added floor after floor, finally topping it all with an audacious spire. For more than fifteen years the community patiently stood by as the architect waxed eloquent on his 'monument of high honour for Italian art, and [for the Jews] of eternal fame for the religiosity of sentiment and the virtue of sacrifice'.[7] And sacrifice it certainly was: the community paid out enormous sums until 1869, when they were unable to raise any more money and were forced to have the work stopped. After a good deal of polemic, the building – more a monument to the architect than anything else – was sold to the city of Turin and it bears his name: the Mole Antonelliana. The Jewish community then hired a less ambitious architect and instructed him to build them a synagogue in prosaic Moorish style.

Antonelli's original plan was an eclectic assembly of neo-classical com-

The east front of the synagogue built by F. W. Scholander at Stockholm, Sweden, in 1878 illustrates the truly eclectic nature of its design.

t the time the synagogue at Trieste, aly was being built, the fourth-·ntury mosaic floor of the nearby isilica of Aquileia was discovered. ne of its motifs, the interlaced oval, as used on the side door of the nagogue by the Berlam brothers. It so appears in the fifth- to sixth-·ntury mosaic floor of the synagogue Aegina, Greece.

PPOSITE Built as a synagogue for the ·ewish community of Turin, Italy, by ie architect and engineer, Alessandro ntonelli, the Mole Antonelliana, ·gun with much promise in 1863, roved to be such a costly monument iat it was sold to the municipality 'hen the funds were exhausted in 869.

ponents, square in plan with a central dome surmounted by a pointed tower 167 m high (one-half the height of the Eiffel Tower). The hall of worship on the second floor was to have an impressive twenty-column peristyle carrying a spacious women's gallery, and above that another gallery where visitors to the synagogue might look on without disturbing the services or the worshippers.[8] The architect's early drawing shows the columned and porticoed base with a simple onion-shaped dome and a pointed finial; the four corners appear to have minaret-like spires. He retained the massive neo-classical base but completed the building with a high, elongated dome and a tall spire.

The Tlomacka ulica Temple, erected in Warsaw between 1875 and 1877, was also an eclectic work by an Italian, Leandro Jan Marconi (1834-1919), one of a family of artists and architects resident in Poland since Enrico Marconi (1792–1863), father of Leandro Jan, had been brought there to build a country house for a Polish nobleman in 1822. The Warsaw synagogue design employed the elements of classical style in a graceful Palladian plan. The main building with its imposing temple-front had flanking pavilions connected by colonnades. In variance with the Palladian style, however, the three buildings bore oriental domes – apparently an effort of the architect to give the building a Jewish aspect. This synagogue, with its lavishly decorated interior, was blown up by the Nazis in 1943.

By the final decades of the nineteenth century there was an increasing tendency for European Jews to build synagogues that openly proclaimed their use and origin, a natural outcome of the ongoing process of emancipation since the beginning of the century. Jews played an active part in the *Risorgimento*, the independence movement in Italy. When Rome itself was seized by Garibaldi's forces in 1870, the oldest Jewish community of the west was given a new lease of life.

The Roman community, conscious and proud of their situation in the capital of a newly united Italy, were happy to clear away the old to make way for the new. Under a municipal plan of redevelopment to accommodate Garibaldi's noble scheme to embank the Tiber, the insalubrious, overcrowded ghetto on the banks of the Tiber was all but demolished and the buildings on the edge of the river, which had been subject to annual flooding, were cleared. Unfortunately, the Cinque Scuole (see p. 85) was demolished during this rebuilding of the former ghetto. In its place the community decided to erect a temple where all five congregations could worship together.

The architects of the new Temple were Osvaldo Armanni and Vincenzo Costa. The centrally planned building is beautifully situated on the Tiber, its square aluminium dome rising confidently among the many church domes in this capital of Catholic Christianity. Though frequently described as being in 'Assyrian-Babylonian' style, the design is basically neo-classical with oriental overtones. Local wits have dubbed its style as 'Mesopotamian Municipal'. The pedimented entrance façade has prominently displayed emblems: lulavim, the Tables of the Law, and a menorah. Some justification for describing the style as 'Assyrian-Babylonian' rests in the liberal use of rosettes and palmettes as well as in the splendour achieved by the multiplication of units rather than by a bold overall design. The interior has sumptuous decoration which employs the same motifs as the exterior; the dome is painted with a background that is clearly of biblical inspiration, resembling peacock feathers and trees.

Another Italian synagogue of eclectic design is that of Trieste, built in 1908–12 by the local architects Ruggero and Arduino Berlam for a prosperous and cultured community which included the family of the author Italo Svevo and the poet Umberto Saba. One of the most interesting synagogues of the period, this finely executed building in Istrian limestone displays a kinship with the art of fourth-century Syria; Berlam uses the repertory of Romanesque and Classical elements but the masterly wielding of smooth undecorated surfaces and simple 'streamlined' geometric forms gives his work a modernity which points forward to similar buildings in the United States thirty years later. The spacious interior, perhaps the most successful modern one in Italy, has sumptuous wallcovering of dark green marble and gold mosaic.

There were interesting eclectic synagogues among the great number constructed in Hungary after the emancipation of Jews in that country in 1867. Just as in Italy, they felt free to build large, impressive synagogues that made no attempt to conceal their identity. Some of these, like the Dohany utca synagogue (see p. 160), were Moorish buildings, but as the vogue for this style waned, new styles were sought. This quest motivated much of the work of Lipót Baumhorn, who was born at Kisbér in 1860 and studied in Vienna and Budapest. He planned no fewer than twenty-four synagogues, the first of which, Esztergom (1890), drew heavily for its inspiration on the Dohany utca synagogue, especially in the use of Moorish banding and detail. Baumhorn's most successful synagogue was the one built at Szeged in southern Hungary, where the town was extensively replanned and rebuilt following a devastating flood in 1879. The centrally planned synagogue, standing in a garden in a residential neighbourhood, was built in 1900–3 and has been classified as a national monument; it replaced a modest neo-classical building depicted in one of the stained-glass windows. Baumhorn's delightful exterior is in the Hungarian Neo-Gothic style of Imre Steindl's monumental parliament building at Budapest which was under construction at the same time. The four gabled façades are heavily adorned with trefoil windows, Gothic cresting, sprockets and spires. The decorative ribbed dome rests on an octagonal base with gables and triple-light windows. Though Baumhorn adapted a style associated both with Christian cathedrals and the nineteenth-century Nationalist movement in Hungary, he ingeniously emphasized its oriental aspects to keep the associations essentially Jewish rather than Christian. The interior, with its restrained palette of grey, ivory, blue and gold, evokes the spiritual richness of the Talmud. The hall of worship, with galleries along three sides, has as its focus the Ark, crowned by a lacy Gothic cupola, and above and beyond it the dimly lit apse with ranks of organ-pipes arranged in gabled cabinets on either side. The door of the Ark is of Nile acacia with a metal inlay representing hyssop, symbol of spiritual purity. No doubt the then Chief Rabbi, Immanuel Loew, a noted botanist and scholar, assisted Baumhorn in his genial conception and in the symbolic references. The women's gallery was decorated with drawings of plants mentioned in the Talmud – water-lilies, oleander and roses; each of the four cross-vaults underneath has a drawing of a plant to represent a part of scripture – the nut orchard from the Song of Songs (6:11); the burning bush (*rubus sanctus*) of the Pentateuch; the wild vine of the first prophets (II Kings 4:39); the tree of Jonah for the last prophet (Jonah 4:6–11); the castor-oil plant. The stained-glass windows represent the holidays.[9] The pendentives of the cupola are inscribed in cobalt blue with the cornerstones of Judaism: Parental Honour, Charity, Peace, Study of the Torah. The proscenium is similarly inscribed with 'Love thy Neighbour as thyself' in Hebrew and Hungarian.

Baumhorn continued to design synagogues up until his death in 1932 and although none surpassed Szeged or equalled its inventive eclecticism, many of them were interesting. The once fashionable synagogue in the elegant Arena ut, Budapest (now renamed Dózsa György ut), built in 1909 with a square plan, single nave and two aisles, is more staid than Szeged, while the Csaky utca synagogue of 1927, first of a series planned in conjunction with György Somogyi, is dull in comparison. The site of the Páva utca synagogue in Budapest, planned in 1923, presented Baumhorn and Somogyi with a spatial problem: their solution was an interesting hexagonal plan, in fact a square with two lateral triangles to accommodate the women's galleries.

Hungarian architects showed considerable enthusiasm for the avant-garde possibilities inherent in the eclectic style. The architects Béla and Sándor Löffler designed the Kazincy utca synagogue for an Orthodox community in Budapest, built in 1911–13. The spacious single-nave interior owes its unusual shape to the use of reinforced concrete; it is lit by geometric, flower-shaped windows filled with coloured glass. The architect Lászlò Vàgó made a project for a Jewish museum and a memorial synagogue complex adjoining the Dohany utca synagogue to commemorate the Hungarian Jews killed in World War 1. The Heroes synagogue was actually built between 1929 and 1931 to the plans of the architects Deli and Faragó.[10] In this experiment with modern classicism the designers reduced a combination of Moorish and neo-classical motifs to absolute geometric forms: square base, circular dome and hemispherical arches. It is a harmonious neighbour to the Dohany utca synagogue and the stark, arcaded courtyard which precedes it now serves as a mass grave for the victims of the 1944–5 Nazi reign of terror in the city.

English Jews had never sought to parade their foreignness; throughout the nineteenth century their native conservatism had found a comfortable berth in the building trends of the times. It is this eminently rational point of view, together with the growing need for all-purpose buildings, that produced the Stoke Newington synagogue, built by Lewis Solomon in 1903 in an eclectic style with a long, red-brick façade. It no longer functions as a synagogue owing to the exodus of the once numerous Jewish population from the area. The prosaic fenestration, consisting of coupled round-headed and Gibbsian-surround windows, belies the mixed origins of its ancestry. The interior, because of the use of slim cast-iron columns, is light and spacious. The classrooms in the courtyard have a movable glass skylight so that *succoth* booths could be erected in the space

Erected in 1913 by a community of fewer than five hundred persons, the synagogue at Nijmegen, Netherlands is a striking building in which the architect combined disparate stylistic elements in an effort to break with traditional designs.

OPPOSITE

ABOVE Temple Mount Sinai, El Paso Texas (1962), from below the soaring arched sanctuary.

BELOW The marvellous window entitled *The Journey of a Mystic*, designed by Abraham Rattner in 1960 for the entire east wall of the Loop synagogue, Chicago, Illinois.

FOLLOWING PAGES The mosaic-mural entitled *The Call of the Shofar*, designed by Ben Shahn in 1959 for Temple Oheb Shalom, Nashville, Tennessee. It measures 2.45 × 4.30 m

below. While Stoke Newington was a successful building from a practical standpoint, it was an aesthetic failure, indicative of the stylistic disintegration only too common at the time in Europe.

In South Africa, the Great Synagogue of Cape Town (1905) is in a style which has been described as '1900-Spanish Colonial', favoured for palatial hotels on the French Riviera.

Holland's vigorous Jewish communities built a number of new synagogues. The prosperity of the community of Eindhoven had increased considerably since the first Jews had moved there at the beginning of the century. Their first small synagogue had been replaced in 1810 by a larger building for which King Louis Napoleon had contributed 500 guilders. It was when the community outgrew this building that they entrusted the task of designing a new one to P. J. H. Cuijpers (1827-

THE SEARCH FOR A STYLE

1921), the master of Dutch eclecticism and designer of the Rijksmuseum. Cuijpers had already undertaken to build a church in the town and his synagogue is a charming building with an onion-domed steeple; rather surprisingly, it is Gothic, with only the Moorish windows of the nave to distinguish it from the churches of the town. Another eclectic synagogue, that of Nijmegen, erected in 1913, has local Dutch, Classical and Romanesque elements. The synagogue of Enschede, built in 1926, achieved a remarkably modern look by the simplified use of domes and patterned red brick.

Finland did not become an independent state until 1918, and then full rights and citizenship were granted to the Jews who were settled there. Prior to this, while it was still a Russian province, two Jewish communities had managed to build synagogues. In 1904 the Orthodox community of Helsinki commissioned the well-known architect Jac Ahrenberg to draw plans for a new synagogue building. One of the two he submitted was chosen and the building contract given to the firm of J. and E. I. Johansson, with a stipulation that no work would be done on Sabbaths or Jewish holidays. As a result of this clause the workers went on strike, demanding compensation for their loss of earnings, and the building was not finished until 1906. In that year Helsinki was host to the Russian Zionist Congress. The Jewish Colonization Association in St Petersburg contributed over a quarter of the cost on condition that the community raised the balance in advance: this they did by auctioning the seats. A cantor and choir came from St Petersburg for the ceremonial opening by Senator Otto Donner in the presence of the representative of the Russian governor-general. The plain building betrays only the slightest traces of modern neo-classicism; it has a central dome and a functional if somewhat drab façade. The stern interior is relieved by eclectic columns with fanciful capitals supporting the women's galleries which flank the Ark. The tympanum of the arch over the Ark area is painted with stars, as is the wall around the Ark itself. Ahrenberg may have based the arrangement of the interior on that of the Copenhagen synagogue. In Turku (Abo), for the small Orthodox community, the architect Krook built a tiny, simplified Romanesque synagogue on a plot donated by the government.

The centrally planned, domed synagogue in simplified Romanesque style was widely adopted by Jewish communities after the turn of the century. In Johannesburg, South Africa, the large community erected a new synagogue in 1914 that occupied an entire city block. Designed by Theodore Schaerer in red brick, it has a central plan with a flat dome, a wide, twin-towered entrance with flanking towers, and apse-like projections. The interior is decorated with marble and mosaic.

The Classical style enjoyed a special significance in the work of the first American-born Jewish architect, Arnold Brunner, at the turn of the century. Born in 1857, Brunner, a graduate of the Massachusetts Institute of Technology, was one of the leading figures of his profession. His numerous achievements include Lewisohn Stadium in New York, Columbia University School of Mines, the Cleveland Courthouse and the Educational Alliance Building on East Broadway, New York.

His first synagogue was an impressive eclectic temple, built to house the congregations of Anshe Chesed and Adas Jeshurun, which had

...açade of the Great Synagogue in ...ape Town, South Africa.

...PPOSITE The world-renowned artist ...arc Chagall executed the radiantly ...eautiful series of windows ...presenting the twelve tribes of Israel ...r the synagogue of the Hadassah ...ospital, Ein Karem, Jerusalem in ...61. Each round-headed window is ...ver three metres in height and about ...vo-and-a-half metres in width. This ...e depicts the tribe of Issarchar.

merged in 1874. The newly amalgamated communities had used the Moorish building at Lexington Avenue and Sixty-third Street, and the congregation may not have felt strange in Brunner's Beth-El Temple at Fifth Avenue and Seventy-sixth Street, completed for them in 1891, because the simplified corner pinnacles and the orientalizing ribbed decoration of the dome were direct references to the congregation's previous house of worship. The decorative shell of the auditorium, however, was a mixture of Byzantine, Romanesque and Venetian Gothic, the emphatic use of round arches stressing the Romanesque element.

Arnold Brunner, an architect at the forefront of his profession, must have been aware of the urge to change synagogue design. He must also have been aware of the currents in his field, which in the last decade of the nineteenth century tended to divide into two camps: 'form-follows-function' and correct 'Beaux Arts' classicism. Both of these were to play an important role in twentieth-century architecture, but it was to the latter of these movements that Brunner turned for the Shearith Israel synagogue on Central Park West in New York City, a new house of worship for North America's oldest congregation. This aristocratic Sephardi community had had a preference for neo-classical: their Crosby Street synagogue (1834) had been Greek Revival and their synagogue on Nineteenth Street had been stately Roman baroque. Now Brunner designed a sleek, proud building, best described as 'Roman Revival'. He argued the suitability of this choice for a Jewish building by pointing to the Greco-Roman style of the Galilean synagogues (see Chapter 2) recently excavated by the Palestine Exploration Fund, but there are stronger and more striking resemblances between the handsome temple-like front of the Shearith Israel synagogue and that of Charles B. Attwood's immensely popular Fine Arts Building (1892-3) for the Chicago World's Fair. The Shearith Israel interior, with its heavy coffered ceiling, pink and ox-blood marble, dark-red velvet and damask is even more sumptuous than the exterior promises, a worthy setting for the nameplates that evoke some of the most glorious pages in American Jewish history.

In 1901, Brunner again employed the neo-classical style for the Harry S. Frank Memorial synagogue in the grounds of the Jewish Hospital in Philadelphia. In this building, on a much smaller scale than the Shearith Israel synagogue, Brunner was more direct in his reference to the Galilean synagogues, and in particular to that of K'far Birim (see pp. 34-5). On the sides of this now disused small synagogue Brunner combined elements from the ancient houses of worship in the three transomed bipartite windows. He expressed his conviction about the aptness of the Greco-Roman style in *The Brickbuilder* of March 1907:

Some years ago, when what was known as the 'Richardson Romanesque' was apparently becoming the expression of American ecclesiastical architecture, it seemed that in a slightly modified form it would be appropriate for the synagogue. When I built the Temple Beth-El in New York, I so believed. After Richardson's death, when his methods were not successfully continued by his followers and imitators, the Romanesque practically disappeared and the choice for architects by now, broadly speaking, lies between the two great styles, Gothic and Classic. I am unhesitatingly of the opinion that the latter is the one that is fit and proper for the synagogue in America. With the sanction

ABOVE Arnold Brunner's sumptuous interior of the synagogue built on Central Park West in 1897 for congregation Shearith Israel, the oldest in the United States. The architect justified his use of 'Roman Revival' by the architecture of the early synagogues discovered in Galilee.

OPPOSITE In a style which departed drastically from all precedents, the architect Dankmar Adler built a synagogue in 1891 on Indiana Avenue Chicago for his own congregation, K. Anshe Maariv in collaboration with his partner Louis Sullivan. This old photograph shows the building when it was still a Jewish house of worship. It is now a Baptist church.

of antiquity it perpetuates the best traditions of Jewish art and takes up a thread, which was broken by circumstances, of a vigorous and once healthy style.[11]

The congregation Beth-El in Detroit might have been reading Brunner's mind when, four years before his article appeared, they commissioned the architect Albert Kahn to build a neo-classical synagogue in place of the existing Gothic Revival one. Kahn, a member of the congregation, was born in Germany in 1869 and emigrated to the United States in 1881. Best known for his brilliant career as an industrial architect, he anticipated many of the styles of the 1950s. The pantheon-like classical Beth-El 'temple' was far removed, however, from the style of the sweeping factory buildings of steel and glass that a later generation would adapt for halls of worship. The eclectic use of neo-classical styles for synagogues in the United States prevailed until well into the twentieth century. As late as 1922 Albert Kahn built a second synagogue for the Beth-El community with a long, colonnaded front concealing the broad hall of worship. Other eclectic structures with classical preferences built in the 1920s were the Temple Israel Meeting House in Brookline, Massachusetts, with a sedate entrance front of four Doric columns, and the Temple Emanu-El in Greensboro, North Carolina, with a six-columned pedimented portico complete with oculus, in the colonial classical style, built by Hobart B. Upjohn.

If Brunner, in his magazine article of 1907, had been of the opinion that 'Richardson Romanesque' was no longer feasible as a synagogue style, there were others who thought differently. When Dankmar Adler was commissioned to build a new synagogue in Chicago he chose to collaborate with his partner, Louis Sullivan, on a design which recalls Richardson's work in its use of arches but which departed drastically from any previous Jewish religious building. Adler, who became President of the Western Association of Architects, was born in Saxe-Weimar in Germany in 1844; he came to America at the age of ten and in 1861 his father became the first rabbi of the Kehilath Anshe Maariv in Chicago. Adler married the daughter of Abraham Kohn, founder of the congregation, and remained a faithful member until his death in 1900: his funeral services were held in the synagogue which he designed with Sullivan. Dankmar Adler designed public buildings in Pueblo (Colorado), St Louis, New Orleans, Buffalo and New York, besides several of importance in Chicago including the Stock Exchange and the Grace Methodist Episcopal church. At the time that the Anshe Maariv synagogue was being built, the young Frank Lloyd Wright was working in Adler and Sullivan's Chicago office.

The Anshe Maariv building was originally designed to be entirely executed in ashlar stone and was so depicted in a watercolour by Paul Lautrup. This design with battered walls, extravagantly heavy window mullions and transoms, broad arches and stark massive simplicity, has a force and stony power far surpassing that of the finished building. Lack of funds prevented Adler and Sullivan from finishing the synagogue as planned and the result is an unhappy compromise of Joliet stone and pressed sheet metal. The horseshoe-shaped interior with its dramatic parabolic-arch ceiling was largely the work of Adler and as a feat of engineering was much praised at the time. The building is now a Baptist church.

Detail of the interior of Alschuler's imposing Temple Isaiah (1924) on Hyde Park Boulevard, Chicago.

One of Cleveland's handsomest buildings, the synagogue of congregation Tifereth Israel (1924) was built by Charles R. Greco to accommodate two thousand persons.

While it did not achieve the stark originality of Anshe Maariv, Temple Tifereth Israel (1894) in Cleveland, Ohio, by Lehman and Schmitt, did exercise a considerable influence. Roughly based on Richardson's Trinity church in Boston, it is more dramatic and less picturesque, with a square dome capping a weighty central block. The Euclid Avenue Temple on East Eighty-second Street by the same firm, built in 1912, is far less grim, its grandeur replaced by red-brick suburban cheerfulness and a more restful, lower profile which shows a pronounced Byzantine influence. Both these synagogues are now used as churches.

Another Cleveland synagogue with strong Byzantine influence was begun in 1924 by Charles R. Greco. This was the temple of congregation Tifereth Israel at East One-hundred-and-fifth Street and Ansel Road. With its striking entrance arch and polygonal-based dome, it is one of the city's handsomest buildings. The fine interior has a central plan which seats 2000 persons within a 27.7-m diameter; the dome rises to almost the same distance from the floor.

In Chicago, Alfred Alschuler (1876–1940) proposed his own interpretation of the Byzantine style for Temple Isaiah (1924) on Hyde Park Boulevard; he explained its use by referring to the remains of a synagogue unearthed in Tiberias that displayed motifs closely resembling those used in the architecture of the Byzantine period. But Alschuler's essay in the style of San Vitale in Ravenna needed no justification. It is a fine eclectic building which incorporates many Jewish symbols in the beautifully decorated interior and ingeniously houses its smoke-stack (for the central heating plant) in a minaret.

ved from destruction by the Nazis
cause it would have been too costly
demolish, the Essen synagogue,
ilt in 1913, was praised for a quality
sanctity achieved by the architect in
design.

Perhaps Alschuler in Chicago was influenced by some of the spectacular German synagogues built before World War I. Assimilation in Germany had reached a very advanced point and many Jews whose families had lived there for centuries certainly felt much more German than Jewish. Relatively few interpreted the signs, already present, of the impending ferocity. Jews in every walk of life, the nobility, the army, the magistrature, the university and the government, in the theatre, in music, medicine, architecture and literature, scoffed at what they considered the puerile and pseudo-scientific theories of racial purity that were being bruited about. In this atmosphere of opulent and sometimes complacent bourgeois conservatism, Jewish congregations chose to build synagogues in an eclectic style sometimes described as 'free traditionalism'. In Frankfurt-am-Main, the architects Peter Jürgenson and Jürgen Bachmann built the Friedberger Anlage synagogue in 1907.

The highly successful partnership of Jürgenson and Bachmann had been formed in 1903 when they were only thirty, and together they won many prizes for a series of Protestant churches constructed of brick in a simple but elegant Romanesque and characterized by their barrel vaults. The twin-towered façade of their Frankfurt synagogue had a large circular window that recalled the west front of a Gothic cathedral: this was preceded, however, by an entrance court closed by a stout gateway with Romanesque arches flanked by cottage-like pavilions.

Three years later, in 1910, the West End synagogue was erected in Frankfurt by Franz Roeckle. Although its design, consisting of a low-domed square central tower with projecting classical temple-fronts at its

four arms, is far more conservative, this dignified, if somewhat dull building, similar in plan to the synagogues of Basle and Rome, seems like a
reaction against the extravagant Friedberger Anlage. Both these synagogues were destroyed, but the later one was restored by the German
government in 1950.

Shortly after the Frankfurt buildings, in 1912, another important hall
of worship, the Fasanenstrasse Temple, was erected in Berlin. The architect Ehrenfried Hessel drew on two well-known Italian Romanesque
monuments for his design: St Mark's in Venice and the Sanctuary of
St Anthony in Padua. Much admired in its time, the dignified limestone
entrance porch decorated with crouching lions was a landmark in this
smart neighbourhood near the Kurfürstendamm. The spacious interior
seated close to 2000 people on its main floor and two-tiered gallery. The
wedding chamber in the basement was decorated with tiles from the imperial factory, a gift from the Kaiser, who had also taken a personal interest in the building of the Neo-baroque synagogue at Potsdam in 1901.

The most ambitious pre-World War I synagogue was undoubtedly that
built in 1913 to the prize-winning design of Edmund Körner in Essen.
Some idea of its grandeur can be gathered from the fact that the Nazis
deemed it 'zu teuer niederzureissen' (too costly to raze) which accounts for
its structure being intact today. Like the Friedberger Anlage synagogue
in Frankfurt, the Essen temple had a forecourt with twin pavilion-like
buildings joined by a pillared gateway. The difficult triangular plot, which
varied considerably in level, was used with great ingenuity by Körner,
later the municipal architect of Essen. The architect intended that the
worshipper in the Steelerstrasse synagogue should be touched by his
subtle theatrical sense as he passed from the narrow entrance under the
ponderous Neo-Romanesque façade, across the forecourt, and up a
broader flight of steps through the spacious lobby and into the vast ever-
broadening hall of worship, dimly lit by stained glass and glowing with
mosaic. Indeed, an account of the building published in 1919 described
it as a kind of *Gralstempel* or Temple of the Holy Grail.[12] The reference,
of course, is to Wagner's opera *Parsifal*, and the architect may well have
been among those cultured Germans who were awed by the romantic
mysticism of that work, which was first performed in Bayreuth in 1889.
The great hall could seat 1500 and had an organ loft and choir balcony
above the entrance lobby. Behind the Ark were changing-rooms for the
rabbi and cantor; below and beyond the Ark area, at the lowest and widest
end of the plot, were arranged the week-day chapel, meeting-hall, library,
ritual bath, offices, classrooms, caretaker's and rabbi's living quarters.

Though synagogue architecture progressed from nineteenth-century
eclecticism to turn-of-the-century 'free traditionalism' in the period
before World War I, it was not before building could begin again in the
period between the two wars that the nineteenth-century image was entirely displaced.

9 *The Modern Synagogue*

This century, and particularly the period after World War I, has been a supremely dramatic one for the Jewish people. It would be hard to imagine greater extremes of sorrow and exultation, despair and youthful optimism. The established freedom of communities in the Americas, South Africa and Australia could not be in greater contrast to the harassment and cruelty of the eastern European pogroms; only divine wisdom could have foreseen the *aliya* and the establishment of the independent state of Israel during the darkness of the Nazi Holocaust.

It is not surprising that during this time synagogue architecture has shown a distinct tendency to reject the various 'revival' experiments of the nineteenth century in favour of a more authentic expression for the gathering-place of a Jewish community. The period of the Weimar Republic was a fecund one, not only for the development of the modern synagogue, but for the course of twentieth-century architecture. Until 1933, when Hitler put the cultural clock back, Germany led the world in architectural development. Already before World War I, German architects working in an Expressionist style had created buildings that were to become classics of modern architecture. Peter Behrens (1868–1940) built the startling AEG Turbine Factory in Berlin in 1909–10; his most successful pupil, Walter Gropius (1883–1969), designed the Fagus Works at Alfeld near Hanover, built in 1911–14. This building especially marked a considerable advance in its use of steel and glass. The Vienna Post Office Savings Bank (1904–6) by Otto Wagner (who as a young man had designed a Moorish synagogue in Budapest), and the elegant modern Brussels mansion, the Palais Stoclet, by his pupil Josef Hoffman (1870–1956), focused international attention on the architecture originating in German-speaking Europe.

After World War I, German Jews played a considerable role in the national public life. Over 100,000 Jews had served in the German army during the war and 12,000 of them had fallen in battle for the fatherland. With the establishment of a democratic republic the Jews felt that any remaining obstacles to complete emancipation had fallen. The government of the Weimar Republic did remove all restrictions, and in fact it was a Jew, Hugo Preuss, who drafted the constitution of the new regime. Another Jew, Walter Rathenau, served first as minister of reconstruction and then as foreign minister. In the large cities the Jewish communities were almost all composed of members of the middle class and in spite of the generally gloomy economic picture they were mostly prosperous: one-third of the lawyers and doctors in the country were Jews and almost one-half of all Jewish marriages were mixed. Many Jews were involved in the arts and some like Erich Mendelsohn (1887–1953) and Richard Neutra (1892–1970) were prominent architects. Neutra's design for a synagogue in Hietzing, a suburb of Vienna, closely resembled the plan for a business centre in Haifa which he conceived working with Mendelsohn in the latter's Berlin studio: the design was not accepted – Neutra's bold concept, a prophetic composition of low-slung rectangles around an open court, cannot have been easy to understand. As early as 1919, Erich Mendelsohn had used steel and reinforced concrete as materials for his industrial and commercial projects. It was not until after World War II, however, that he was to bring this experience to bear on synagogue

PREVIOUS PAGE Eisenshtat relied on the strong verticals and horizontals of his design to give dramatic impact to the entrance of Temple Mount Sinai, built in 1962 at El Paso, Texas.

architecture when he was residing in the United States.

By no means all synagogue commissions were given to Jewish architects. Communities frequently held competitions and awarded the contract to the architect who submitted the best design. Such was the case
with the community of Zilina (Sillein) in Czechoslovakia. In 1926 the
Jewish community in this small city was determined to have a modern
synagogue and invited architects of considerable reputation to submit
plans. Among them were Josef Hoffman of Vienna and Peter Behrens
of Berlin, both non-Jews and at the zenith of their profession. The architectural critic Max Eisler commented adversely on this in *Menorah* and
took the Zilina community to task for ignoring Jewish architects such
as Oskar Strnad (1879–1935) and Josef Frank (born 1885) who he felt
could have made valuable contributions.[1]

Josef Hoffman became very interested in the Zilina synagogue project
and his sketches reveal a mind at work on a spiritual as well as material
level to produce a building entirely suited to its mission. In the first of
these sketches, the synagogue is conceived as a hemispherical dome resting on a very low base. In the second sketch the dome has been replaced
by a tent-like pyramid of glass with a high surrounding wall – a reference
to the Tabernacle in the Wilderness. Neither of Hoffman's plans was
used, but it is fascinating to note that with some variation both these concepts were eventually executed in the United States: the dome by Erich
Mendelsohn, the tent by Frank Lloyd Wright.

The design by Hoffman's chief competitor, Behrens, was finally
chosen, and the synagogue building was erected in 1931. It is a low-
domed, squarish structure which could pass for a neat civic auditorium:
only a Magen David perched on each corner and on the summit of the
dome identify it externally as a Jewish building.

During the early 1920s, the extreme economic hardships in Germany
together with the sudden explosion of liberal ideas under the Weimar
Republic led architects into flights of inventive fancy. As there was little
money for the realization of high-flown projects, many architects continued to design in the Expressionist vein of the period before the war.
Later in the decade, when economic conditions had improved, a new and
more functional architecture emerged which was responsible for such
masterpieces as Walter Gropius' Bauhaus in Dessau (1925–6), which gave
its name to a whole artistic movement, and Mies Van der Rohe's German
pavilion at the Barcelona Exhibition of 1929, a work which more than
any other of its time proved, with its lyrical simplicity, that modernity
was not synonymous with brutality. A few notable synagogues were built,
but before the fruit of this rich period could be culled in terms of synagogue architecture, Hitler rose to power and no further Jewish building
took place.

The German synagogue which most closely reflected the spirit of the
Bauhaus School was built at Plauen (1929–30) by the architect Fritz Lan-
dauer (born 1883). The long, plain, rectangular block is raised on stilts
at one end (possibly the influence of Le Corbusier can be detected here)
and has a carefully considered fenestration which combines flush
'punched-out' rectangles with a long, framed window composed of
squares. High above the inconspicuous entrance, to the right of the long,

framed window, is a recessed circle containing a Magen David. The synagogue, now destroyed, had an austere hall of worship with 9.7-m-tall recess for the Ark.[2]

The Israelitische Tempel in the Oberstrasse in Hamburg was another of the pre-Hitler period synagogues. Built in 1930–1, it was designed by the engineers Felix Ascher and Robert Friedmann. Like the Essen synagogue (see p. 190) it survived because it was too costly to raze, and it was occupied by the German radio network. The symmetrical plan provided a main hall of worship with two projecting wings which housed a week-day chapel and an assembly hall. The monolithic façade is stark and rhetorical: a stylized menorah in sharp relief is over the central entrance.

Dutch architects were not far behind their German colleagues at the forefront of the profession in the 1920s. Two belonging to the Dutch Progressive school designed synagogues of a most elegant and original character. Both were built in quiet suburbs of Amsterdam: the earlier, the Linnaeus Straat synagogue, erected in 1927–8 to the design of Jacob S. Baars (1886–1956), is no longer standing. Although it relied to some extent on Dutch church tradition, Baars' building had a rustic cottage-like appearance with a pitched roof over the main hall and adjoining edifices. The tall tower further broke the skyline, perhaps in deference to the Halakah ruling on synagogue height, and the off-centre entrance added to the whole informal and 'homely' character. The interior of the hall of worship had a novel diagonal layout in which the Ark and entrance were at opposite corners of a square plan, with the bimah in the centre. Baars made liberal and effective use of parabolic arches in the entrance and over the Ark and its flanking recesses.

The Jacob Obrechtplein synagogue, built in 1928, in Amsterdam-Zuid, was designed by Harry Elte (1880–1945). It has some elements in common with Baars' building, notably the studied irregularity of elevation and skyline, but is more consciously 'modern'. The interior of the hall of worship, with blue and gold mosaic tiles and black marble, is particularly fine. The stained-glass windows which have unfortunately suffered from vandalism, portray scenes from the Old Testament. Elte, like Baars, used a parabolic arch over the Ark: his treatment is most effective, for the division of the broad soffit of the arch into three glazed channels provides a pale, dreamy lighting for the Ark area.

In England the first really significant synagogue building of this century was the Dollis Hill synagogue in Cricklewood, London, built in 1937 to a design of Sir Owen Williams (born 1890). Here he cleverly contrived to do away with the gallery supports by resting the cantilevered galleries against the corrugated (and thus greatly strengthened) walls; the interior space is free of pillars or supports because Williams also designed a corrugated roof. The striking exterior has hexagonal and shield-shaped windows to represent the Magen David and the menorah.

The abandonment of historical associations made it comparatively easy for the modern synagogue to adapt to its social and climatic environment. Two synagogues built in Israel during the 1930s were designed to protect their congregations from both the glaring sun and possible enemy attack. In Hadera, a pioneering town of Israel, established in 1891 at the dawn of modern Zionism, where many early settlers perished before the vast

The genteel modernism of Hendon, a respectable London suburb, extended to this discreet red-brick synagogue, built there in 1935.

malaria-breeding swamps were replaced by citrus groves, the settlers purchased the ancient Arab caravanserai in the centre of the town as their home. In 1935 a large synagogue was erected on this site within the caravanserai: this impressive building, designed by Judith Stolzer, revived the centuries-old concept of the fortress-like Polish synagogues (see Chapter 5). The tall tower served as a lookout over the surrounding countryside and the courtyard could harbour 2000 people in case of attack. In Jerusalem the architects Friedman, Rubin and Stolzer designed the large Jeshurun synagogue in King George Avenue in 1934–5. Because of the strong sunlight the windows were reduced to mere slits.

Jewish communities in the United States did not adopt the functional styles that were being developed in Europe until after World War II, when building recommenced and American architectural ranks had been filled by brilliant immigrants from Germany and Austria. An exception, perhaps, was the interior of Yeshiva University auditorium-synagogue in New York, designed in 1928 by Charles B. Meyers and Henry B. Herts. The spiky decoration is basically a re-thinking of details of the ubiquitous Moorish Revival, but the result was fresh and new, especially such features as the mirror-faceted Art Deco lighting fixtures.

Once the evil reputation of Adolf Hitler had been spread abroad there was little enthusiasm to continue the bold experiments of the 1920s. The little building that necessity demanded was carried out in simplicity: the red-brick, rather 'suburban' modernism of Hendon synagogue (1935) in London is a good example. Cricklewood synagogue is another.

World War II put an end to synagogue-building because of anxiety and financial pressures, and the diabolically efficient Nazi plan to eradicate Judaism resulted in the destruction of many synagogues. Vienna, for instance, which had fifty-nine synagogues before the war, was left afterwards with only seventeen; forty-two were destroyed in the single greatest episode of destruction and desecration of synagogues on 9–10 November 1938, the infamous *Kristallnacht* or Night of the Broken Glass. Earlier that week Herschel Grynzspan, a seventeen-year-old Jewish refugee in France, half-crazed at reports of his parents' ill-treatment in Poland, where they had been deported by the Nazis, shot and killed Ernst vom Rath, a secretary in the German Embassy in Paris. The party leaders gleefully seized this opportunity to organize a 'spontaneous' mass outbreak of anti-Semitism. While the Nazi party bosses, headed by Hitler and Goering, concluded the annual celebration of the Beer Hall Putsch in Munich, hoards of young Nazis ransacked, burned, destroyed, desecrated and looted Jewish homes, businesses and synagogues. Official figures record '119 synagogues burned and another 76 completely destroyed'[3] but this was a conservative estimate. Cecil Roth reports that 'with hardly a single exception, all of the 600 synagogues in the country [Germany] – including ancient buildings which had formerly been regarded as national monuments – were gutted.'[4] Nazi thugs broke $1,250,000 worth of window glass and Goering was piqued to learn that it could not be replaced except by costly imports, paid for with valuable foreign exchange.[5]

The Holocaust experience indicated to Jews that they might be safe nowhere. In past centuries they had been persecuted for their religion but now they were inexorably hunted down and exterminated because of their race. Jews who were converted to Christianity or had long ceased the practice of their faith were not spared the hysterical ferocity of Nazi racial hatred. At the end of the war the stocktaking was chilling: six million Jews had been systematically eliminated from Germany, Italy and German-occupied Europe.

The Jewish people and Judaic thought and culture rose out of the ashes like a phoenix. In 1948 the eminent Jewish art historian, Helen Rosenau, was pessimistic about the modern synagogue when she wrote: 'Jewish distinctiveness almost disappears in the cosmopolitanism of contemporary art, which is super-national and technological in its tendency.'[6] This was true in England and its former colonies like South Africa, where synagogue architects made use of all the technological advancements of recent years in large and commodious buildings such as the Bloemfontein and Springs synagogues, but had scant sucess in achieving a specifically Judaic architectural expression. It was in the United States within two decades of the end of the war that a number of synagogues were built which represent something of a culmination in Jewish cultural history.[7]

In 1945 the B'nai Amoona congregation in St Louis, Missouri, gave the commission for their new synagogue to Erich Mendelsohn, an immigrant Jewish architect of whom Bruno Zevi (an Italian Jewish architect and one of that country's major architectural writers) has written, 'Architectural expressionism found its major exponent in Erich Mendelsohn, whose buildings and whose visions seem to free themselves from an earthquake, boiling matter, like lava, that spurt from the earth and rise with their own force, caught in an instant of their dramatic self-creation. In this moment, Judaism found a Jewish architect.'[8] Mendelsohn, who left Germany in 1933, had settled for a time in England and then spent some years in Palestine designing a variety of buildings, but no synagogues. In March 1941 Mendelsohn – who had few business prospects left in an economically insecure country – emigrated with his wife and family to the United States, where he was able to give free rein to his considerable creative powers, as the seven synagogues and community centres which he designed bear ample witness.

The commission for the St Louis synagogue was Mendelsohn's first in the United States. In 1945 Jewish communities still clung tenaciously to the traditional styles. Mendelsohn, with courageous simplicity, set out to reverse this attitude. His basic plan for the B'nai Amoona synagogue takes into account the differing spatial requirements of the normal Sabbath worshippers and the enormously increased congregations on high holidays. His solution, which he employed in one form or another in all his synagogues, was to design movable partitions, sliding doors or disappearing walls, which when opened could join the hall of worship, entrance foyer and community hall. The B'nai Amoona synagogue, completed in 1950, has a majestic parabolic roof that rises up over the main hall of worship. The lighting is most delicately judged: it comes from behind and, indirectly, from the glazed sides of a channel in the arched ceiling which houses the Ark at its base. The Ark is imposing yet fragile, with a grille of finely worked bronze – the 'golden fence' around the Torah.

Designs for the Park synagogue, for the Hebrew congregation of Cleve-

Erich Mendelsohn began designs for the Park synagogue at Cleveland, Ohio in 1946. The building, with a domed hall of worship and adjacent administrative offices, was completed in 1952.

land, Ohio, were begun in 1946, and the building was completed in 1952. Mendelsohn's design made the maximum advantage of the beautiful site, on a wooded ravine. The plan is a long triangle with the domed hall of worship filling the narrow end and the administrative and social services housed in the wider section around an open patio. Both within and without, the adventurous use of space is masterly: there are surprises round every corner and unexpected vistas at every turn. Walter Gropius said, 'It is important to walk round a building in order to grasp its shape and the function of its parts': the complex spaces of the Park synagogue seem to unfold effortlessly to the viewer, like the strains of the Bach fugues which Mendelsohn liked to listen to while he worked at his drawing-board. Nikolaus Pevsner has suggested that a religious building should 'convert visitors into worshippers'.[9] This is the effect Mendelsohn has tried to achieve in the Park synagogue.

Of Mendelsohn's other American synagogue designs, only those for congregation Emanu-El, Grand Rapids, Michigan (1952) and Mount Zion Hebrew congregation, St Paul, Minnesota (1954) were actually built. The Grand Rapids building has a particularly ingenious solution to the expandable seating problem: the hall of worship and the social hall are in parallel and can form one large room with a unifying tapestry-covered Ark wall when the dividing wall is taken up into its track in the ceiling. The Mount Zion Temple declares itself clearly and proudly with a rectangular roof over the main hall which recalls the five books of the Pentateuch. Mendelsohn's death in 1953 was a blow to the development of a unique synagogue style, but his influence is still strongly felt.

Percival Goodman is a contemporary architect who has had more opportunities to build American synagogues than most. However, he is one whose style owes little to Mendelsohn. While it is perhaps an exaggeration to call it 'playful', as Rachel Wischnitzer has done,[10] it is true that his synagogues have neither the drama nor the monumentality of Mendelsohn's. Goodman's synagogue for congregation B'Nai Israel at Millburn, New Jersey (1951) exactly suits the pleasing suburb in which it is situated. The lively façade, which has a projecting bay to house the Ark, the soft colours and the gentle profile all give it a welcoming and homely air pertinent to its function as the heart of the community. The interior, following Goodman's practice of commissioning prominent artists, has decorations by different hands. The Ark curtain was designed by Adolph Gottlieb and worked by the ladies of the congregation; the abstract mural in the entrance hall was painted by Robert Motherwell.

In the synagogue that Percival Goodman designed for congregation Beth El, Rochester, New York (1962) red brick is treated almost like cloth to form an exterior curtain that wraps the congregation in its folds and forms an undulating backdrop for the Ark; the Ark itself, in an envelope of Galilean marble, dominates the interior space with hieratic grandeur.

More striking is Goodman's design for congregation Shaarey Zedek, Southfield, Michigan (1963), with a steeply pitched roof rising up to a craggy pinnacle over the Ark. The result, somewhat grandiloquent, is nevertheless highly individual.

An eminent Jewish architect, Louis Kahn (born 1901), who came to the United States from his native Estonia, was only involved in designing synagogues late in his career, and owing to practical difficulties neither of the two was realized. His design of 1963 for a new synagogue for the Orthodox congregation Mikveh Israel in Philadelphia is outstanding: while retaining the traditional western Sephardic arrangement of Ark and bimah, he employed a sculptural series of cylinders perforated with arched openings to provide an almost mystical sense of amorphous space. His project for the Hurvah synagogue in Jerusalem is an exciting solution to the problems involved, showing an understanding of religion, the liturgy and the idea of God.

American congregations did not always choose Jewish architects, but few of those who were not Jews came as close to the spirit of Judaism as Frank Lloyd Wright (1869–1959) in his marvellous design for Beth Shalom congregation, Elkins Park, Pennsylvania. Wright, the son of a Unitarian minister, had a profound knowledge of the Bible; his biographer, Finis Farr, has remarked,

As a non-Jew designing a synagogue, Wright could not claim to be learned in the Torah, but he applied himself so diligently to the client's problems that the correspondence over several years filled many folders. Wright's interest, in fact, was so great that the Rabbi has been compelled to deny the persistent story that he got approval of the plans from his trustees by insisting, 'We pray the way Mr Wright *says* we pray.'[11]

It may be assumed that this wealthy suburban congregation also paid as Mr Wright said they should pay. Wright's design, which was first published in 1954, was for a soaring pyramidal structure with a translucent plastic covering. The hall of worship is reached by an ingenious arrangement of ramps; space is provided below it for a chapel and two meeting-rooms. Everywhere, the detail is superb and the endlessly re-iterated triangular motif lends the interior a restless, searching urgency that is tremendously effective. It is precisely Wright's destruction of the old comfortable forms in favour of a tense, questioning spirit that is central to Judaism; his detestation of neo-classical architecture is well-known and perhaps Beth Shalom synagogue represents, in Bruno Zevi's words, 'the victory of time over space that is the architectonic incarnation of Jewish thought, all the more significant because it has been realized by a non-Jew'.[12]

Other architects were not as successful as Wright in creating true expressions of the spirit of Judaism. In 1954 Philip Johnson (born 1906) built a synagogue for the Kneses Tifereth Israel congregation of Port Chester, New York, in a refined manner that has been described as Johnson's 'Ballet School period'.[13] The main hall is a stately rectangle on to which is stuck the entrance foyer in the form of a saucer-domed oval. The interior can be divided to provide the necessary extra seating for high holidays and is treated much as the architect did the guest bedroom of his own house at New Canaan, Connecticut. In the synagogue Ibram Lassaw's metalwork, which creeps over the Ark wall, recalls a similar sculpture over Johnson's guest bed. The effect in Kneses Tifereth synagogue is awkwardly theatrical, too much like 'interior decoration'.

In Waltham, Massachusetts, at Brandeis University, the architectural firm of Harrison and Abramowitz built an interesting small synagogue

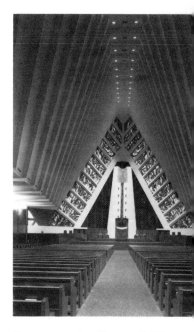

For congregation Shaarey Zedek at Southfield, Michigan, Percival Goodman executed one of his most successful synagogue designs in 1963. The steeply pitched roof lends a soaring majesty to the interior.

as part of an inter-denominational complex that also included Catholic and Protestant chapels. In the synagogue two curved windowless walls surround the congregation and focus attention on the Ark and the view of trees and sky through the window behind it.

The Ark as the focus of the synagogue worship is splendidly treated in Temple Emanu-El, Dallas, Texas (1957) by the architects Howard K. Meyer, Max M. Sanfeld and William Wurster, who called in the artist Gyorgy Kepes to decorate the domed interior. The dominating feature is a huge expanse of Mexican brick with gold tiles used in the interstices to form the outline of a menorah. The Ark screen is a glistening woven tapestry by the artist Anni Alpers.

The interior decoration of synagogues at the hands of some of America's greatest Jewish artists has been a characteristic of the modern temple. The need for liturgical ornaments, eternal lights, candelabra and Ark curtains has provided the United States with an outstanding quantity of excellent Jewish works of art. The coincidence of the post-war synagogue-building boom with a flowering of non-figurative art which fitted comfortably into the Jewish non-representational tradition was a happy one, but figurative wall decorations have also been used. For the Temple Oheb Shalom at Nashville, Tennessee, where Nathaniel Kaz executed a 3-m-high limestone sculpture on the façade, representing Truth, Justice and Peace, to a design of Raymond Katz, the artist Ben Shahn (1906–69) made a splendid mosaic mural, 2.46 × 4.3 m, for the vestibule. Entitled *The Call of the Shofar*, it illustrates Malachi 2:10, 'Have we not all one father? Has not one God created us? Why then are we faithless to one another, profaning the covenant of our fathers?' The sculptor Seymour Lipton, who was commissioned to work on Temple Israel, Tulsa, Oklahoma (1955), made for it a massive but supple menorah in nickel-silver and a great *ner tamid* in the same material. Among the many other successful artists who have worked for synagogues are Boris Aronson, who executed sculptures in teak and bronze for Temple Sinai at Washington DC, Adolph Gottlieb, who designed the stained-glass wall of the Milton Steinberg House attached to the Park Avenue synagogue, New York, and the sculptor Milton Horn whose work can be seen at Har Zion Temple, River Forest, Illinois and Temple Israel, Charleston, Virginia.

The Israeli artist Amiram Shamir was commissioned to decorate the small circular place of worship for the children inside the school building of the Salanter Akiba Riverdale Academy (1974), at Riverdale, a suburb of New York City. The exterior is decorated with symbolic designs in plexiglass, wrought iron, stained glass and stainless steel. The Ark is placed at the eastern end of the circle which has carpeted steps around in tiers to provide seating for the children. The colourful needlepoint paroketh and the *ner tamid* of carved wood provide a lively focal point.

Perhaps the most beautiful synagogue interior in the United States is that of the Loop synagogue, Chicago (1960). Its single feature is the magnificent stained-glass east wall over the street, designed by Abraham Rattner and entitled *The Journey of a Mystic*: the composition includes mystic symbols from the Cabbala and Hebrew calligraphy. The Ark is set against the glass and the ravishing effect of light thrown in great washes of colour over the marble north wall behind the bimah justifies the utter

OPPOSITE Herbert Ferber was one of the artists invited by Percival Goodman to participate in the decoration of the synagogue of congregation B'Nai Israel, Millburn, New Jersey. His *Burning Bush* in copper, brass and lead was made in 1951 to embellish the façade behind the Ark.

simplicity of the rest of the interior. Rattner also designed tapestries for the synagogue of congregation Anshe Chesed in Cleveland, Ohio (1956).

The renowned American artist Louise Nevelson executed a huge steel sculpture to decorate the entrance of Temple Israel at Brookline, Massachusetts. Her assembly of boxes with abstract shapes helps to tie the starkly modern synagogue building of 1973 to the previous one in neoclassical style which adjoins it. In 1962, the architect Sidney Eisenshtat, who had built the Temple Emanuel at Beverly Hills, California, in 1955, designed a dramatic modern building for the Mount Sinai congregation at El Paso, Texas. The synagogue with its soaring arched shell seems to spring out of the rocky Texas soil. This theme is repeated in the interior, where the congregation can see the distant mountains through the high glazed arch behind the Ark.

Another important synagogue is one designed by the Seattle-born architect Minoru Yamasaki (born 1912) for North Shore congregation Israel in prosperous Glencoe, Illinois (1964). This large, shell-like structure is supported by a series of arches that seem to dissolve into gossamer-light panels of glass. The pointed arches at the base of the side walls provide a strong rhythmic underpinning to the long narrow bays that arch over the worshippers like hands folded in prayer. The unusual Ark of gilded teak is long and narrow, shaped like a pen-nib, perhaps symbolic of the calligraphic Torah; partially enfolding the Ark is a graceful form that symbolizes the traditional prayer-shawl.

Marcel Breuer (born 1902), the eminent follower of Gropius and member of the Bauhaus, was commissioned by the B'nai Jeshurun congregation of Short Hills, New Jersey, another prosperous community, to build a synagogue that could accommodate 2500 persons on high holidays and about 1000 on a normal Sabbath. Built in 1966, this imposing complex of schoolrooms, auditorium and majestic hall of worship has an arrangement of sliding panels that can be moved to provide much greater space. The interior of the sanctuary has a nicely calculated sense of drama, though the extensive use of close-carpeting is claustrophobic.

World War II left Europe tired and broken. The once flourishing Jewish communities had been decimated by the Holocaust and by the *aliya* of their members to Israel or emigration to new homes in the United States, Canada, South Africa, Australia and South America. As a result there was no widespread need for new synagogues, and where they replaced ones destroyed in the war the designs were usually modest.

The modern synagogue of Milan, the Tempio Israelitico, was built in 1953. It has a handsome, functional interior with much use of pink and dark-red marble. The bimah is placed in the centre and there is a balcony for the choir above the women's gallery, which is screened by blue shutters. At Livorno, a new synagogue was commissioned from Angelo di Castro to replace the old one which had been destroyed in a bombing raid. The synagogue was completed in 1962 in the daring style of Pier Luigi Nervi as a single-room hall of worship of tent-like construction with strongly projecting stanchions and ribs to strengthen the roof. The layout, with a central bimah and women's gallery, is handled in an angular, modern manner, while the octagonal windows, recalling those of the previous building, provide a link with the past.

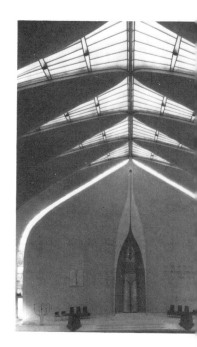

For the children of the Salanter Akiba Academy in the New York suburb of Riverdale, this colourful little synagogue was designed like a theatre in-the-round. The intimacy of the arrangement in no way detracts from the importance of the Ark.

The rhythmic lines of Minoru Yamasaki's synagogue of North Shore Congregation Israel at Glencoe near Chicago, built in 1964, draw the attention of the worshippers toward the Ark.

Post-war synagogue building in most European countries has usually been modest and none of the communities has been as ambitious as those in the United States. The St John's Wood synagogue, London, and the Liberal synagogue in Amsterdam are examples. In France, one notable modern synagogue is that of Strasbourg, a large basilical-style building designed for the community by Claude Meyer-Lévy, Jean-Paul Berst and René Heller. Although it employs modern technology in its structure, the style of the building is neo-classical. The rectangular hall, which seats 1700, has a two-tiered gallery at the entrance end and slightly lower single ones along either side. Twelve tapered columns, 18.5 m high, support the segment-arched barrel roof.

While rich congregations continue to build glamorous and impressive synagogues there are still in urban America small congregations who are happy to meet in an upper room or a converted shop or house that recalls the *shtibl* of the Hassidim of the eastern European *shtetl*. In these unpretentious synagogues *minyanim* of friends and neighbours meet for the services. They feel no need of a particular religious building to convert them into worshippers (see p. 197); they regard the luxurious synagogues without jealousy but are apt to describe their style wryly as 'meshugothic'.

The post-war German state assisted communities to rebuild their synagogues but the Jewish population of the country in the late 1950s had dwindled to about 27,000 – a dramatic drop from the pre-war half-million. So the need for these new synagogues was sometimes more symbolic than real. One architect, Helmut Goldschmidt (born 1918), has built a number of these post-war German synagogues. Beginning with his functional 'community centre' synagogue at Dortmund (1956) he continued with the more exciting synagogue of Bonn (1959), with its staggered louvre-like walls moving towards the eastern end. He also planned the stark remodelling in 1959 of the old Byzantine-style Roonstrasse synagogue in Cologne. The Ruhrallee synagogue in Hamburg, built in 1959 to the design of the architects Knoblauch and Heise, looks back to the pre-war design for a domed synagogue in Zilina by Josef Hoffman (see p. 193). The hall of worship, a copper-clad concrete hemisphere with rectangular areas of circular windows, is somewhat 'arty'. At the dedication in 1958, the entire Hamburg community numbered 254 members. Before the war it had been 4,500. In Berlin the same firm of Knoblauch and Heise built a synagogue and community house on the site of the Fasanenstrasse synagogue of 1912. They deliberately made the regular, functional façade very simple as a foil for the ruined doorway of the previous synagogue which is set in it. The long, narrow interior has a series of saucer domes with small circular windows. Willy Brandt, then the Mayor of Berlin, attended the ceremony when the cornerstone was laid in 1957. In his speech he urged his fellow-countrymen not to try to hush up the past but to have the courage to face it. In most cases Jewish architects have been chosen to design the synagogues built in post-war Germany; generally they are restrained and often drab. Alfons Leitl, a non-Jewish architect, built the synagogue at Trier.

Important synagogues are not a feature of modern Israel. The priorities in building are houses, factories, hospitals, roads and defence installations. Little can be spared for luxurious synagogue-building, although precious funds have been spent on the beautiful restoration of the old synagogues in the Jewish quarter of Jerusalem which were wrecked during the period of Jordanian rule.[14] In many places, a simple spare room or an unpretentious building has been adapted as a place of worship. The need for a community centre in connection with the religious place of assembly has not, as yet, been felt in Israel, where the land itself is the place of assembly of the people. In time to come this may change if the religious authorities find a need to attract the young to study Torah and worship, through the provision of social amenities in the same place.

Two notable exceptions to the utility synagogue in Jerusalem are the curious, domed, windowless synagogue at the University and the simple, dignified synagogue of the Hadassah Hospital, by the architect Joseph Neufeld. It has a central 'lantern' that contains a series of glorious stained-glass windows, each 3×2.5 m, designed by Marc Chagall and representing the Twelve Tribes of Israel.

Lovingly, the holy Arks of many desecrated or abandoned synagogues have been brought from many countries to Israel, gathered to the homeland along with the scattered children of Israel and set up in new synagogues where they may remind the new and future generations of their forefathers' veneration of Torah in the communities of the Diaspora – those forefathers who made or gave these shrines to the houses of worship which they cared for so dearly, and which so often were the centre of their social life and of their unity as well as of their cherished hopes until the Day of Return dawned.

Notes

THE ORIGINS OF THE SYNAGOGUE

JOSEPHUS, *Apion*, 2:175.
Acts 15:21.
WEINGREEN, J., in *Hermathena*, 98 (1964).
FRIEDLANDER, M., *Synagoge und Kirche* (1908).
HERFORD, Robert T., *The Separation of Christianity from Judaism* (New York, 1927).
FREY, J.-B. (ed.), *Corpus Inscriptionum Judaicarum*, 1440, 36352 (Vatican City, 1952).
III Maccabees 7:20.
TCHERIKOVER, V.A. (ed.), *Corpus Papyrorum Judaicarum*, ol. I, 127 (1957).
TCHERIKOVER, V.A. (ed.), *Corpus Papyrorum Judaicarum*, ol. I, 134 (1957).
Mishnah, *Sot.* 7:7.
JOSEPHUS, *Vita*, 54, 56.
Talmud, *Meg.* 3:1; *Ket.* 1052.
Mishnah, *Sot.* 7:7–8.
Talmud, Josef, *Meg.* 3(2):6; T.J. *Meg.* 3:1, 73; *Meg.* 262.
Acts 6:9.
Patrologia Graeca, 43, 259–62.
BALDI, D., *Enchidrion Locorum Sanctorum* (Jerusalem, 55).
BAGATTI, Bellarmino, OFM, *The Church from the Circumcision: History and Archaeology of the Judaeo-Christians*, rans. Eugene, Hoade, OFM, Jerusalem, 1970).
FREY, J.-B. (ed.), *Corpus Inscriptionum Judaicarum*, 1404.
JOSEPHUS, *Wars*, 2:285–9; *The Antiquities of the Jews*, :305; *Vita*, 280.
Matthew 13:53; Mark 6:1; Luke 4:16–17.
Mark 1:21; Luke 4:31; Luke 7:1, 5; John 6:59.
Matthew 4:23; Matthew 9:35; Mark 1:39; Luke 4:14–15.
Mark 1:21; Mark 3:1; Mark 6:1; Luke 4:16; Luke 6:6; uke 3:10.
Luke 4:16–17, 20–22.
Luke 13:10–14.
Luke 7:1–5.
Matthew 6:2–3, 5.
James 2:2–3.
JOSEPHUS, *The Antiquities of the Jews*, 14:24.
Acts 16:13.
PHILO, *Legationem ad Gaium*.
Talmud, Suk. 51b.
SUKENIK, E.L., *Ancient Synagogues in Palestine and Greece* ondon, 1934).
I Maccabees 15:16–23.
JOSEPHUS, *The Antiquities of the Jews*, 14:24.
Louis M. Rabinowitz Fund for the Exploration of Ancient ynagogues, Bulletin I (Hebrew University, Jerusalem, 1949).
BOECKH, A. (ed.), *Corpus Inscriptionum Graecarum*, Vol. I, 5361 *et seq.*
PHILO, *Legationem ad Gaium*.
JOSEPHUS, *Wars* 7:43–6.

41 JOSEPHUS, *The Antiquities of the Jews*, 14:24.
42 Acts 9:20, 22.
43 Acts 13:14–15.
44 Acts 13:15–16.
45 Acts 19:9.
46 Acts 14:1.
47 Acts 17:1.
48 Acts 17:10.
49 Acts 17:16.
50 Acts 18:4.
51 FREY, J.-B. (ed.), *Corpus Inscriptionum Judaicarum*, 71b.
52 Acts 13:5.
53 EUSEBIUS, *Ecclesiastical History*, IV:5, 2.
54 EUSEBIUS, *Ecclesiastical History*, IV:5, 3.
55 This opinion of Jacob Pinkerfeld is reported by E.L. Sukenik in Bulletin III of the Louis M. Rabinowitz Fund for the Exploration of Ancient Synagogues (Hebrew University, Jerusalem, 1960).
56 Acts 1:12–13.

2 THE PATRIARCHATE AND THE EXILARCHATE

1 PINKERFELD, Jacob, *Synagogues of North Africa* (Jerusalem, 1974, in Hebrew).
2 ROTH, Cecil, *A History of the Jews* (revised edition, New York, 1970).
3 *Meg.* 4:23.
4 *Ber.* 34b.
5 *Meg.* 4:21.
6 *Meg.* 4:22.
7 VITRUVIUS, *Architectura*, IV, 5.
8 *Patrologia Latina*, II, 580.
9 *Didaskalia*, XII.
10 *Patrologia Graeca*, XXXII, 189 f.
11 *Patrologia Graeca*, XLIV, 1184.
12 BRANDT, Wilhelm, *Elchasai, ein Religionsstifter und sein Werk* (Leipzig, 1912).
13 EUSEBIUS, *Biography of Constantine*, III, 37.
14 DU MESNIL DU BUISSON, R., *Les Peintures de la Synagogue de Doura-Europos* (Rome, 1939).
15 KRAABEL, A.T., *Judaism in Western Asia Minor under the Roman Empire with a Preliminary Study of the Jewish Community at Sardis, Lydia* (Harvard University Divinity School, unpublished Ph.D. thesis, 1968).
16 FLORIANI SQUARCIAPINO, Maria, 'La Sinagoga Recentemente Scoperta ad Ostia', in *Atti della Pontificia Accademia Romana di Archeologia*, Series III, Vol. XXXIV (Vatican City, 1962).
17 FLORIANI SQUARCIAPINO, Maria, 'La Sinagoga di Ostia, Seconda Campagna di Scavo', in *Atti del VI° Congresso Internazionale di Archeologia Cristiana, Ravenna, 23–30 Settembre 1962* (Vatican City, 1965).
18 *idem*.

19 FLORIANI SQUARCIAPINO, Maria, 'Ebrei a Roma e ad Ostia', in *Studi Romani*, anno XI (Rome, 1963).

20 HENGEL, Martin, 'Die Synagogenschrift von Stobi', in *Zeitschrift für die neutestamentliche Wissenschaft*, 57 (1966).

21 FREY, J.-B. (ed.), *Corpus Inscriptionum Judaicarum*, Vol. II (Vatican City, 1952).

22 *Israel Exploration Journal*, Vol. 19 (Jerusalem, 1969).

23 FREY, J.-B. (ed.), *Corpus Inscriptionum Judaicarum*, Vol. II.

24 AVIGAD, N., 'A Dated Lintel Inscription from the Ancient Synagogue of Nabratein near Safed', in Bulletin III, Louis M. Rabinowitz Fund for the Exploration of Ancient Synagogues (Jerusalem, 1960).

25 FREY, J.-B. (ed.), *Corpus Inscriptionum Judaicarum*, Vol. II.

26 CORBO, Virgilio, OFM, LOFFREDA, Stanislao, OFM, and SPIJKERMAN, Augusto, OFM, *La Sinagoga di Cafarnao dopo gli Scavi del 1969* (Jerusalem, 1970).

27 BALDI, D., *Enchiridion Locorum Sanctorum* (Jerusalem, 1955).

28 CORBO, Virgilio, OFM, *The House of St Peter at Capharnaum* (trans Sylvester J. Saller, OFM, Jerusalem, 1969).

29 *Patrologia Graeca*, XLVIII, 844–940.

30 *Patrologia Graeca*, XLVI, 1009–24.

31 TESTA, E., OFM, *I Graffiti della Casa di San Pietro* (Jerusalem, 1972).

32 LOFFREDA, Stanislao, OFM, *A Visit to Capharnaum* (5th edition, Jerusalem, 1977).

33 LOFFREDA, Stanislao, OFM, *A Visit to Capharnaum*.

34 CORBO, Virgilio, OFM, LOFFREDA, Stanislao, OFM, and SPIJKERMAN, Augusto, OFM, *La Sinagoga di Cafarnao dopo gli Scavi del 1969*.

35 EUSEBIUS, *Onomastikon*, 174:25.

36 FREY, J.-B. (ed.), *Corpus Inscriptionum Judaicarum*, Vol. II.

37 FREY, J.-B. (ed.), *Corpus Inscriptionum Judaicarum*, Vol. II.

38 *Israel Exploration Journal*, Vol. 12 (Jerusalem, 1962).

39 *Qadmoniot*, Vol. I (Jerusalem, 1968, in Hebrew).

40 FREY, J.-B. (ed.), *Corpus Inscriptionum Judaicarum*, Vol. II.

41 FREY, J.-B. (ed.), *Corpus Inscriptionum Judaicarum*, Vol. II.

42 AVI-YONAH, M., DUNAYEVSKY, I., HIRAM, A.S., LEVY, S., RAHMANI, L.Y., and YEIRUN, S., 'The Ancient Synagogue of Ma'on', in Bulletin III, Louis M. Rabinowitz Fund for the Exploration of Ancient Synagogues.

43 *Av. Zar.* 3:4, 42d.

44 *Jahrbuch des Archaeologischen Instituts des Deutschen Reichs* (1932).

45 SUKENIK, E.L., *Ancient Synagogues of Palestine and Greece* (London, 1934).

46 IBARRA, Pedro, *Elche, Materiales para su Historia* (Cuenca, 1926).

CANTERA, F., and MILLA, J.M., *Las Inscripciones Hebraicas de España* (Madrid, 1956).

SCHLUNK, Helmut, 'La Sinagoga de Elche ...' in *Cronica del III Congreso Arqueológico del Sudeste Español* (Murcia, 1947).

47 SCHAPIRO, Meyer, preface to *Israel: Ancient Mosaics* (New York Graphic Society by arrangement with UNESCO, n.d.).

3 THE MIDDLE AGES

1 ADLER, Elkan N. (ed. and trans.), 'Itinerary of Benjamin of Tudela', in *Jewish Quarterly Review*, Vols. XVI and XVIII (London and Philadelphia, 1904–6).

2 Records of the Cancelleria cited by Giovanni di Giovanni in *L'Ebraismo della Sicilia* (Palermo, 1748).

3 *idem*.

4 *idem*.

5 *idem*.

6 *idem*.

7 *idem*.

8 *idem*.

9 MILANO, Attilio, *Storia degli Ebrei in Italia* (Turin, 1963).

10 ADLER, Elkan N. (ed.), *Jewish Travellers* (London, 1930).

11 KRAUTHEIMER, Richard, *Mittelalterliche Synagogen* (Berlin, 1927).

12 HÖNIGER, R., 'Das Judenschreinsbuch der Laurenzpfarre in Köln', in *Quellen zur Geschichte der Juden in Deutschland*, Vol. I (Berlin, 1888).

13 AGUS, I.A., *Rabbi Meir of Rothenburg* (Philadelphia, 1947).

14 ELBOGEN, I., *Der jüdische Gottesdienst und seine geschichtliche Entwicklung* (Leipzig, 1913).

15 ELBOGEN, I., FREIMANN, A., and TYKOCINSKI, H. (eds), *Germania Judaica*, Vol. I (Breslau, 1934).

16 KRAUTHEIMER, Richard, *Mittelalterliche Synagogen* (Berlin, 1927).

17 HALLER, Imre and VAJDA, Zsigmond, *A Magyarországi Zsinagógák Albuma* (The Synagogues of Hungary, an Album) (New York, 1968).

18 BLUMENKRANZ, Bernhard, *Les Auteurs Chrétiens du Moyen Age sur les Juifs et le Judaisme* (Paris, 1963).

19 BLUMENKRANZ, Bernhard, *Histoire des Juifs en France* (Toulouse, 1972).

20 KAHN, S., 'Thomas Platter et les Juifs d'Avignon', in *Revue des Etudes Juives*, Vol. XXV (Paris, 1892).

21 DEPPING, G.B., *Les Juifs dans le Moyen Age* (Brussels, 1844).

22 LUARD, H.R. (ed.), *Mattaei Parisiensis monachi Sancti Albani, Chronica majora* (London, 1872–3).

23 Ms. 13089, Biblioteca Nacional, Madrid.

24 CANTERA BURGOS, Francisco, *Sinagogas Españolas* (Madrid, 1955).

25 Archivo de Protocolos de Zaragoza, Protocolo of 1485 cited by Francisco Cantera Burgos in *Sinagogas Españolas*.

26 BOFARULL Y SANS, Francisco de Asis, *Los Judios en el Territorio de Barcelona* (Barcelona, 1910).

27 ALVAREZ DE LE BRAÑA, R., 'La Sinagoga de Bembibre y los Judios de Léon', in *Boletin de la Real Academia de la Historia*, Vol. XXXII (1898).

28 BALLESTREROS, A., *Sevilla en el siglo XIII* (Madrid, 1913).

29 FITA, Fidel, *La Sinagoga de Cordoba* (1884).

30 FITA, Fidel, *Actas Ineditas de Siete Concillios Españoles* (Madrid, 1882).

31 CZEKELIUS, Otto, 'Antiguas Sinagogas de España', in *Arquitectura*, Vol. XIII, (1931).

32 KRAUTHEIMER, Richard, *Mittelalterliche Synagogen*.

33 ROTH, Cecil, 'A Hebrew Elegy on the Martyrs of Toledo', in *The Jewish Quarterly Review*, N.S. Vol. XXXIX (Philadelphia 1948).

34 LAMBERT, Elie, 'Les Synagogues de Tolédo', in *Revue des Etudes Juives*, Vol. LXXXIV (Paris, 1927).

35 GONZALES PALENCIA, *Mozarabes*, p. 583, document 1144, cited by Francisco Cantera Burgos, in *Sinagogas Españolas*.

36 Documents cited by Francisco Cantera Burgos, in *Sinagogas Españolas*.

37 CANTERA BURGOS, Francisco, *Sinagogas Españolas*.

38 DE ESPINA, Alonso, *Fortalitium Fidei* (Lyon, 1511).

FITA, Fidel, 'La Juderia de Segovia', in *Boletin de la Real Academia de la Historia*, Vols IX and X (1886, 1887).

39 British Museum, Oriental Ms. 14761 (Barcelona Haggadah).

0 British Museum, Oriental Ms. 2884 folio 17v. ('Sister' to
the Golden Haggadah.)

1 Library of the Hungarian Academy of Sciences, Budapest,
Kaufmann Collection, Ms. A422. (Facsimile edition, ed.
Alexander Schreiber, Budapest, 1957).

2 ROTH, Cecil, 'Las Inscripciones históricas de la Sinagoga
el Tránsito de Toledo', in Sefarad, Vol. VIII (1948).

3 ADLER, Elkan N. (ed.), Jewish Travellers.

4 SAFIR, Jacob, Eben Sappir (Luck, 1866).

5 ADLER, Elkan N. (ed.), Jewish Travellers.

THE RENAISSANCE IN ITALY

ADLER, Elkan N. (ed.), Jewish Travellers (London, 1930).
RODOCANACHI, Emanuele, Le Ghetto à Rome (Paris, 1891).
Acts of the Otto di Guardia, State Archive, Florence, cited
Umberto Cassuto, Gli Ebrei a Firenze nell'età del
Rinascimento (Florence, 1918).
    Kid. 4 :14.
    Kid. 82a.
VASARI, Giorgio, Le vite de' più eccellenti architetti, pittori e
scultori italiani (Florence, 1550).
RODOCANACHI, Emanuele, 'La communauté juive de Rome
au temps de Jules II et Léon X', in Revue des études juives, Vol.
XI (1911).
CANCELLIERE, F., Storia de' solenni possessi de' Sommi
Pontefici detti anticamente processi o processioni (Rome, 1802).
MILANO, Attilio, Il Ghetto di Roma (Rome, 1964).
MILANO, Attilio, Storia degli Ebrei in Italia (Turin,
1963).
MILANO, Attilio, Storia degli Ebrei in Italia.
HUELSEN, Christian, Le Chiese di Roma nel Medio Evo
(Florence, 1927).
MILANO, Attilio, Il Ghetto di Roma.
ARMELLINI, Mariano, Le Chiese di Roma dal Secolo IV al
XIX (new edition, ed. Cecchelli, C., Rome, 1942).
PINKERFELD, J., The Synagogues of Italy (Jerusalem, 1954,
Hebrew).
The description is based on a photograph taken before the
demolition.
MILANO, Attilio, Il Ghetto di Roma.
See illustrations in a work published prior to the
demolition of the Cinque Scuole building – BERLINER, A.,
Geschichte der Juden in Rom (Frankfurt-am-Main, 1893).
This Ark and the seats are now preserved in the basement
of the Rome synagogue.
The Tables of the Law appeared about this time as a
decorative element on the Arks of the Spanish synagogue,
Venice (c. 1655–75), London (1674) and Amsterdam (1675).
PINKERFELD, J., The Synagogues of Italy.
FREIMANN, A.H., Seder Kidushin ... (Jerusalem, 1945).
BALLETTI, Andrea, Gli Ebrei e gli Estensi (Reggio Emilia,
1930).
State Archive, Florence, Mediceo 45c 502a.
ABOAB, Immanuel, Nomologia o Discursos Legales
(Amsterdam, 1629).
See SERMONETA, Josef B., 'Sull' origine della parola
ghetto', in Studi sull' Ebraismo Italiano (ed. E. Toaff, 1974),
originally published in Tharbiz, Vol. 32 (1962).
CORYAT, Thomas, Coryat's Crudities (1611).
OTTOLENGHI, Adolpho, 'Leon da Modena e la vita ebraica
nel ghetto di Venezia nel secolo XVII', in Rivista di Venezia
(Venice, July 1929).
PIATTELLI, Abramo A., 'Un arazzo veneziano del XVII

secolo', in La Rassegna Mensile di Israel, Vol. XXXVI (Milan,
July–September 1970).

30 PACIFICI, Riccardo, Le iscrizioni dell'antico cimitero ebraico
a Venezia, Vol. I (Alexandria, 1936).

31 ZANOTTO, F., Novissima Guida di Venezia (Venice, 1856).

32 SEMENZATO, C., L'Architectura di Baldassare Longhena
(Padua, 1954).

33 Rachel Wischnitzer confused these two synagogues when
she stated that the Italian was destroyed and the Spanish
continued in use. The contrary is true. See WISCHNITZER,
Rachel, The Architecture of the European Synagogue
(Philadelphia, 1963).

34 BIRNBAUM, Eduard, 'Musicisti ebrei alla Corte di Mantova
dal 1542 al 1628', in Civiltà Mantovana, No. 9 (Mantua, 1967).
    GHIRARDINI, Gherardo, 'Musicisti israeliti alla Corte dei
Gonzaga', in La Rassegna Mensile di Lsrael, Vol. XLI, No. 2
(Milan, February 1975).

35 State Archive, Florence, Privilegi granducali, Vol. I, c. 946.

36 ABOAB, Immanuel, Nomologia o Discursos Legales.

37 CASSUTO, Umberto, Gli Ebrei a Firenze nell'età del
Rinascimento.

5 THE RENAISSANCE IN POLAND

1 KOPERA, F., 'Jan Maria Padovano' in Prace Komisji Historii
Sztuki, Vol. 7, (Warsaw, 1937).

2 LEPSZY, L., Krakau ((Leipzig, 1906).
    THIEME-BECKER, Lexikon der Bildenden Künstler, Vol. XII,
p. 184.

3 BALABAN, Majer, Zabytki Historyczne Zydow w Polsce
(Warsaw, 1929).

4 Encyclopaedia Judaica, Vol. XV, p. 606 (Jerusalem, 1972).
    THIEME-BECKER, Lexikon der Bildenden Künstler, Vol. XXVI,
p. 5.

5 VOLAVKOVA, Hana, The Pinkas Synagogue (trans. Greta
Hort, Prague, 1955).

6 MARK, Bernard, and KUPFER, F., 'Zydzi polscy w okresie
Odrodzenia', in Biuletyn Zyd. Inst. Hist., Vols 2–3 (Warsaw,
1953).
    WEINRYB, Bernard D., The Jews of Poland, Appendix 3
(Philadelphia, 1973).

7 BALABAN, Majer, Zabytki Historyczne Zydow w Polsce.

8 idem.

9 idem.

10 idem.

11 DUBNOW, Simon, Pinkas Medinat Lita (Berlin, 1925).

12 BALABAN, Majer, Zabytki Historyczne Zydow w Polsce.

13 BALABAN, Majer, Zabytki Historyczne Zydow w Polsce.

14 SCHORR, M., Aus der Geschichte der Juden in Przemysl
(Vienna, 1915).

15 BALABAN, Majer, Zabytki Historyczne Zydow w Polsce.

16 BALABAN, Majer, Przewodnik po żydowskich zabytkach
Krakowa (Cracow, 1935).

17 BALABAN, Majer, Przewodnik po żydowskich zabytkach
Krakowa.

18 KOPERA, F., 'Jan Maria Padovano'.

19 Psalms 130, 1.

20 CZERPAK, Stanislaw (ed.), Stara Boznica Kazimierska
(Cracow, Muzeum Historyczne Miasta Krakowa, n.d.).

21 BALABAN, Majer, Przewodnik po żydowskich zabytkach
Krakowa.

22 BALABAN, Majer, Zabytki Historyczne Zydow w Polsce.
    BALABAN, Majer, Die Judenstadt von Lublin (Berlin, 1919).

23 BALABAN, Majer, Zabytki Historyczne Zydow w Polsce.

24 *idem.*

25 *idem.*

26 THIEME-BECKER, *Lexikon der Bildenden Künstler*, Vol. XXVI, p. 213.

27 BALABAN, Majer, *Dzielnica zydowska joj dzieje i zabytki*, Vols 5 and 6 (Biblioteka Lwowska, Lvov, 1909).

28 SCHORR, M., *Aus der Geschichte der Juden in Przemysl.*

29 Municipal Acts, Przemysl, Vol. XX, no. 56.

30 BALABAN, Majer, *Zabytki Historyczne Zydow w Polsce.*

31 BEHRSON, Mattias, *Dyplomatarusz dotyczacy zydow w dawnej Polsce* (Warsaw, 1910).

32 BALABAN, Majer, *Dzieje Zydow w Krakowie i na Kazimierzu* (Cracow, 1912).

BALABAN, Majer, *Zydzi w Krakowie* (Cracow, 1932).

33 BALABAN, Majer, *Przewodnik po żydowskich zybytkach Krakowa.*

34 ROSENAU, Helen, *A Short History of Jewish Art* (London, 1948).

35 *Enclyclopaedia Judaica*, Vol. XV, p. 608.

36 BALABAN, Majer, *Zabytki Historyczne Zydow w Polsce.*

37 BREIER, Alois, EISLER, M., and GRUNWALD, M., *Holzsynagogen in Polen* (Baden-bei-Wien, 1934).

38 BREIER, Alois, EISLER, M., and GRUNWALD, M., *Holzsynagogen in Polen.*

39 LISSITZKY, Eliezer, *The Synagogue of Mogylev* (in Hebrew, Rimon Vol. 3, 1923).

40 PIECHOTKA, Maria and Kazimierz, *Bóznice Drewniane* (Warsaw, 1957).

41 SZYSZKO-BAHUSZ, A., 'Materialy do architecktury boznic w Polsce', in *Prace Komisji Historii Sztuki*, Vol. 4, no. 1 (Warsaw, 1927).

42 ZAJCZYK, S., 'Architektura Barokowych boznic murowanych w Polsce', in *Biuletyn Naukowy Zaklad Architektury Polskiej*, No. 4 (Warsaw, 1933).

43 LUKOMSKI, Georgii K., *Jewish Art in European Synagogues* (London and New York, 1947).

44 *Bayrische Kunstdenkmale* (*Kurzinventar, Landkries Feuchtwangen*) (Munich, 1964).

45 *Monumenta Judaica* (Exhibition, Stadtmuseum Köln) (Cologne, 1964).

46 Toeplitz, E., 'Die Malerei in den Synagogen', in *Beiträge zur Jüdischen Kulturgeschichte*, No. 3 (Frankfurt-am-Main, 1929).

ECKSTEIN, A., 'Die Synagogenmalereien von Horb in der Städtischen Gemäldesammlung zu Bamberg', in *Bamberger Blätter für Fränkische Kunst und Geschichte*, Vol. 7 (1924).

47 *Monumenta Judaica.*

48 HELLER, Imre, and VAJDA, Zsigmond, *A Magyarországi Zsinagogak Albuma* (*The Synagogues of Hungary, an Album*) (New York, 1968).

6 WESTERN TASTE AND FASHION

1 VOLAVKOVA, Hana, *The Pinkas Synagogue* (trans. Greta Hort, Prague, 1955).

2 Diary of Charles Ogier in Latin, Egerton Ms. 2434, British Museum.

3 THIEME-BECKER, *Lexikon der Bildenden Künstler*, Vol. XXI, p. 454.

4 BRUGMANS, H., and FRANK, A., *Geschiedenis der Joden in Nederland* (Amsterdam, 1940).

5 DA SILVA ROSA, J.S., *Geschiedenis der Portugeesche Joden in Amsterdam, 1593–1925* (Amsterdam, 1925).

6 MEIJER, J., and DECASTRO, D.H., *De Synagoge der Portugees-Israelitische Gemeente te Amsterdam* (Amsterdam, 1950).

7 SCHWARZ, Karl, *Die Juden in der Kunst* (Vienna, 1936).

8 Letter of John Greenhalgh to Thomas Crompton, 22 April 1662, published in *Transactions of the Jewish Historical Society of England*, Vol. X, pp. 49–57 (London, 1924).

9 BARNETT, L.D. (trans.), *El libro de los Acuerdos, Being the Records and Accounts of the Spanish and Portuguese Synagogue a London from 1663 to 1681* (Oxford, 1931).

10 MEIJER, J., *Encyclopaedia Nederlandica Sefardica* (Amsterdam, 1949).

11 BARNETT, L.D. (trans.), *El libro de los Acuerdos.*

12 BARNETT, L.D. (trans.), *El libro de los Acuerdos.*

13 GASTER, Moses, *The History of the Ancient Synagogue at Bevis Marks, London* (London, 1901).

14 GASTER, Moses, *The History of the Ancient Synagogue at Bevis Marks, London.*

15 WILLIAMS, Temple, 'A Description of the Furniture', in *Treasures of a London Temple*, 250th Anniversary Catalogue (London, 1951).

16 FISKE, Kimball (Director of the Philadelphia Museum of Art), 'Peter Harrison', in *Touro Synagogue of Congregation Jeshuat Israel* (The Society of Friends of Touro Synagogue National Historic Shrine Inc., 1948).

17 GUTSTEIN, Morris A., 'The Jews of Newport, R.I., in Pre Revolutionary Days', in *Touro Synagogue of Congregation Jeshuat Israel.*

18 HALLO, Rudolf, *Jüdische Kunst aus Hessen und Nassau,* (1927).

19 LANSBERGER, Franz, History of Jewish Art (Cincinnati, 1946).

20 LEVI, Giuseppe, *Le Iscrizioni del Sacro Tempio Israelitico a Casale Monferrato* (Casale Monferrato, 1914).

21 *idem.*

22 *idem.*

23 *idem.*

24 POLLAK, Manó, *Zsidó templomépités Magyarországon* (Budapest, 1935).

25 WISCHNITZER, Rachel, *The Architecture of the European Synagogue,* (Philadelphia, 1963).

26 BENEZIT, E. *Dictionnaire des Peintres, Sculpteurs, Dessinateurs et Graveurs*, Vol. I (new edition, Paris, 1976).

27 Published by DUMOULIN, André, as Document-Annexe No. 3 in *Un Joyau de l'Art Judaique Français, La Synagogue de Cavaillon* (Paris, 1970).

28 *A Guide to Jewish Monuments in France* (Centre National d'Expansion du Tourisme etc., Paris, n.d.).

29 Published by DUMOULIN, André, as Document-Annexe No. 3 in *Un Joyau de l'Art Judaique Français, La Synagogue de Cavaillon.*

30 HALLO, Rudolf, *Kasseler Synagogengeschichte* (Kassel, 1932).

31 POLLAK, Manó, *Zsidó templomépités Magyarországon.*

32 WOLF, G., *Geschichte der Juden in Wien, 1156–1876* (Vienna, 1876).

33 Reports of Alfred Bendiner to the American Philosophical Society (1954 *et seq.*).

34 WISCHNITZER, Rachel, *Synagogue Architecture in the United States* (Philadelphia, 1955).

35 KAELTER, R., *Geschichte der Jüdischen Gemeinde zu Potsdam* (Potsdam, 1903).

36 KAELTER, R., *Geschichte der Jüdischen Gemeinde zu Potsdam.*

THE ORIENTAL INFLUENCE

CARMOLY, E., and LELEWEL, L., *Notice Historique sur
njamin de Tudèle* (Brussels, 1852).

DE LOS RIOS, José Amador, *Estudios historicos, politicos y
erarios sobre los Judios en España* (Madrid, 1848).

KATONA, Jozsef, *A 90 Eves Dohany-utcai Templom*
udapest, 1949).

KATONA, Jozsef, *A 90 Eves Dohany-utcai Templom*.

For example in PEREZ DE VILLA-AMIL., Genaro, *España
tistica y Monumental (3 vols. Madrid, 1842–56).

HALLO, Rudolf, *Kasseler Synagogengeschichte* (Kassel,
32).

The Israelite (22 April 1864).

HELLER, J.C., *As Yesterday when it is Past* (Cincinnati,
42).

The Occident (August 1816).

The Occident (August 1816).

Harper's Weekly (6 July 1872).

RYBAR, Ctibor, *Prague: Guide, Information, Facts* (Prague,
73).

ANON., *Ricordo della Comunità Israelitica di Firenze
lorence, n.d.).

PINKERFELD, Jacob, *The Synagogues of North Africa
erusalem, 1974, in Hebrew).

THE SEARCH FOR A STYLE

PEVSNER, Niklaus, *An Outline of European Architecture
ondon, 1943).

CLARK, Kenneth, *The Gothic Revival* (New York, 1950).

ROSENGARTEN, Albrecht, *Architektonische Stilarten* (1857);
nglish translation by W. Collett-Sanders as *A Handbook of
rchitectural Styles (New York, 1894)).

MEEKS, Carroll L.V., *Italian Architecture 1750–1914* (New
aven and London, 1966).

CASELLI, Crescentino, *Il Tempio Israelitico in Torino* (Turin,
$75).

CASSELLI, Crescentino, *Il Tempio Israelitico in Torino*.

MILANO, Attilio, *Storia degli Ebrei in Italia* (Turin, 1963).

CASELLI, Crescentino, *Il Tempio Israelitico in Torino*.

LOEW, I., 'Glasmalereien der Neuen Synagoge in
egedin', in *Mitteilungen für Jüdische Volkskunde*, Vol. XIII,
0. 1 (1904).

10 GRUNVALD, Fülöp and NAMÉNY, Ernö, *Budapesti
Zsinagogak* (Budapest, 1949).

11 BRUNNER, Arnold W., 'Synagogue Architecture', in *The
Brickbuilder*, Vol. XVI, No. 3 (1907).

12 KLAPHECK, R., 'Die Neue Synagoge in Essen a.d. Ruhr
erbaut von Prof. Edmund Koerner', in *13. Sonderheft der
Architektur des XX Jahrhunderts* (Berlin, 1919).

9 THE MODERN SYNAGOGUE

1 EISLER, Max, 'Vom Neuen Geist der Jüdischen Baukunst',
in *Menorah*, Vol. IV, No. 9 (Vienna, 1926); and 'Kunst und
Gemeinde', in *Menorah*, Vol. VI, No. 2 (Vienna, 1928).

2 EISLER, Max, 'Neue Synagogen', in *Menorah*, Vol. VIII,
Nos. 11–12 (Vienna, 1930).

3 See report of Reinhard Heydrich to Goering, 10 November
1938, Nuremberg Document 3058–PS published in *Nazi
Conspiracy and Aggression*, Vol. V, p. 854 *et seq.* (Washington,
1946).

4 ROTH, Cecil, *A History of the Jews* (New York, 1954).

5 *Trial of the Major War Criminals before the International
Military Tribunal*, Vol. 9, p. 358 (Nuremberg).

6 ROSENAU, Helen, *A Short History of Jewish Art* (London,
1948).

7 See KAMPF, Avram, *Contemporary Synagogue Art,
Developments in the United States, 1945–1965* (New York,
1966); and BLAKE, Peter (ed.), *An American Synagogue for
Today and Tomorrow* (New York, 1954).

8 ZEVI, Bruno, *Ebraismo e concezione spazio-temporale nell'arte*
(Rome, 1974).

9 Quoted in SHEAR, John Knox, and DODGE, F.W., *Religious
Buildings of Today* (New York, 1957).

10 WISCHNITZER, Rachel, *Synagogue Architecture in the
United States* (Philadelphia, 1955).

11 FARR, Finis, *Frank Lloyd Wright* (London, 1962).

12 ZEVI, Bruno, *Ebraismo e concezione spazio-temporale
nell'arte*.

13 TOMKINS, Calvin, 'Profile (Philip Johnson)', in *The New
Yorker* (23 May 1977).

14 See BEN-ELIEZER, Shimon, *Destruction and Renewal, the
Synagogues of the Jewish Quarter* (2nd revised edition,
Jerusalem, 1975).

Glossary

AGORA An open space used as a meeting-place in Ancient Greece and the Hellenistic cities.

AMBRY (pl. ambries). Recess in a wall used as a cupboard for storing sacred vessels or objects.

ARCHISYNAGOGUE The ruler of a synagogue.

ARCHON (Greek). Chief Magistrate.

ASHKENAZIM Jews who lived originally in the Rhineland and spread through central and eastern Europe; the term eventually was used to include all Jews who observe the 'German' synagogue ritual.

BALDACHIN (in Italian, *baldacchino*). A canopy, suspended or placed on columns, set over an altar, a venerated place, a throne, or even a bed.

BETH MIDRASH Place where rabbinical literature is studied; meeting-place of a study group.

BIMAH The platform from which the Torah is read to the assembly and Benediction is recited.

COLOBIUM A long tunic, usually sleeveless or with short sleeves, worn for ecclesiastical rites and for ceremonies.

COPTIC Of, or pertaining to, native Egyptian Christianity.

CROCKETING Continuous carved decoration of leaves projecting from the edges of a spire or pinnacle.

DIASPORA Term used to describe the dispersion of the Jews outside Erez Israel; from the Greek word for dispersion.

DOMUS-ECCLESIA (Latin). Literally 'house-church'. A house used for religious worship by the early Christians.

EREZ ISRAEL (Hebrew). Literally 'Land of Israel', ie the promised land, The biblical territory of Israel.

ESTRANGELO SCRIPT An archaic form of the Syriac alphabet.

ETROG (Hebrew). Citron.

FRAUENSCHUL (German). The women's prayer-hall.

GAON (Hebrew, pl. *gaonim*). Title of the head of a Jewish academy, formerly the highest authority on Jewish law.

GERUSIARCH (Greek). The president of an assembly of elders.

HAFTOR or HAFTARAH (Hebrew). Selected reading from the prophets recited in the synagogue on Sabbath and festival mornings and fast-day afternoons.

HAGGADAH (Hebrew). Book which is read at the *Seder*, the festive home service of Passover.

HAHAM or HAKHAM (Hebrew). Title given to rabbinical scholars; originally inferior to 'rabbi', later used for ordained scholars. Used for their local rabbi by the Sephardi communities of Amsterdam and London.

HALAKAH (Hebrew). The laws, rules and regulations which govern Jewish life.

HASSIDISM A popular religious movement which began about 1740 in southern Poland as a reaction against rabbinical intellectualism. It stresses faith, trust in God, religious emotion and ecstatic prayer as the principal way to approach God.

HAZZAN (Hebrew). Cantor or Reader who leads the congregation in prayer in the synagogue.

HEREM (Hebrew). A rabbinical interdict intended to assure conformity to the laws; sometimes a sentence of expulsion from the community for disobedience.

HOSHAN RABBAH (Hebrew). The seventh day of the festival of *Sukkot*, the harvest festival of thanksgiving, on which there are processions in the synagogue.

ICONOSTASIS (Greek). The screen separating the sanctuary from the main body of the church.

INTARSIA Inlaid decoration, often pictorial, in which small pieces of wood chosen for their varied colour and texture are used.

LAMBREQUIN Short curtain or drape, usually with jagged or scalloped hem.

LAVER Vessel, basin or cistern for washing.

LULAV (Hebrew). Palm branch.

MA'AMAD One of the twenty-four groups of Jewish laymen who attended at the Second Temple for one week by rota to witness the daily sacrifices.

MAGEN DAVID (Hebrew). The so-called 'Star of David', superimposed triangles forming a six-pointed star.

MARRANO Name used for the Jews of Spain and Portugal and their descendants who were converted to Christianity to escape persecution but continued to adhere secretly to Judaism.

MEGILLOT (Hebrew). The five scrolls of the Song of Songs, Ruth, Lamentations, Ecclesiastes and Esther.

MERLON The raised part of an indented parapet.

MIDRASH (Hebrew, pl. *Midrashim*). Rabbinical literature containing homilectic interpretations.

MIHRAB (Arabic). Niche in the *qibla* wall (q.v.) of the mosque, indicating the direction of Mecca.

MILLENNIUM Period of one thousand years when, according to Christian belief, Christ will return and establish his reign on earth.

MINBAR (Arabic). Seat or pulpit in the mosque to the right of the *mihrab* (q.v.).

MINYAN (Hebrew). Ten Jewish males over the age of thirteen, the minimum attendance required for congregational worship.

MISHNAH (Hebrew). The authoritative digest of the oral Torah, elaborating and interpreting the laws of the Pentateuch.

MUQARNAS An Arabic term, derived from the Greek, for

cales used in roof tiles. It is used to describe what are also called stalactite or honeycomb vaults.

NARTHEX Vestibule or portico stretching across the main entrance of a church.

NER TAMID (Hebrew). The lamp which burns continually before the Ark. It is commonly called the Eternal Light.

OPUS RETICULATUM Ancient Roman form of wall-work in which pyramid-shaped stones with square bases were set diagonally and wedged into the wall.

OPUS SECTILE Type of mosaic work in which stone pieces of varying shapes, sizes and colours are used to compose the pattern or figure.

OSTRACON Inscribed fragment of pottery.

PARNASSIM (Hebrew). Presiding leaders of the community. Usually elected for a term of office but sometimes appointed for life.

PAROKETH (Hebrew). Curtain hanging in front of, or sometimes inside, the doors of the Ark.

PAROUSIA The second coming of Christ.

POLITEUMA A corporate body of foreign residents with their own internal administration, living in a Greek or Hellenistic city.

PORTE-COCHERE Carriage entrance.

PRESBYTER Officer of the congregation who was responsible for the management of local affairs.

PROPYLAEUM Entrance to a temple or sacred enclosure.

QIBLA (Arabic). The direction of prayer, hence the wall of the mosque which was directed towards Mecca.

RIMMONIM (Hebrew). Finials, frequently decorated with bells, which are placed on top of the staves of the Torah.

SANHEDRIN (Hebrew, from Greek). The Supreme Jewish tribunal of seventy-one sages which had authority in matters of civil and criminal law and religious observance.

SHEWBREAD The twelve loaves which were placed each Sabbath on a table in the Temple before the Altar of Incense.

SHOFAR (Hebrew). Ram's horn. It symbolizes the call to repentance.

SHOHET (Hebrew). Man trained and authorized to slaughter beasts and poultry according to Judaic law.

SHTETL Jewish village community or small-town Jewish community in eastern Europe.

SHTIBL Hassidic prayer-room.

STOA A colonnaded roofed hall.

TALMUD The encyclopaedic collection of the decisions and arguments of the Jewish sages from the close of the biblical era to the seventh century CE.

TESSERAE Small cubes of stone, glass or ceramic used to make up a mosaic.

TEVAH Term used by the Sephardim for the reading platform or bimah.

TORUS Convex moulding at the base of a column.

TOSEFTA A collection of traditions related to Judaic oral law similar to but sometimes contradicting the Mishnah.

TRABEATED Of doorways, built on the post and lintel principle instead of using the arch.

VOUSSOIR A wedge-shaped brick or stone component-piece of an arch.

WARDEN'S TRIBUNE Bench for the presiding elders or officers of the congregation.

YESHIVA (Hebrew). Theological academy for mature students.

YOM KIPPUR (Hebrew). The feast of man's reconciliation with God – the holiest festival of the Jewish calendar.

ZIYADAH (Arabic). The outer enclosure of the mosque.

Bibliography

The very informative works of Dr Rachel Wischnitzer on synagogue architecture in Europe and the United States proved invaluable in my research. I am also indebted to other scholars, especially to Professor Richard Krautheimer without whose book *Mittelalterliche Synagogen*, published before the Holocaust, our knowledge of the early synagogues of Germany would be incomplete, and to Maria and Kazimierz Piechotka who published their own and the late Szymon Zajczyk's researches on the wooden synagogues of Poland together with valuable architectural plans of these buildings, all victims of the destructive zeal of the Nazis.

Extensive bibliographical references will be found with the notes for each chapter. The following are some works on the subject in English.

WISCHNITZER, Rachel, *The Architecture of the European Synagogue*, The Jewish Publication Society of America (Philadelphia, 1963).

Synagogue Architecture in the United States, The Jewish Publication Society of America (Philadelphia, 1955).

KAMPF, Avram, *Contemporary Synagogue Art*, Union of American Hebrew Congregations (New York, 1966) (3rd printing, New York, 1976).

BLAKE, Peter, *An American Synagogue for Today and Tomorrow*, Union of American Hebrew Congregations (New York, 1954).

KAPLOUN, Uri (compiler), *The Synagogue*, Leon Amiel Publisher (Jerusalem, 1973).

KOHN, Joshua, *The Synagogue in Jewish Life*, KTAV Publishing House (New York, 1971).

PIECHOTKA, Maria and Kazimierz, *Wooden Synagogues*, Arkady (Warsaw, 1959).

SALLER, Fr Sylvester J., OFM, *Second Revised Catalogue of the Ancient Synagogues of the Holy Land*, Franciscan Printing Press (Jerusalem, 1972).

EISENBERG, Azriel, *The Synagogue Through the Ages*, Bloch (New York, 1974).

BEN-ELIEZER, Shimon, *Destruction and Renewal, the Synagogues of the Jewish Quarter*, Rubin Mass (Jerusalem, 1975).

VENICE JEWISH COMMUNITY (ed.), *Jewish Art Treasures in Venice*, International Fund for Monuments Inc., New York (Venice, n.d.).

VOLAVKOVA, Hana, *The Synagogue Treasures of Bohemia and Moravia*, Sfinx (Prague, 1949).

GUTMANN, Joseph (ed.), *The Dura-Europos Synagogue: A Re-Evaluation*, American Academy of Religion, Society of Biblical Literature (Missoula, Montana, 1973).

HELLER, Imre and VAJDA, Zsigmond, *The Synagogues of Hungary, an Album*, World Federation of Hungarian Jews (New York, 1968).

GANS, Mozes Heiman, Memorbook, *History of Dutch Jewry from the Renaissance to 1940*, Bosch & Keuning (Baarn, Netherlands, 1977) (English translation by Arnold J. Pomerans).

ROTH, Cecil, *Jewish Art, an Illustrated History* (revised edition by Bezalel Narkiss), Valentine, Mitchell (London, 1971).

Israel, Ancient Mosaics, preface by Meyer Shapiro, introduction by Michael Avi-Yonah, Unesco World Art Series, New York Graphic Society with UNESCO (Paris, 1960).

Acknowledgments

Most of the black-and-white photographs and all of the colour (except page 54 which was supplied by the Royal Library, Copenhagen) were taken specially for this book by George Mott. Specific permission for photography was granted by the Jewish Museum, New York (pages 142 and 146), the Association for the Administration of the Sephardi Synagogues in the Old City, RYBZ, Jerusalem (page 77), the Israel Museum, Jerusalem (pages 121 and 124), and Hevrat Yehude Italia Lif'Ula Ruhanit, Jerusalem (pages 100–101).

The architectural plans were drawn by John Redmill.

Illustrations supplied by other sources are as follows: Biblioteca Apostolica Vaticana, Vatican City: 61, 93; Bildarchiv Preussischer Kulturbesitz, West Berlin: 166; Cape Archives, Cape Town: 185; Chicago Public Library: 187; Congregation Shaarey Zedek, Southfield, Michigan (photo by Balthazar Korab, Troy, Michigan): 198; Congregation of the Great Synagogue, Sydney: 153; Ecole Française d'Archéologie, Athens: 15; Gemeentelijke Archiefdienst, Rotterdam: 138; Herzog August Bibliothek, Wolfenbüttel: 135; Israel Museum Photo Archives: 11, 41, 66, 105, 114, 116, 126, 127; Keckenburg Museum, Schwäbisch Hall: 127; A. F. Kersting, London: 68–9; Kultur Institut, Worms: 62; Landeshauptarchiv, Koblenz: 60; Museo di Roma, Archivo Fotografico: 85; Photo Christophe, Lunéville: 138; Pontifical Commission for Sacred Archaeology, Vatican City: 18; Réunion de Musées Nationaux, Paris, Documentation Photographique: 58; Rijksdienst v.d. Monumentenzorg, Ziest: 180; Rijksmuseum, Amsterdam: 134; Sardis Research & Publications, Busch-Reisinger Museum, Fogg Art Museum, Harvard University: 29; Staatliche Museen, Berlin: 27, 38; Staatliche Museen Preussischer Kulturbesitz, Kupferstichkabinett, Berlin: 63; Staatliche Schlösser und Gärten, Wörlitz (Foto Huebbe, Wörlitz): 148; Stadtbildstelle, Essen: 189